ALL FOR LOVE

ALL FOR LOVE

*A study in
soap opera by*

PETER BUCKMAN

"Witness, ye days and nights, and all your hours,
That danced away with down upon your feet."

—Dryden, All For Love, II, 1.

SALEM HOUSE

Copyright © Peter Buckman 1984

First published in the United States in 1985 by
Salem House, 47 Pelham Road, Salem, New Hampshire

Library of Congress Catalog Card Number: 84-52466

ISBN 0-88162-083-1

Printed and bound in Great Britain

For Val and Charles,
who suggested it,
and for Tom
ubi os, ibi aes

CONTENTS

ACKNOWLEDGEMENTS

I would like to thank, in England, Clare Paterson for advice and the loan of invaluable research material; John Michael Phillips, for his detailed and constructive comments; Peter Ling; the late Alan Melville; Lord Ted Willis; Adele and Brian Winston; Dr Kenneth Short, Editor, *Historical Journal of Film, Radio, and Television*; H. V. Kershaw; Bill Ash; Norman Frisby; Bruce Purchase; Elspeth Sandys; in their various departments of the BBC, Gerald Glaister, Christopher Lewis and Eileen Mullen; the BBC Written Archives Centre; Gillian Hartnoll, Librarian of the BFI Book Library; Lucy Douch of BFI Information; the Bodleian Library; the London Library; and the Writers' Guild of Great Britain. In America I am indebted to Manuela Soares; Hugh Franklin; Jacqueline Babbin; Kerry Edwards; David O'Brien; Peggy O'Shea; Barbara Duggan; Cheryl McFadden; Allen Potter and the Procter & Gamble Company; Dr Mary Cassata; Karen Russo; the State Historical Society of Wisconsin; and Corinne L. Notkin of the Writers' Guild of America, East, Inc. I am very grateful to Laura Morris and Alison Samuel, most generous and most punctilious of editors; to Helen Burnett, for her high-speed typing; and lastly to my wife and two daughters, for their enthusiastic involvement in the business of watching and commenting on as many soaps as we could get our eyes and ears on.

INTRODUCTION

Soap opera is like sex outside marriage: many have tried it, but most are ashamed of being caught.

There are millions, of course, who regard it as a healthy activity to be indulged, without shame, as often as possible. I shall address myself to both these attitudes. But first, a definition.

By soap opera I mean a continuous serial of contemporary life, where traditional moral values (I shall define those later) are asserted. Each episode in a soap opera advances the plots and sub-plots, but does not resolve them (that is what series do: serials drag it out for as long as possible).

I exclude from the genre thrillers, situation comedies, police sagas, and period drama. But I shall be flexible. The serials I shall consider range from daily to weekly examples, from day-time to prime-time (evening). To exclude *Dallas* (because continuity is broken between series) or *Coronation Street* (whose producers object to the "soap" label) would be ridiculous.

I shall confine myself to the soaps of England and America, though as these sell all over the world, I shall be dealing with attitudes that transcend those two cultures.

No one knows who coined the term "soap opera", but it came about because the soap manufacturers Procter & Gamble sponsored so many serials on American day-time radio in the 1930s. The "soap" part is therefore easy to explain; the "opera" came, I imagine, from the melodrama and romantic entanglements that were common to all the serials, and which played such an important part in the complicated plots of Grand Opera. As an alternative, it has been suggested that "opera" attached itself to the name because of the sung jingle that opened and closed each episode.

I listened to my first day-time serial, *Mrs Dale's Diary*, on British radio when, as a small boy, I was supposed to be having my rest. No doubt that is where my guilt sprang from—just as, when we got our first television set, to see the Coronation in 1953, I felt a twinge when shutting out the light to watch, when I should probably have been doing my homework. I drag in these secrets from my past to illustrate something of my attitude to the subject. I am not an out-and-out addict of the form: I can live without it. But I have been exposed to it since childhood – like most people – and I get hooked on the story-telling at the root of its appeal.

The genre has quite suddenly become almost respectable, after years of being derided by reviewers. The British radio serial *The Archers* received a pretty poor press when it began in 1951, but four million people rapidly became regular listeners, rising to twenty million in the show's heyday, and it is still going, the only continuous day-time serial in Britain. The television serial *Coronation Street*, mocked when it opened, has been running twice weekly on the British commercial network for nearly 25 years, and is usually in the top ten programmes, often at number one. In America no reviewer noticed *The Guiding Light* when it began on radio in 1937 and then ran simultaneously on television from 1952: it is still showing on television to huge and faithful audiences after 45 years. Such staying power and popularity must in the end be acknowledged by the media. Which is why day-time serials now get the cover of glossy magazines; why college students are suddenly proud to proclaim themselves fans; why housewives, shift-workers, and those at home during the day for whatever reason (usually unemployment) are now coming out of the closet and admitting to watching or listening to what was once a private obsession. The survival of the form, and the enormous cash-flow it generates, have made it fashionable – perhaps only temporarily, except with the millions of regular fans who don't give a hoot about fashion, and have always liked what they have known.

You will say I am jumping on an already fast-moving bandwagon. Yes and no. When I started my research, it seemed that there was very little in print about the subject, and most of that was either academic, or designed for addicts (offering synopses of plots going back to the very beginning and gossip about the stars).

Even the popular press's interest concentrated on who was bedding whom. Everyone was prepared to have a guess at why shows produced so quickly and cheaply appeal to so many people. But no one seemed to have investigated what working in such a high-pressure business does to all those involved: the writers, actors, directors, technicians, producers, reviewers and critics, and – not least – the public. That is what I intend to do.

The sub-culture of the continuous serial has flourished for half a century, from one Depression to another, through a world war and the largest and fastest expansion of mass communications in history. Why should that be? Who runs this industry, what kind of people work in it, how do they operate? Is it, like the old Hollywood, a sweat-shop cranking out fantasies (and what could be more interesting than a history of popular fantasy)? Or is it a form of neo-realism, reflecting some of our longings and most of our frustrations?

That is the sort of thing I am going to write about. I should say at once, however, that this is not going to be a comprehensive history: those exist already, at least in America. What I am offering will be selective, partisan, and personal: an exploration of how we see and hear ourselves.

Oxfordshire
May, 1984

1

INVENTING THE CONVENTIONS: A HISTORY FROM EAR TO EYE

In the beginning was the word, and the word was on radio.

On American radio, anyway: the BBC under its first Director-General, John Reith, was opposed to serials in general, and soap opera in particular. It was felt that the form encouraged "mindless listening", whereas Reith's ambition was to elevate public taste.

"The BBC must lead, not follow, its listeners," Reith wrote in 1931, though he had the sense to add that "it must not lead at so great a distance as to shake off pursuit". During his first decade, the Corporation offered the public a menu of which 80% consisted of serious drama, classical music, and talks. "Entertainment" filled up the other 20%. The public, according to the Radio Manufacturers' Association (not perhaps the most objective of bodies) would have preferred the proportions reversed: 80% "entertainment", 20% "highbrow" material. Reith was unmoved. His BBC was a public corporation with monopoly powers, and he saw it as his duty to serve the "public interest" – which meant no "trivializing" of the air-waves.

No such inhibitions dogged the Americans. Market forces determined programme policy from the first, and soon advertisers hoisted themselves into the driving seat. In 1922 the American Telephone and Telegraph Company (AT&T), who held the monopoly over the American telephone system, announced that they were making available air-time for anyone who wanted to buy it. They were not going into programme production; merely providing the channels for others to use. Programme makers would pay to entertain the audience and to advertise their products.

First reactions to AT&T's proposal were not exactly rapturous. The trade magazine *Radio Dealer* denounced the company's "mercenary advertising purposes". The whole idea of "ether advertising" was condemned by the Washington Radio Conference. Even Herbert Hoover—

the American Canute who tried to keep back the tide of the Depression with the phrase "business as usual" – maintained that "it is inconceivable that we should allow so great a possibility for service to be drowned in advertising chatter".

It is interesting to recall these fine sentiments when you look at American broadcasting now, entirely dominated by advertisements (originally called "plugs", a term soon dignified into "commercials"). As a matter of fact, within six months of AT&T's announcement, it had sixteen sponsors for programmes. The future paths of American and British broadcasting were set within a year or two of their foundation in the early 1920s. In America, programmes would be paid for by advertisers; in Britain, through the revenue from the public's purchase of "licences" to listen. There soon grew up a class of radio writers and producers, on whom the broadcasters relied to provide them with programmes. (Many of the early programmes were simply cobbled together by station managers and their assistants, and for a long time they resisted the idea of paying for ideas, much less scripts – a notion still dear to some in broadcasting.) But the assumptions of the programme makers on either side of the Atlantic were different. Both said they wanted to stimulate, educate and entertain their audiences. However, in America, where there was fierce competition between stations for listeners, what mattered in the end was the quantity of those who tuned in. In Britain, where there was no such competition, what mattered was quality.

This situation was altogether new. Here was a public medium attempting to grab the attention of millions of private people for several hours a day, seven days a week. The sheer effort involved in filling so much time meant, on the one hand, that all sorts of novelties could be tried out (as long as they were cheap) and, on the other, that whatever worked in getting listeners hooked was liable to be repeated endlessly, in one form or another. But, before going further, perhaps I ought to make clear my position in this quantity versus quality debate.

In a medium like radio, the public only learns what it wants from what is offered. And those who offer it are just as much monopolists as were the programme makers of the old BBC. The cost involved in putting programmes on meant (and still means) that only people with cash can do it. They expect a return (in terms of high audience figures), which "unpopular" programmes – those that are difficult or serious – do not deliver. Thus the commercial type of monopoly restricts choice as much as the more public-spirited kind. And no writer is in favour of such a restriction.

But were Reith and his colleagues successful in elevating public taste? They had a fair crack of the whip: how far did they get?

Not very far. Radio is, like television, a powerful and persuasive medium – otherwise advertisers and politicians would not have embraced it with such enthusiasm – but it does not have the power, alone, to persuade people to like something they don't like. Reith's attempt to "improve" the intellectual calibre of the British came to grief because of the intractable British public. As early as the 1930s millions of them perversely tuned in to foreign stations whose commercial operators offered precisely the kind of "entertainment" (often American) that Reith denied them. They chose, in fact, to go elsewhere.

But at least the British had more choice of quality programmes than their American cousins, because of Reith's policy. And it cannot be denied that, as the advertisers tightened their grip around the throat of American broadcasting, their listeners received *less* choice. So if you believe in choice, as I do, then you have to believe (as many American critics have long believed) that a publicly owned broadcasting system offers at least more choice than a privately owned one. I would say this is still true, even though the BBC now plays the ratings game just like all the others.

Where, then, do I stand? With that critic – it was Milton Shulman – who described British television as "the least worst in the world".

The need to fill the hours of broadcasting was what brought about the birth of soap opera in America. Manufacturers responded to the fall in demand brought by the Depression by pushing their products even more stridently. The restraint that had marked the early years of sponsored broadcasting gave way to ads like "There is no spit in Cremo!", bellowed by a voice plugging the purity of Cremo cigars. Millions of listeners, their anxieties raised and their resistance lowered by the economic climate, responded to appeals from drug companies and quacks to send in coupons or box-tops in order to have their problems solved. The radio audience turned out to be infinitely larger, and infinitely more receptive, than the audiences for theatre, cinema or music hall. The sponsors fell over themselves to get its attention – and to find programmes that would sell their products.

Radio drama had been around since 1922, but it was never as popular as music (especially jazz). Not until 1928 – the year of the first experimental *televised* play – was drama a smash hit with CBS's *True Story*. Significantly for the future form of soap opera, these were cleaned-up versions of magazine stories, well greased with moralizing, and sponsored by Macfadden Publications. But even this success was eclipsed by that of a pioneering series which ended up closing churches and stopping film shows while its 40 million listeners tuned in: *Amos 'n' Andy*.

Amos 'n' Andy featured two white actors who portrayed blacks in comedy situations. It was the first radio show to employ the device on which all soap opera was – and is – based: the continuing narrative, where plot situations are only resolved over a period of weeks. This was new only to radio: it has been the mainstay of story-tellers from Homer to Dickens, and made fortunes for the publishers of pulp fiction (which has a claim to be called the first mass medium). It also made *Amos 'n' Andy* a fortune, and turned them into a national institution; as well as selling a lot of toothpaste for their sponsor, Pepsodent.

Soon the sponsors came to replace the American networks as the producers of programmes, and in turn they relied on their advertising agencies to come up with the programme ideas that would find the big audiences. The networks were happy with this arrangement, as long as they were provided with, and paid for, programmes to fill their air-time. The sponsors were happy as long as the programmes sold their products. And the agencies were happiest of all, because they took a 15% commission from the networks for bringing in sponsors and 15% from the sponsors, on the costs of putting together the necessary programmes: hiring writers, organizing production, booking actors, and so forth.

Very quickly the agencies started coming up with programme ideas to sell to sponsors and networks, instead of waiting to be asked. And one such idea was the continuing daily serial, fifteen minutes in length like *Amos 'n' Andy* (or its comic Jewish equivalent *The Goldbergs*), but based, like the popular magazine romances of the time, on the problems faced by modern men and women, especially in their love-life. If any single individual could claim the credit for getting this idea onto radio, it would be Frank Hummert, of the advertising agency Blackett, Sample and Hummert.

Imagine the Depression, a term that applies to your mental state and your bank balance. There are few jobs, less money, little to live on but rhetoric and promises. The shops are full of goods, so somebody must be buying; only rarely is it you. You become oppressed by a feeling of waste: wasted talents, wasted resources, wasted lives. You can't afford to go out much, and you've cut right down on the entertaining, so there are fewer and fewer opportunities for the comfort of neighbourly gossip. You turn in on yourself, and you worry. Where do you look when you want a bit of understanding and an escape?

Now you turn to your television; in the 1930s it was to your radio. As you went about your household chores – the routine that both kept you going and drove you mad – you could hear a voice, a rich man's voice as solidly dependable as home-made fruit cake, telling you of "The real-life drama of Helen Trent who, when life mocks her, breaks her hopes, dashes her against the rocks of despair, fights back bravely, successfully, to prove what so many women long to prove in their own lives, that because a woman is 35, or more, romance in life need not be over, that romance can begin at 35."

That was one of Frank Hummert's. A modest man – although reputed to be the highest paid writer in the world – he disclaimed all credit for inventing the form of soap opera which is still going strong. It was only a guess, he wrote to Raymond W. Stedman (the authoritative historian of the American serial in all its forms): "not a flash of so-called genius, but a shot in the dark". Lots of people, especially women, lapped up the serials that appeared in magazines: why shouldn't they follow them equally avidly if they were dramatized, on radio?

It must be said that there was precious little entertainment for women who were home during the day. Then as now, the major resources of broadcasting went on the evening programmes, which got the biggest family audiences. Day-time radio consisted of easy music and talks on beauty, better laundering methods, and how to make lighter pastry. The advertisers were not slow to realize that these captive women – the domestic slave market – were also the main buyers of household goods. Procter & Gamble, the long established soap and cooking oil conglomerate, were among the first to advertise on radio, and they sponsored talks by experts on etiquette like Emily Post. They could also take advantage of the cheap rates charged by the networks for day-time radio: half that levied on evening broadcasts. Cheap air-time for a huge potential market: it only needed someone like Frank Hummert to come up with a formula for entertaining the depressed masses. Something like the formula that kept them at home in the evenings (only cheaper): a continuing story of contemporary folk, divided into fifteen-minute daily episodes five days a week, opened, closed and punctuated by messages from the sponsor. Thus was soap opera born.

Of course, there were plenty of serials on American radio (not, as I've said, in Britain, where even classic detective fiction got only a rare look-in). *Amos 'n' Andy* spawned scores of imitations, as sponsors all over the country demanded "family entertainment" for their customers. Most of these were comedies, though they differed from what we know as "situation comedy" in keeping the plot bubbling for several episodes. Most revolved around that central and familiar institution, the family, and most allowed Ma to be the one who put everything right. Finally, most of them were set in small towns. In part this was because many of the sponsors involved had headquarters outside New York (P&G's was, and is, in Cincinnati, a town named for the Roman hero who turned his back on success in order to return to the plough). It was cheaper to produce programmes in Chicago or Cincinnati than it was in New York, and the grip of the unions was looser (all of which

explained the burgeoning of Hollywood as a centre of movie-making).
But above all it catered for the nostalgia felt by most Americans (and
the rest of us, for that matter) for the small, friendly, manageable
community, where you were never alone with your problems, and
where there was always somebody's Ma (or someone's widowed
Grandpa) ready with sympathy, understanding and bucketsful of traditional wisdom.

So Frank Hummert was just building on existing models when he
came up with the idea of a continuing serial. Where he and his wife
Anne – and their romance is a soap opera in itself (tall, courteous,
quietly spoken Frank is persuaded to employ as his assistant small,
elegant Anne Ashenhurst, who has never worked in advertising, but
whose remarkable competence soon makes her indispensable, so that
within a few years of the death of Frank's wife, Anne becomes the
new Mrs Hummert . . . but this isn't that kind of book) – where the
Hummerts actually revolutionized the process was in the way they
exploited it.

Having realized that one serial idea was not going to make them and
the agency rich, they organized themselves into a machine for the
production of plot ideas. Their working method was a streamlined
version of agency practice. The Hummerts dreamed up the story: say,
that of a simple secretary called Betty who ended up marrying her rich
boss Bob. They sold the idea to a sponsor – in this case, the cereal firm
General Mills, who were actually the first to pay for a networked
day-time serial. Had they invested as heavily as Procter & Gamble, the
form would no doubt have been known as "cereals" (I take no credit
for this pun).

Once the sponsor was signed up, the Hummerts would outline each
episode in some detail, to make sure it conformed to the sponsor's
expectations. Then they would hand over the drudgery of actually
writing the words the characters were to speak to "dialoguers". The
Hummerts thus kept total control of characters and plot – and incidentally of the rights in each serial. Writers were paid a standard fee (in
1938 it was $25 per script, or $125 per week) and did what they were
told. There is a celebrated story of the writer Manya Starr, to whom
Anne Hummert said, "I want you to put God on every page." When
Miss Starr asked who would play the part, she was immediately dismissed. None of the Hummert serials were noted for their humour.

Undoubtedly the Hummert method worked. Soon they had their
own production organization, Air Features, which included a clutch of
six "script readers" who liaised between them and the writers, and who
read every script to ensure consistency. This is precisely how soap
opera is organized today. But there are very few today capable of

creating, and keeping alive, as many serials as the Hummerts did. Between 1932 and 1940 they invented more than thirty. More than twenty were on the air together at the end of the decade. (Only Britain's Ted Willis, who among his other credits was one of the original writers of the soap opera *Mrs Dale's Diary*, surpasses the Hummerts' output.) None of these have worn well – but then neither Frank nor Anne Hummert claimed to be creating literature. They were simply proud of giving housewives harmless escapist pleasure at a time when there was little enough pleasure around; and of giving work to so many writers and actors, when employment in either profession was even more of a problem than usual.

Frank Hummert told a *New York Times* reporter in 1938 that he and Anne created people who were human, lovable, logical and believable when performing actions "painted against the canvas of everyday American life". The characters also had to be "uniformly consistent and high-principled". Why was high moral tone so necessary? Mr Hummert's answer was that his characters were close enough to their listeners to form "part of their daily lives" – a justified claim that shows how quickly the continuing serial insinuated itself into its listeners' routine. Such a thing was only possible in a medium as instantly and continuously available as radio. No wonder the *New York Times* felt Mr Hummert worth interviewing.

But to show goodness at its best, you need a villain to vanquish. The Hummerts didn't go in just for soppy sentiment or pious preachifying – though, looked at fifty years on, their heroines seem insufferably sanctimonious. They filled their serials with solid, juicy scoundrels, forever doing the dirty on those who thought them friends. Thus they added one more item to the formula, an item all story-tellers down the centuries had relied on, but which in the 1920s seemed confined to gangster tales: the battle of good against evil. With, of course, good always proving victorious in the end. No serial then was complete without a villain, just as no modern soap is any good without a bitch.

Consider an event in the life of Mary Noble, heroine of *Backstage Wife*, a Hummert creation which ran from 1935 to 1959, "the story of a little Iowa girl, who married Larry Noble, handsome matinée idol, dream sweetheart of a million other women, and her struggle to keep his love in the complicated atmosphere of backstage life". A single episode was summed up by the announcer thus:

Mary has been the victim of a false friend, Armand Delubeque, who took her diamond engagement ring with the promise of having it repaired. But instead Armand pawned the ring and tried to blackmail Mary and Larry. And when Marcia Mannering tried to make it appear that Mary was in love with Armand, and had given the ring to him, she turned Larry violently against her. And thereupon Marcia conspired with Armand to get even with Mary and Larry. When Mary and Larry later discovered that the ring had disappeared from the shop, Mary is heartbroken, and Larry resolves at last to notify the police.

Here are several elements common to all the Hummert canon. There is the perennial fantasy of the pauper marrying the prince, updated to the modern corporation in *Betty and Bob*, and given the glamour of theatrical life in *Backstage Wife*. There is the snobbery about class and breeding: poor Mary's is always an uphill struggle because she was just an Iowa girl, while Larry was the suave man-about-everywhere. (Compare the Hummerts' *Our Gal Sunday*, the story of an orphan girl from "the little mining town of Silver Creek, Colorado, who in young womanhood married England's richest, most handsome lord, Lord Henry Brinthrope. The story asks the question: Can this girl from a mining town in the West find happiness as the wife of a wealthy and titled Englishman?")

There is the untrustworthy foreigner, Armand Delubeque, and the even more untrustworthy woman "friend" Marcia (the bitch figure, although the term would never cross a Hummert pen-nib). Finally there is the indomitable strength of American womanhood: Mary always behaved well, whether extricating her jealous and insecure husband from trouble (and if Larry wasn't bad enough, Lord Henry Brinthrope was a pathological case of marital suspicion), or saving herself from men who thundered in her wake going crazy – often literally – over her charms.

American men were weak, selfish, uncertain, petty, cowardly, and pretty silly on the whole – or at least many of the Hummerts' leading men were. Their women, by contrast, were always beautiful, strong, faithful, loving, capable and, above all, virtuous. Helen Trent never got between the sheets with a man in twenty-seven years, even with her long-standing fiancé, whom she once informed that being engaged was not a licence to hold her hand. Mary never even considered leaving the foolish Larry, nor Betty the lecherous Bob (who was originally played by the smooth Don Ameche, giving soap its first heart-throb), nor Our Gal Sunday the idiot Brinthrope. Why? Because the serials never pretended to reflect everyday reality. Instead they invented, and sustained, a reality all their own, a peculiar blend of fantasy and traditional morality (which is the kind most people follow. I'd place it chronologically as being ten or twenty years behind the behavioural standards of the trend-setters).

Most of the housewives who quickly identified with these faithful radio heroines were themselves prevented, by circumstance and inhibition, from committing adultery. And before you think that serial listeners were a group of provincial, dowdy, frustrated, ill-educated, spineless housewives, let me assure you that research established that those who listened to the American soaps in the 1930s and 1940s differed very little in age, education, or social standing from those women who listened to other programmes.

We are talking here about a public attitude to morality shared by the majority. Sex was a private matter, love a noble aspiration, adultery difficult to forgive. The Hummerts were not in the business of trying to create a new moral climate. They were trying to sell soap, or whatever their sponsors produced. Procter & Gamble invested two million dollars in soap operas in 1935. By 1939 the company had no less than twenty-one serials under its sponsorship, worth 8¾ million dollars. You can see why the label "soap" stuck so firmly. Naturally they reflected mainstream opinion: no serial that was after success would presume to do otherwise. Neither they nor their audience felt defensive about believing in such values, which were the hardcore in the foundations of all those cherished institutions that even the Depression could not destroy. In uncertain times, most people cling even more fervently to what they know (even if they don't like it). The serials gave them all hope that in the end these values would see them through, and bring them love, prosperity and – just possibly – happiness.

The Hummerts were not alone in their field. Another name to rank alongside theirs is that of Irna Phillips. A graduate of three universities, in 1929 she found herself working in a radio station run by the Chicago *Tribune*. Since the station, like most others, was desperate for material to keep going, Miss Phillips suggested a day-time serial aimed at women, which would feature Mother Moynihan, her lodging-house, and her grown-up children. With a change of station came a change of name: Mother Moynihan became Mother Moran (a part Miss Phillips often played herself, basing it on her own mother), and the serial was called *Today's Children*.

It bore a curious resemblance to the Hummerts' most famous creation, *Ma Perkins*, which was first broadcast in 1933, and written for years by a Chicago-based writer called Orin Tovrov. Now it is not unthinkable that the Hummerts were guilty of plagiarism, for advertising people are celebrated for that very quality. But more likely is that serial ideas featuring a widowed Ma struggling to keep her family together were floating around every station in the nation. It is one of the peculiar features of broadcasting that a whole lot of people seem to have the same idea at once, without consciously copying each other. I speak from personal experience. It may be deplorable, but there's no copyright in ideas. Widowed Mas popped up all over the place. Miss Phillips just seemed to have been there first.

Where the Hummerts specialized in romantic fantasy, Miss Phillips embroidered from life, taking her characters from the circle of professional people she moved in. Again, I must stress that she wasn't trying to be "realistic" in the documentary sense: rather she, and the Hummerts, sought to invent people with whom their listeners could identify, and who would behave with credible consistency. Where Miss Phillips took a giant step forward was in realizing that, if there was anything more fascinating than other people's problems with love and money, it was other people's illnesses. She invented – yes – the medical soap, starting with *The Road of Life*, which ran from 1937 to 1959, and was the pattern for Britain's *Mrs Dale's Diary*, as well as for all those hospital serials now on television.

Another thing Irna Phillips chanced upon was the use of illness for dramatic effect. She made amnesia respectable – as a serial device that gave you two story-lines for the price of one. The first story concerned the impossible situation the victim had got himself (or herself) into, with grieving spouse and shattered family; the second was about the new life he or she created once all memory of the old was effaced. Clever stuff, and a brilliant addition to the array of cliff-hangers with which each episode had to end (without them, who'd bother to tune in tomorrow?). Naturally it was immediately copied, and is still a strong favourite in the repertoire (even Meg Mortimer of the British serial *Crossroads* had a bout of amnesia, which strangely never recurred).

Miss Phillips also appreciated her listeners' appetite for gossip about the private lives of those entrusted with the mission to cure, and *The Road of Life*'s formula – the rivalries and jealousies of the hospital world, the cravings of its staff for promotion and each other, contrasted with their divine gift of healing – this was the stuff of myth (which is after all only tittle-tattle about the failings of the gods). It was loved by the audience and copied by everyone in the business.

The Guiding Light is the most celebrated Phillips creation, simply because of its survival. Sponsored by Procter & Gamble, it was first networked in 1937, moved without strain to television (while continuing on radio as well until 1956), and is still going happily on CBS. Among Miss Phillips' many claims to fame (she was also the first to extend the soap opera to half an hour on television), the longevity of *The Guiding Light* must rank as a record. It still has one of the original cast in it – Charita Bauer, who plays the matriach Bert, and who gets letters from people who have followed her fortunes for half a century.

Of course the serial has changed – Bert, once the mainstay of the programme, now makes only occasional appearances, since all American soaps have come to concentrate on the younger characters, with the soap audience itself grown younger – but Miss Phillips was there to preside over its fortunes until her death in 1974. She was notoriously difficult to work with, telephoning actors after a screening to complain that they had altered one of her lines, taking writers to task for presuming to tinker with her concept. The Hummerts did things more discreetly, but then radio was a more discreet medium than television.

The Hummerts and Phillipses of soap shared the supervision of every script with the sponsor's representative, who was careful to see that nothing was included that would either offend the audience or give comfort to a rival. So important was the sponsor that he was even provided with his own little booth in the recording studio, from which he could oversee, and if necessary override, the producer. But that wasn't the only pressure on those who made the programmes.

The writers had to produce some 75 minutes of script to the creators' and the companies' exacting demands, once a week, every week. The money was good but the pace was killing. The only way writers managed to take a holiday was by writing several weeks ahead of transmission. Women writers who got pregnant were wheeled into the delivery ward still scribbling on their notepads.

The actors and actresses had a brief rehearsal, and then went straight on to the air, with no chance of a "second take" and no editing. Mistakes in picking up cues or delivering lines could not be put right, and were a source of much amusement to hard-worked players landed with solemn scripts. The audience cherished them too. Some of the cast found their lines so deadly they would mess around during performance, pulling down their colleagues' trousers and playing other jolly japes – though not when the sponsor was in his little booth. And far from relaxing after the show over a drink or a cup of java, many of these players would rush off to appear in another soap. The work may not have been glamorous, and was not all that well paid, but an actor or actress who pleased the Hummerts (Anne did the casting) could be signed up for several of their series, which bumped up the money considerably.

Some did as many as ten a day, which says much for their stamina and professionalism, and a fair amount about the status of such acting. To change from one character to another in the space of a few minutes meant either that the parts were all very similar (which of course they were), or that the player could not take them very seriously (also true). Nevertheless many of the leading players stayed in their parts for years, from beginning to bitter end. And the listeners got so used to them they would write in to the actress or actor involved as if she or he *was* the character. To which the production company, keen to maintain the illusion, would respond with a letter and a photograph of the player got up to look like what it was hoped the public thought the character looked like. "Ma Perkins", for example, was pictured as a little old lady with her hair in a bun and steel glasses on her nose, to show she was mature, knowledgeable and wise. The actress who played her for all 27 years of her fictional life, Virginia Payne, went along with this: she even agreed to appear in public dressed as the old biddy, an act of considerable self-sacrifice for an attractive actress. Thus did radio embody its listeners' fantasies.

The production of each soap was as economical as could be. Soulful music was used to introduce and bridge each item, and sound effects were, in these early days, limited virtually to the opening and closing of doors. When Gertrude Berg, creator, writer and leading actress in *The Goldbergs*, wanted Molly Goldberg to fry an egg, she brought in egg and pan and did it herself. That whole richness of sound and effect that the more highbrow radio drama was beginning to explore was too expensive for the soaps. Anything that couldn't be done by the cast themselves was out. Thus the background noises that gave a sense of reality to other plays – the traffic noise, for example, of the gangsters' getaways – was missing on the soaps. From the very beginning they were cheap and lacking in veracity, at least as far as "realism" is concerned. In many cases this is still true.

The soaps nevertheless succeeded in creating a world of their own, based on widely cherished fantasies. And the sponsors nurtured the idea that the characters were real: it made them better selling agents. This can be seen as sinister manipulation, or as a benevolent indulgence of harmless escapism. What cannot be denied is the persuasive and convincing power of the serial form. Something that is relayed up to five times a week, fifty-two weeks a year, gets a pretty firm grip on its audience. But what they were hooked by was the *story*, which provided a sorely needed escape into romance, and the pleasurable tension of wanting to know what would happen next.

It could be claimed that the serials were (and are) used to hoodwink the public into putting its faith in fantasy stereotypes which are dangerously removed from reality. Certainly in their *commercials*, the advertisers assume women to be helplessly house-proud, and incapable of making up their minds without the firm guidance of a man – as personified by the announcers who put the message across in those rich, reliable, manly voices.

But the heroines of these American radio serials did not, as a rule, conform to the stereotypes of the ads. Most of the leading characters were professional women, often busy running a business, and quite capable of taking decisions on their own – except where affairs of the heart were concerned. The woman of the story was in complete contrast to the woman of the commercial. It was this that prevented them becoming propaganda for the product pure and simple – although I would not deny that they were conceived purely as aids to selling. The Hummert agency, for example, was desperate to get its hands on P&G's Oxydol account. *Ma Perkins* – known as "Oxydol's own Ma" – was what did it for them. But then cash has always been a great stimulus to invention.

What the Hummerts, Irna Phillips and their peers did was to invent and refine a *form*, and supply the elements that have sustained it for half a century. The form was the unending story, tailored to the needs of an audience assumed to be doing something else – such as housework – while listening. It could not be assumed that this audience, though faithful, would tune in every day: the story had to be told with enough repetition and recapitulation to allow the fans to catch up easily with anything they might have missed (as well as abolishing any bafflement or bewilderment felt by a new or casual listener).

Gilbert Seldes, the distinguished American critic, called this form "the great invention of radio". He maintained that it was the popular arts like the serials that "create the climate of feeling in which all of us live. The other arts are private and personal, they influence the lives of those who enjoy them; the effect of the public arts cannot be escaped by turning off the radio or television set, by refusing to go to the movies: neither our indifference nor our contempt gives us immunity against them." If you think he was mistaken, try pretending you've never heard of *Dallas* in any public place.

And what, you will ask, of Britain? Indeed, of the rest of the world? There the soap opera slumbered, to be awakened by the trumpets of war.

Meanwhile those starved of narrative tension could be satisfied by turning to the European commercial stations like Radio Luxembourg, to whom the Hummerts had sold several of their shows. The BBC could only stamp a well-shod foot at the activities of these "pirates". The British public, at least, was not entirely satisfied with the "entertainment" output of the Corporation, even though a brand new Variety Department had been set up in 1933. Its first Director, Eric Maschwitz, was accused of "rabid pro-Americanism", though nothing remotely resembling either the serials or the slick comedies that had made

George Burns and Gracie Allen household names ever sullied our pre-war air-waves (not legally, anyhow). The Variety Department was constantly sneered and sniped at, especially by its big sister the Drama Department. Maybe that was why listeners gave ear, in such large numbers, to the output of Radios Normandie and Luxembourg. On Sundays in the late 1930s, when Reith's religious principles ensured that "trivia" was banned altogether, more than 80% of Britain's radio listeners tuned in to foreign stations. Radio Luxembourg's Sunday audience alone was greater than that of the entire national and regional audience of the BBC.

The outbreak of war in Europe saw blatant propaganda break out on the air-waves. With German bombs devastating our major cities, the British were keen to tell the world how well they were "taking it" – and to persuade the Americans to join in the fight against Hitler. It was, indeed, a bombing raid that was responsible for the birth of Britain's very first soap opera (the term was now well established on both sides of the Atlantic). Alan Melville, who had been transferred as script writer from the BBC's Variety Department to the North American Service, which aimed programmes at the USA and Canada, found himself sheltering from a raid under a restaurant table, in the company of a man from the Canadian Broadcasting Corporation. The pair of them hatched the idea of a daily serial that would show "a gallant little London family 'taking it'." Melville came up with the title *Front Line Family*. His bosses gave him six weeks and a severely limited budget to try out the idea. It ran (with a post-war change of title to *The Robinsons*) for almost six years.

Recognizing that the genre was entirely alien to British broadcasting, Melville's superiors obtained for him recordings of American serials, for use as models. Melville listened, and rejected them with horror. To adopt their technique for something "tremendously London, tremendously British, tremendously United Kingdom taking the war" would, he felt, have made the whole thing sound false. Nevertheless, since the serial was aimed primarily at American audiences, there had to be the ingredients they would recognize. There had to be romance, which was provided in the person of the Robinsons' daughter Kay; there had to be action, for which the Robinsons' two sons Dick and Andy were created. Andy served in the Royal Air Force, and was forever being shot down or going missing. There had to be something approaching a bitch (a character the British have never taken to their bosoms): this was the Robinsons' neighbour Mrs Bowker, one of those domineering and complaining women who make everyone else seem wonderful. And there had to be a Mother (not to mention Father – Mr Robinson served quietly in the Home Guard): Helen Robinson, who had a "nice warm

Scots accent" and a very British catch-phrase – "I'd give anything for a nice cup of tea" – that brought crates of the stuff pouring in from generous and well-supplied listeners the world over.

There also had to be a daily cliff-hanger, and to make this sound both familiar and dramatic to North American audiences, the BBC agreed to hire a Canadian to introduce and close each episode ("Will the bomb be a direct hit? Tune in tomorrow!"). This device increased the murmurings within the Corporation about the Americanisms Melville sometimes had to use in order not to baffle his trans-Atlantic audience. His superiors also complained about slapdash production – hardly surprising considering that each fifteen-minute episode was rehearsed and recorded in less than three hours – and about a lack of continuity. Since for the first six months Melville alone wrote, produced, and directed the serial, it is amazing that it had as much consistency as it did. He wrote his scripts three weeks ahead of recording with a lack of gravity the Hummerts would have deplored (Melville was always ready, for example, to write in parts for acting friends of his who were on leave or temporarily jobless – and there were lots of them, since most theatres were closed).

For all the carping, *Front Line Family* was recognized as a valuable contribution to propaganda – and as a popular entertainment that quickly built up a following on the BBC's Overseas Programmes. Although it contained far less of the love-interest that was the mainstay of American serials, its characters were immediately accepted as convincingly real. People wrote from all over the place expressing their appreciation and offering food parcels for the beleaguered characters – something familiar in America, but entirely without precedent in British broadcasting. When Mrs Robinson was made to fall ill, the BBC received a number of threatening telegrams warning them not to let her die – an indication of audience involvement again without precedent. When the serial was dropped from the BBC's Eastern Service, so much protest poured in that it had to be reinstated. British National Films were interested in filming the scripts, an American publisher was mentioned, and the Ministry of Information wanted to do a documentary. Though none of these came to anything, that such a cheap and (by the hierarchy) little regarded programme could arouse such enthusiasm was a tribute to its creator, and to the soap opera form.

The American soaps also responded to the war, with as much alacrity as other branches of the entertainment industry. Despite criticism from certain "experts" that the serials sapped the nation's moral fibre – criticisms that were instantly answered by other "experts" commissioned by the networks (and anyway if Ma Perkins and Helen Trent and Stella Dallas and all the others weren't steeped in moral fibre up to their ear-lobes, who was?) – despite the carping, the creators and sponsors were keen to be seen Doing their Bit. Indeed, even before America's entry into the fighting, Procter & Gamble's head of programming commissioned a serial whose characters warned the world of the menace of Fascism. This was Sandra Michael's *Against the Storm*, and it became the first day-time serial to receive critical approval. John K. Hutchens wrote in the *New York Times* that it was "remarkable for its literate writing, excellent characterization and sensitive concern with political and cultural problems".

Of course it didn't last. *Against the Storm* had characters who were articulate, even poetic, and who openly discussed politics, poetry and art, as well as the everyday gossip of family life. The public liked it for a while – which just shows how discriminating listeners were – and the show won a Peabody Award, in 1942, as "radio's finest drama". But that same year the show was cancelled. P&G were worried about falling listening figures, and tried to persuade Sandra Michael to make the show more like its sisters – in other words, drop all the political guff and concentrate on the domestic drama. She refused, and the only soap to feature writers like Edgar Lee Masters and John Masefield, reading their work to the "students" of the fictional Harper University where the serial was based – and which had booked President Roosevelt to appear in a guest spot, that had to be cancelled when Pearl Harbor was bombed – the soap found itself following the words of its own epigraph: "Against the storm keep thy head bowed/For the greatest storm the world has ever known/Came to an end one sunny morning."

By 1942 no American soap listener could have been unaware that there was a war on. Like the comedians whose routines were filled with references to saving gasoline and buying war bonds, the serials incorporated the war into their background. Ma Perkins' son joined up and was killed in combat. Matinée idol Larry Noble joined the Coast Guard. Ma Goldberg's son Sammy was called up because the actor who played him received his draft papers – and with her insistence on realism, Gertrude Berg insisted on having the departure recorded in Pennsylvania Station, as the troop train left.

It was not just the script writers' patriotic fervour that brought forth such generous helpings of broadcast public spirit. The government recognized the soaps' unique influence, and approached the serials' creators to try and persuade them to include items of war propaganda. Alan Melville was similarly approached by the British government. The writers tried to be obliging within the limits of dramatic credibility. For example the United States War Department was worried about the low esteem in which black soldiers were held. There they were, fighting for democracy in an army that was segregated. Agitation for change was blocked at every level: what was needed was a campaign of persuasion that would also allay the fears of conservative whites who, it was believed, were amongst the most fervent addicts of soap opera.

The Hummerts tried. Helen Trent, heroically stopping a truck full of war goods from falling into an abyss, fell in herself, and was rescued by a black doctor. Helen's gratitude stretched over several weeks, and gave rise to many a discussion of black patriotism, blacks' qualities and capabilities, and their patience in the face of white persecution. Helen repaid her debt by getting the good doctor a job as staff physician in a war factory.

Irna Phillips reported to the Third Regional Conference on Broadcasting that she actually plotted her stories with help from a host of official organizations, from the American Medical Association to the Veterans' Administration. In Britain Alan Melville was not always so ready to swallow the official line – though he did prepare an outline for a "Russian interlude" for *Front Line Family*, aimed at getting across "the ordinary people of Russia to the ordinary people in the States", once the former enemy had become one of the Allies. The Director of the North American Service sounded a warning: "the thing to avoid is boosting Russia in such a way that will give American critics a chance to mock us for turning round and praising this Bolshevik state after knocking it for years". But although the "Russian interlude" never got off the ground, the lengthy memos from various official bodies showed, just as they did in America, how seriously the authorities took the serial's persuasive powers.

Knowing that their first duty was to entertain, the serial writers used the war as they had the Depression, as yet another trial to be undergone and (in the end) triumphed over. Love stories continued to blossom in the unlikeliest places, but tragedy loped by their side. When Ma Perkins lost her son, she could find comfort only in the thought that life went on around her. Death was not made comfortable, for the soaps had always had their fair share of it – more than their fair share, indeed, as those reviewers who chanced upon the form revelled in pointing out. Melodrama, murder and mayhem had always been soap staples, as they were in most romantic fiction. Nobody could call the soap opera world either safe or comfortable. But what always counted (something the casual listener may well have missed) was not the *incident*, but the characters' *reactions* to it. Action was only put in to provoke reaction. Irna Phillips' Young Doctor Malone was sent to England and somehow got commissioned as a British officer. He was despatched to Russia, shot down, and presumed dead. His grief-stricken wife transferred her attentions to a shell-shocked Navy pilot she was nursing back to health. Dr Malone, however, had survived as a prisoner of the Nazis, from whom he finally escaped . . .

The serials had always relied on the most outrageous coincidence to keep their plots going, though in war-time perhaps these looked a little more credible than usual. But there was more than coincidence in the American sponsors' heavy war-time investment in the soaps. Congress had put through an excess-profits tax up of to 90% to prevent profiteering. Rather than give money to the tax-man, the big companies were advised to spend it on advertising. The agencies, always anxious for work, persuaded companies that it was important to keep their products before the public, even if they had few to sell (and sales were confined to the domestic market, with the closure of export markets because of the war). Radio advertising poured into the networks – and was deducted from taxable income. When this loophole was discovered, there were howls of protest. The advertising industry proclaimed its innocence. Weren't the soaps helping to put across the government's message? Was not the great American public being persuaded to perform vital war duties – saving tin cans, using less sugar, adopting a healthier diet, helping with nursing, blacking out windows, writing to soldiers, becoming air-raid wardens, buying war bonds – because they were set an example by Ma Perkins and her ilk? You bet they were. Advertising costs were allowed to be deducted from taxable income. The soaps, and their sponsors, continued to flourish.

There is one other curious fact about the use of soap opera as propaganda. The American Office of War Information, in conjunction with the NBC and CBS networks, decided to put on an *extra* dose of soaps, in addition to those already established. These would have the same characters, but a different announcer and a different plot, specifically related to the problems of the war. The special plot, instead of being developed at the leisurely pace that was the hallmark of the genre, was to be completed over five days – a narrative haste that, to addicts, appeared positively unseemly.

In the autumn of 1942, therefore, fans of NBC soaps like *Ma Perkins* and *Stella Dallas*, and CBS shows like *Our Gal Sunday*, found themselves with *two* weekly sets of plot to deal with. One – the story that had been unfolding for a decade – had the usual narrator and was preceded and followed by sponsors' messages; the other – specifically related to the war – was narrated by Clifton Fadiman, chairman of the War Writers' Board, who ended each programme by reading out government messages.

This experiment lasted less than two months. Its failure must be

ascribed to the understandable confusion of listeners, and to the violence
done to the form by the need to get a specific story over (in both senses)
so quickly. The "message" contained in the *real* soaps (apart from plugs
by the sponsors) was always hinted at, rather than being directly blurted
out. It was allowed to emerge from the speech and behaviour of the
principal characters in a crisis; it was a matter of *personal*, rather than
political, concern. The soaps could not bear too much reality: they
were dragged along by a kite of fantasy, anchored to the lines of
traditional wisdom. And to cram an entire story into a mere week was
too crude for the listeners who were used to the raising of expectations,
the teasing tensions, the rewards and disappointments that were the
genre's specialities.

So soaps as propaganda pure and simple were a failure with the
audience. In part this was due to the clumsiness, and condescension,
of those who understood little of the form and cared nothing for its
conventions. They – the committee men in the Ministries of Information – saw the genre as something to use, or rather abuse, to put
across a specific message. The sponsors were a lot more subtle. Though
their commercials were blatant enough, they did not try to insinuate
them into the stories themselves (or only rarely, in the early days). Nor
were they concerned to hurry things along: anything that kept the
listeners tuned in regularly was fine. This is one reason why it is hard
to imagine the serials being used for overtly political purposes.

One of the criticisms levelled at the form is that it is reactionary.
These critics pay tribute to the persuasive power of the soaps, but some
think this power could and should be used for progressive purposes.
War-time experience, on both sides of the Atlantic, showed such an
attempt failing. Not because – or not entirely because – the writers
concerned weren't skilful enough: both the Hummerts and Irna Phillips
produced masses of outlines and scripts incorporating government
messages, as did Alan Melville for *Front Line Family*. The chief reasons
for failure were that both the conventions of the genre, and the expectations of the listeners, were opposed to politics. In soaps everything
has to be personalized, so that the characters take responsibility for
their own actions. Politics finds the causes in history, and seeks remedy
in social action. Politics concerns the group, while soaps are concerned
with the individual. That is why I don't believe the form can be used
to put across any *specific* political message, whether progressive or
reactionary.

In a single decade, the conventions governing the soap formula had
become well established. Even Melville, while rejecting American

models, was influenced by what they sounded like and what they contained. Now if you believe in the conspiracy theory of history, you will believe that these conventions were planned and arrived at by a sinister group of people, who were trying to brainwash the public not only into buying more goods, but into accepting the ethic of the society that produced these goods – capitalism. But I do not believe in the conspiracy theory. I think the conventions were arrived at through chance, born of a scramble to fill time and grab audiences, and they stayed because they worked. For all the serials that lasted the decade and beyond, there were scores more that fell on unappreciative ears. Some failed because they were poorly written, some had characters no one could believe in: since all adhered to more or less the same formula, popularity obviously rested on the personal tastes of the audience, and on whether the show was well or badly done. The formula was arrived at through trial and error, more by accident than design.

Speed was of course essential when there was all that air-time to fill. As with any new opportunity, it was important to get something on, to grab the sponsors' and listeners' interest before anyone else did. The details could be worked out later: what mattered was getting the idea across as simply as possible. So the early soaps were simply romantic stories stretched into infinity. And because production was cheap, new ideas could be tried (if they were cheap too), and just as easily dropped if they failed. There was, in the 1930s, still the excitement of being innovators on radio (with television round the corner). The dozens of soaps available on American radio were, each one of them, a testament to some writer's ingenuity.

There was too much hurry – to get things on, and to make money – for there to be time to conspire to brainwash the public into accepting one form of morality over another. The traditional moral values which, on the very first page of this book, I defined the soaps as supporting, just happen to be the easiest and most available to writers in a hurry. That body of collective wisdom built up over generations – the prov- erbial wisdom of everyday experience – is not only the longest-lasting, but also the most accessible form of philosophy. Everybody has grown up with it, everybody recognizes it, even if they don't accept all of it. The writers and producers of the soaps were no exception: in their rush to get something together, and keep it going, something both acceptable and popular, they grabbed at the wisdom they and their audience knew so well, because it was there, because it was easy, because it was something everyone could swallow without effort, because – being based on "good sense" – it was something they could justify, if anyone asked them.

Because something has lasted a long time doesn't necessarily mean it's any good. To take refuge, as the soap writers did – and do – in what is easy, isn't necessarily honourable either. Many writers and artists pride themselves on questioning the assumptions of their society: on the whole (there are notable exceptions) soap writers do not.

I can put forward several explanations for this. The first is that the audiences do not look to the soaps for intellectual stimulation, but for escape and entertainment. Intellectual massage they can get elsewhere.

The second is, that during a Depression (then as now), political challenges seem to come from the extremes. Those in the middle ground – where the soaps were and are firmly encamped – are bogged down and bewildered, their "experts" discredited. Their only solution seems to be to muddle through, to rely on "common sense", which is itself grounded in traditional beliefs and loyalties. The only certainties are those that are so engrained they are uncontroversial. In bad times, everyone needs such certainties, and traditional morality is a never-ending supplier of them.

A third explanation is that bad times reveal the weaknesses of all prophets. They turn out to be as wrong as everyone else. The real suffering caused by poverty, unemployment and the ultimate threat of war makes the predictions of the philosophers – whether Marx, Freud, Barthes or the loonies of the Right – look pathetic, irrelevant, outdated. Shrivelled by contact with reality, they turn out not to be eternal truths, but the products of a mind tied to a particular period, and background, and personality. If, in my view, a Depression does little else, it shines a spotlight on humbug.

Traditional morality, proverbial wisdom, does not of course provide much help in finding a new way forward. On the contrary, it is essentially backward-looking. Revolutionaries of whatever stripe blame this conservatism for everything – but these same revolutionaries are always astonished by the failure of the masses, when suffering, to act on radical ideas. A Depression always involves a giant step backwards – in living standards, as well as in political attitudes – after which any progress (like the New Deal) appears positively salvationary. Traditional wisdom, with its roots in nostalgic times of innocence and apparent prosperity, seems to flourish more in bad times than in good. Which is another reason why the soaps were so successful in peddling it; not simply because the serial makers were dyed-in-the-head conservatives, or that their masters (whether sponsors or committee men) were concerned to stamp out any flickers of radicalism. Soaps were and are a commercial product of a capitalist society whose interests lay in promoting consumption of commercial products. It would be naive to think that their message would be anti-capitalist – but equally naive to think that this message was the product of a sinister and reactionary conspiracy. Naive, because that displays an ignorance of the pressures on the soaps to take the shortest cut to popular acceptance – and because it also shows an ignorance of how very popular traditional morality is, and why this should be so.

And what is traditional morality? It is the puritan ethic militant and triumphant. Goodness is defined by adherence to Biblical precepts. It will always triumph over evil, in the end. It involves devotion to duty (including rotten husband, snotty children, tedious household chores, dependent relatives) and sacrifice – endless sacrifice. The Higher Call of Love can only be answered with a marriage contract: anything less is bound to end in tears. Sex outside marriage is wrong, and will invariably lead to madness, blindness and probably violent death. Anyone who questions devotion to duty is severely lacking in moral fibre, which keeps one regular. Traditional morality is founded on the trinity of Love, Family and Domestic Property. Of these, the last is undoubtedly the greatest.

Having said that, let me add that there were other certainties that the soaps provided. There was certainty of regular listening, a routine needed more than ever in time of war. There was certainty that everything would be explained: not for the soaps any fashionable theories of ellipsis or symbolic allusion: everyone is told everything, and more than once. There was the certainty of a happy ending, at least for the deserving, though this ending could be indefinitely postponed. There was the certainty of action, romance, melodrama (a form that has never lost its popularity) – and a consistency in plotting and characterization, so that whatever happened (and plenty did), it would be in line with what the audience knew of the serial's background. If it wasn't, the listeners would write in to complain, in their thousands. People out there noticed everything that was going on. From the form's earliest days, the public took a proprietary interest in every detail. Their comments played a more important part in future plotting and plans than in any other popular genre. It was, and remains, a partnership peculiar to soap opera: one founded on the certainties it embodies.

The serial world was unreal in at least two respects: money was rarely a major problem to its chief characters, and good always triumphed. But as I have said, "reality" was not the chief concern of the creators of the serials. It was at best a background – one that changed with the times – against which listeners' fantasies were projected. Radio, is, of course, the perfect medium for fantasy, since it allows so much room for the listener's imagination to do its own conjuring. The letters from listeners with which the producers were inundated shows how imaginatively they responded to the stimuli the soaps provided.

What people escape to is a comment on what they are escaping from. Serial listeners lived in a world where raising a family could be physically exhausting, mentally draining, emotionally unrewarding and politically uncertain. They might have fled to an imaginary land eternal happy-ever-afters – but instead they chose a place (or a number of places: most addicts listened to more than one serial when they got the chance) not too unlike their own (and not too like, either). The same goals – love, marriage, house, and family – brought the same problems and disappointments; the same morality brought the same lack of fulfilment. What was attractive was the glamour – either of a romance, or of the setting.

Glamour was something post-war consumers seemed to need more than ever. It was, of course, the glamour of the old rather than the new. The war shook up so many expectations that an escape into the past was inevitable, at least in soap opera. The old favourites enjoyed a new popularity in peace-time, on both sides of the Atlantic.

If the post-war American soaps followed majority opinion in presenting a world little changed by victory, that is partly because the American political system put great emphasis on continuity. President Truman wanted to show himself as great a statesman as Roosevelt. That meant acting tough, in the time-honoured manner of the American hero, and standing up for tradition. In that, at least, the soaps echoed him.

In Britain, by contrast, a new Labour government had promised a radical break with the past. This aroused the kind of expectation and excitement (or gloom, depending on your convictions) that the New Deal had once stirred up. And although the BBC was not controlled (in party political terms) by the government, even it could not avoid – and would not want to avoid – reflecting the prevailing mood. The challenges and problems of living through the creation of the Welfare State were, it was hoped, to come through the daily serial which, in 1948, replaced *The Robinsons* (the post-war title for *Front Line Family*): *Mrs Dale's Diary*.

The Robinsons were taken off the air, despite strong audience objections and a good "rating", because it was felt the serial was getting stale. In fact the Director of Drama, Val Gielgud, had long been gunning for it. He hated his department being associated with a programme whose production standards were, he felt, so low. As the man who founded the BBC's celebrated Repertory Company, he had the curious notion that serial actors, once they felt themselves indispensable, would operate a "most dangerous sort of petty racket", and end up demanding salaries as great as those paid to "the best people in our Repertory"! He labelled serial actors as third-rate ("no-one above that would accept an engagement of this kind"), and he also had a horror of the form itself, which he described as "deliberately constructed to hit the very centre of the domestic hearth by playing variations upon the theme of all kinds of domestic trivia", which was "bound to achieve a quite unreasonable influence", and (which was worst of all) would "provoke quite irrational criticism in proportion".

This attitude was, and remains, typical where popular drama is concerned, of many within the BBC. Personal taste is one thing, but to apply such prejudice to an entire form is an indication of blind spots, which could well black out many other forms of drama.

Gielgud was nevertheless persuaded to give house room to at least one serial. This was *Mrs Dale's Diary* – though even the original script writers (Jonquil Antony and Ted Willis: a very different pair of writers in background and attitude) were not clear on the differences between it and *The Robinsons*. They pointed out that if the new serial was to appeal to the same audience as had *The Robinsons*, it would have to deal with family problems and with rationing – which had not only provided *The Robinsons* with their most popular scripts, but which no contemporary writer could avoid, "since they are so much a part of the life of any British family and housewife".

The BBC took a serious view of its social responsibilities (it was, remember, still a broadcasting monopoly – there was no challenge from commercial stations, at least not in mainland Britain, and television was still an expensive toy). A document headed "Editorial Policy" from the second year of *Mrs Dale*'s life (she first opened her Diary, to that rippling harp effect, on 5 January 1948) began:

> This serial has a simple object: to hold a mirror to the everyday life of a normal, middle-class family. It is not a soap-opera of the kind which abounds in American day-time radio and is therefore not subject to the restrictive rules and practices of sponsors and their agents. The family members can and should have faults in their behaviour and their characters, although the mistakes they make should obviously be errors of omission rather than commission.

(I take this last point to mean that there should be no extra-marital sex.)

"Social justice," the document continued, "need not necessarily prevail. Womanhood does not have to be demonstrated invariably as the dominant sex and the source of all human virtues. In other words, *Mrs Dale's Diary* should strive to achieve a realism which is specifically withheld from its American counterparts."

But this ringing declaration of the superiority of British radio writing was immediately undercut in the document's next paragraph.

It is the role of the Dale family to act as the representatives of the society we have selected to portray. They are permanent characters and must, therefore, in a dramatic sense, be regarded as symbols. Consequently, unlike their friends, acquaintances, and enemies, they must be denied the privileges of growing older and wiser. They cannot be married: to permit them to do so would mean the loss of one useful permanent character or the addition of one more and this in turn would create an embarrassing rigidity, since the number of permanent characters (6) is regarded as the absolute maximum. They cannot be divorced, have offspring or even die. From time to time they may attempt to break the bonds which hold them to their environment. They may try to increase their wisdom. But in the long run they must remain mentally, physically, and spiritually intact – the same people, in the same stage of development, tied to the same background, inhibited by the same hopes and fears with which they were introduced.

If that was the BBC's idea of not subjecting a serial to "restrictive rules and practices", I tremble to think what they must do when they *really* exert control. In fact, the *Dales* document is a statement of all the ingredients of a classic soap opera. Which is precisely what the *Diary* was. And very popular too – though not with the Drama Department, who refused to do more than tolerate it from a great height, nor with all its writers and would-be writers. Ted Willis got so fed up with trying to play down middle-class attitudes and inject a little working-class reality into his scripts, that he jocularly included with one batch an incident in which the entire Dale family was killed in a charabanc crash. He was fired. Writers of the calibre of Doris Lessing and Olivia Manning, both of whom applied to write for the show (the money was good, even by BBC standards), were turned down as "unsuitable" – though Tom Stoppard got to write a few scripts in the programme's later years.

The uncomfortable fact was that, far from achieving that "realism which is specifically withheld from its American counterparts", *Mrs Dale's Diary* proved most popular when it left all the problems of post-war Britain, and examined at inordinate length the domestic and romantic – especially the romantic – problems of the Dale family. Mrs Dale had a tendency to be nice to gentlemen who turned out to fancy her. Her daughter Gwen had, in the early days, a most convoluted love-life. Her son Bob couldn't settle down. Even when the family moved out of London into the calm of the country – the equivalent of the American small town setting—the ratings rose when these problems worsened. Of the revolution taking place in medical care with the formation of the National Health Service, little was heard. Dr Dale was always rushed off his feet, so naturally Mrs Dale had to cope: the programme's most famous catchphrase was her "I'm worried about Jim". Professional concerns were instantly domesticated: that was the secret of the show's success.

But there was one British soap opera that began with an overtly educational aim, and which is still running more than thirty years later: *The Archers*. Created by Godfrey Baseley, who was producing agricultural programmes for the BBC in the Midlands, its aim was to catch farmers' attention with "an everyday story of country folk", and then indoctrinate them with information on the latest farming methods. There was a desperate need to increase agricultural efficiency and food production in post-war Britain, and Mr Baseley put forward the idea of a "farming *Dick Barton*" – the Special Agent who was a boyhood hero of mine, but whom I cannot, unfortunately, drag in here – to help the modernization campaign. Baseley roped in two writers who were responsible for *Dick Barton*, Edward J. Mason and Geoffrey Webb, and they were so successful that *The Archers* actually replaced the peerless Special Agent within three months of its first broadcast (which was in January 1951).

Baseley and his team stuck closely to the conventions of soap opera. There were the mother and father figures (Doris and Dan Archer), the young lovers (their son Philip and his girl-friend, Grace, whom he later married), the eccentric (Walter Gabriel, a neighbouring farmer who was "agin'" anything new), and a character who did little but interfere and grumble (Mrs P, mother-in-law of the Archers' eldest son Jack). Onto the domestic dramas in which these stereotypes were embroiled the writers grafted information fed them directly by the Ministry of Agriculture: the facts, say, about foot-and-mouth disease or artificial insemination, or the benefits of Friesian dairy cattle over shorthorns. And the audience loved it all: at its peak, one in three of the adult population tuned in every day.

The success of *The Archers* in combining the suspense of daily domestic drama and the facts about farming matters raises the question of whether other soaps could have done the same. Why couldn't *The Dales* have kept the public informed about new medical techniques, as well as entertaining it with Mrs Dale's latest suitor? Why, in America, didn't the serials ease into their tortuous plots the concerns that exercised thinking people – the "Red-baiting" of Senator Joe McCarthy, the war in Korea, the atomic bomb, the research into infantile paralysis? (On McCarthyism, I have to say that, although the serials failed to use their power to spread a little light during a dark period – a period when men and women, especially in the entertainment industry, were condemned as moral lepers by mere innuendo and malicious invention – at least they did not add to the sulphur in the air. No Reds were found under Helen Trent's bed, nor was Ma Perkins branded as a communist for uttering sentiments Thomas Jefferson would have been proud of. If the decent, humane, tolerant, and neighbourly generosity of Ma and her peers was not active in the cause of reason during the 1950s, nor was it active in the cause of unreason. And, let's face it, how many decent, humane, tolerant, neighbourly and generous people stood up for those smeared by the blacklists, in those poisonous times?)

I'd say there were three reasons for this failure of other soaps to be both educational and entertaining. First, that unless politics are personalized, the soaps can't handle them. Second, they led public opinion from behind (which is why they were so popular). And third, *The Archers* could only manage because it operated within a very narrow range of concern. Agriculture was a subject which most people were very ignorant about, though they combined this ignorance with a sentimental "feeling for the land". In farming, life and work, public and private, are very closely linked – more so than in most professions. This link meant that the writers of *The Archers* could slide between work and play without straining credibility. And they also started as they meant to go on, remaining consistent in their double purpose. Consistency, as I have said, is essential to the success of soap opera. You cannot expect a flowering of social concern unless the seeds have been planted at the right season and kept well fertilized.

The first public television service in the world began in Britain, in 1936. The first TV drama production took place in America in the autumn of 1928: it was a melodrama called *The Queen's Messenger*. The BBC's first televised play, by contrast, in 1930, was Pirandello's *The Man with a Flower in his Mouth*.

The pre-war British television audience was so small that its members would have made up a modest party in Alexandra Palace, where the first studios were. They were offered a large number of plays (in 1937 there were 123 drama productions, including repeats), but I need hardly say that soap opera did not get a look in. Nor did it in America, where pre-war programmes consisted of comedians (*Amos 'n' Andy*, of course), singers, jugglers, celebrity appearances and sport.

Television services were suspended on both sides of the Atlantic during the war, but once hostilities ended, the consumer boom began, especially in America. RCA was selling black-and-white sets in 1946, and the same year demonstrated a colour system which, however crude, was compatible with their monochrome. By 1952 fifteen million American homes had television sets, and by the middle of the decade six million Britons could make the same boast. They were, of course, offered limited hours and a limited choice. The new medium was expensive and cumbersome. But its future was not for a moment in doubt.

The main reason, though, why soaps were slow to hit television was cost. It is one thing to contract a bunch of actors and actresses to make regular appearances in front of a microphone, but the prospect of having to pay, not only for the players and writers, but also for the camera, sound and lighting men, the designers and their sets, the director and his assistants (they were all men then, of course), the make-up and the costumes – all that tying up of space and capital was extremely daunting. Especially when the radio habit of listening and working at the same time was deeply engrained, and nobody knew how many people would actually want to sit down in front of their sets, on their own, and give up fifteen minutes of their time. Wouldn't that make them feel guilty?

In the States there was a one-day experiment in 1946, when they televised a single portion of the radio soap *Big Sister*. The next year there was an attempt at a continuing day-time television serial from Chicago (where so many radio soaps had started): *These Are Our Children*. It failed. It was 1950 before the first networked soap hit the screens. Sponsored by Procter & Gamble, put out by CBS, this was *The First Hundred Years* in the marriage of Connie and Chris Thayer, young newly-weds. It just struggled past its first anniversary before being axed. Between 1950 and 1960 forty-one television soaps went into production. A mere six survived the decade – and of those, four are still with us (*The Guiding Light, Search for Tomorrow, As the World Turns* and *The Edge of the Night* – which last is the nearest the genre comes to the thriller).

Though some of the old radio soaps were given a run on American television, most of them didn't work. Though the ingredients were the same for both media, the rhythms of writing, delivery, and direction were very different. And, of course, the picture imagined by a radio listener of an actress in a favourite role might be distinctly out of focus with the televised reality. Just as talkies ended the career of many a good-looking but ill-sounding actor and actress, so television was a threat to those stars who sounded better than they looked.

But the real reason for the decline of radio soaps was the decline of the radio audience, in favour of television. Fewer listeners meant lower advertising rates, which in turn meant that, for the sponsors, the soaps no longer seemed such a good proposition. Their costs remained fixed – all those salaries had to be paid – but there was less profit in it. In 1957 the American Broadcasting Company (ABC) dropped all its radio soaps. By 1960 the National Broadcasting Company (NBC) had also chickened out. Only Columbia Broadcasting System (CBS) kept the radio flag flying, with 6 soaps in 1960, all owned by sponsors who were dying to get rid of them. Rather than go without – each "death" prompted such howls of agony from the fans that the network was convinced the form was worth saving – CBS leased the soaps from Procter & Gamble and other owners, and paid them royalties. They sought new sponsors, breaking the identification that a particular sponsor had with a particular serial. (Television has continued this process: though firms like P&G own several serials, the networks sell advertising space to other sponsors as well.) But even that didn't work. In 1940 there had been no less than 75 hours of soaps available on American radio. Within twenty years, this had come down to one and a half hours, all of them confined to CBS.

An attempt was made to revitalize the genre by dramatizing popular novels under the title *Best Seller*. The Hummerts had done this very successfully as their last fling in the 1940s, starting with the adaptation of popular movies, and ending with a ten-month run of Theodore Dreiser's *An American Tragedy*. It was a formula television has adapted very successfully in our own times. But for CBS radio, in 1960, it was not enough to save soap. The network's affiliated stations wanted to drop them, and use the air-time for local programmes and sales-pitches. In the summer of 1960 CBS announced to a shrunken but grieving public that all their radio serials would come to an end on the last Friday in November.

Of course this posed a problem that had rarely occurred: how, finally, to deliver that happy ending that had been so long delayed. The CBS Press Department released the four concluding story-lines for *The Right to Happiness*, *Ma Perkins*, *Young Dr Malone* and *The Second Mrs Burton*. *The Right to Happiness*, a spin-off from Irna Phillips' *Guiding Light*, ended thus:

Now that Dick Braden has been paroled from prison and his parents have become reconciled, the Braden family is united again. Grace has assured Skip that he is the only boy in her life, and Lee's court case has come to a satisfactory close, even though the missing witness has not been found. Carolyn and Lee now face the future with assurance, the events of the past few weeks having brought them closer than ever before.

Ma Perkins' finale was briefer:

Charlie Lindstrom has accepted a job in the East. He and Mary are taking leave of Ma Perkins and Rushville Center. On Thanksgiving Day, the entire family is gathered at Ma's house. Ma Perkins herself sees happiness ahead, primarily because Anushka and her grandson, Junior, will be married next month.

You will notice that these endings are not so final that the serial could not be started up again if the call came. And of course a few – such as *Young Dr Malone* – had found new life on television, where they continued to run long after their radio ancestors had been laid to rest. Even Ma Perkins herself ended her last appearance – the 7065th – with the call to "write to me, and I'll try to answer you."

The techniques of television may differ completely from radio's, but the soap formula was exactly the same. The domestic concerns of small-town families, the drama of their hopes and despair: these were played out in fifteen-minute episodes, as they were on radio. The sets were kept to a minimum, on grounds of cost and space; the actors and actresses had to be careful not to move their heads too violently, since they were often filmed against a narrow backcloth, and if they went too far, the camera would show the bare walls on either side. Camera shots were extremely limited, and writers had to avoid as often as possible making players appear in consecutive scenes, since rushing around the studio dodging cameras and cables, not to mention changing clothes and make-up, made this a very dangerous business.

Of course these shows went out live, like their radio counterparts, and – again like them – they relied heavily on the "let's have a cup of coffee and catch up on some gossip" routine for a cheap and simple way of filling in new viewers. The pace was extremely slow – slower even than American radio. This was to fill in time, and because nobody knew what subtleties television was capable of. The lingering close-up of a look of horror, bewilderment or melting tenderness was a favourite device for ending a scene on a note of cliff-hanging tension (it still is). This gave added authority to the rule that soap opera is more about reaction than action.

In Britain it was the challenge from commercial television that really persuaded the BBC to give soap opera a try – after it had successfully stolen the publicity from the launch of the rival television service by having Grace Archer die in a fire minutes before the new channel opened (in September 1955). True, BBC TV had a weekly family serial, *The Groves*, in the mid-1950s, but it was not until Granada began *Coronation Street* in December 1960 that the BBC responded with a twice-weekly serial set in a magazine office, *Compact* (written by Hazel Adair and Peter Ling, who later started ATV'S *Crossroads*). The earliest medical soap was ATV'S *Emergency Ward 10*, which ran twice a week from 1957 until the mid-1960s. The BBC countered with two serials that ran on alternate nights of the week – the only time they committed themselves to continuous serials. These were *United* (1965-7), about a football club, and *The Newcomers* (1965-9), which centred on a family who had moved into a new town.

Why has British television never had a daily soap, as there was (and still is) on radio? And why has the BBC, since dropping *The Newcomers*, not committed itself to a continuous serial, like its commercial rivals?

To the first question, the answers are cost, and a great fear of lowering standards. A daily television soap requires a very large team, especially if it lasts half an hour (which soon became the standard time in England and America, where Irna Phillips led the way. Of course that only meant between 20 and 25 minutes of drama, since the rest was taken up by commercials. Maybe that's why the BBC favoured, and still favours, 20 minutes for some of its serials. An hour became the American norm in the 1970s). Long gone were the days when someone like Gertrude Berg could write, act, and direct a daily dose all by herself. Teams of writers were needed, as well as several directors and great numbers of technicians. Television is more demanding than radio – there is more to go wrong, and everything costs more, especially studio time and space – and a daily serial would need an enormous investment of capital to make it work. The committees who run the television companies have always been reluctant to spend more, especially if it cannot be proved that bigger audiences will result. And although there has always been a loyal daily audience for radio serials (when *Waggoners' Walk*, which succeeded *Mrs Dale's Diary* in 1969, was axed on grounds of cost in 1980, the BBC received more letters of protest than on any other subject), it was felt that British viewers were adequately served with a twice- or thrice-weekly portion of television soap (*Crossroads* originally went out four times a week, but the Independent Broadcasting Authority made ATV reduce output to three times a week in 1980).

A jealous regard for the high standards of British television is also behind the decision not to splash out daily. Those few who have seen, and the many more who have heard about, American day-time soaps have a low opinion of their production values. It is felt that they are too hastily slapped together, that the pressure to record some thirty minutes (or more) of television in a single day, five days a week, results in slapdash writing, wooden acting and careless direction.

There is a lot of truth in this, though I have to say that the production standards of the British serials are not noticeably higher than their American sisters. The most obvious difference is in pace: a story told over two or three days does not have to drag itself out in the way a five-times-weekly does, with the result that things happen at a speed which is more naturalistic than the tortoise crawl of American serials. But the pressure is still greater on the British soaps than on any other form of television drama, and the strains show. Not that the fans mind. The essential thing is the continuing narrative and, as long as the viewing public has its curiosity constantly whetted, it will take (or serial addicts will) any amount of banal verbiage or actors causing the set to fall down. Or almost.

As to the second question, why the BBC doesn't have a continuous serial, the answer again, I believe, lies in cost, and attitude. Since the Corporation still depends purely on its licence money, and continues to offer a wider variety of programmes than its commercially-funded rivals, it has to be careful about tying up the large sums of money and scarce studio space a continuous serial would need.

But basically it seems to come back to the Reithian principle of leading rather than being led. It is the urge for self-improvement that is at the root of the guilt many feel at watching soap operas which, however uplifting, are more escapist than educational. The BBC has as great a need of large audiences as anyone, but its traditions dictate that it strive to extend their horizons, rather than letting their eyes and brains glaze over through endless gazing at one familiar sight. That, at least, is the principle: why else would they ignore a form that, however expensive, is still cheaper per programme than any other type of drama, and which – if it is any good at all – never fails to build large and faithful audiences?

Of course the Corporation is delighted to buy in a soap like *Dallas* which, although not continuous like *The Archers* nor appearing more than once a week, has brought a new (and very expensive) glamour to the hallowed soap formula. But *Dallas* and its imitators are made in series – that is, blocks of so many programmes, with large gaps in between each block. The makers may say this is to keep standards up, but it is also on grounds of cost: both reasons the BBC well understands, and is willing to defend. Enormously popular though *Dallas* has been, it could be considered more of a trendy cult than an addictive soap. And the BBC has always wanted to be a trend-setter.

2

THE CHARACTERS:SAINTS, SUFFERERS, AND SINNERS

You know them – or you think you do – as soon as they slide across your screen. The decent husband with a fatal weakness (girls, booze or a passion so blinding he can no longer tell right from wrong). The scheming bitch who does her damnedest to cheat him, or his already mixed-up children, out of his or their rightful inheritance. The long-suffering wife whose love shines through the ordure everybody dumps on her. The "king" or "queen" whose wealth, power, or experience puts them outside conventional morality, and who is the target of every man's envy and (if male) most maidens' desire. The romantic hero who, despite making wrong decisions at crucial times, ends up with the right girl. The innocent heroine, forever endangered by the wrong man. The ruthless villain greedy for anything in skirts or folded into a wallet.

These are the stereotypes of folk myth and soap opera. You may never find out what these characters think about the great issues of our time, but they will always react to given (even preposterous) circumstances exactly as you would expect. The decent husband (Jeff Colby in *Dynasty*, David Hunter in *Crossroads*, Bobby Ewing in *Dallas*) will wrestle with his weakness, succumb, repent, confess – and begin all over again. The bitch (not a character who features so prominently in English soaps as in the American serials, who abound in this type) will bring the family to the brink of total disaster, only to be thwarted at the very last moment. The devoted wife (Rita Fairclough in *Coronation Street*, Krystle Carrington in *Dynasty*) will survive poisonous gossip, social ostracism, adultery, abortion, argument and amnesia (in various combinations) to retain the love of her husband. The "king" or "queen" (Jock Ewing in *Dallas*, *Another World*'s Mac Cory, *Coronation Street*'s Annie Walker) will fight off attempts at usurpation, financial annihilation, assassination, blackmail, entrapment and fraud, to rise triumphant and assert his or her divine invulnerability (only the death of

Jim Davis, the actor playing Jock Ewing, prevented the character's immediate renaissance). So it is with the rest: they behave with welcome predictability. Their ability to astonish resembles that of the marshmallow: a small surprise contained inside the mouth that leaves a sticky residue.

The reason for this predictability – which in any other art form would be ascribed to a dismal lack of invention – is that soap fulfils the function of folk myth: it deals with the victory of old-fashioned and traditional certainties over the evanescent fashions that assail them. As in fairy stories or the dramas of the ancient Greeks, the plot can be complete nonsense, as long as the good guys beat the bad. The characters must be immediately recognizable as symbols of a certain type of action and reaction – but also sufficiently human (i.e. both fallible and perverse) to encourage audience identification. Just as Hänsel saves himself from being insufferably perfect by insisting – when turned into a fawn by the witch – on following the hunt, so the frailties of Miss Ellie, the pillar on which *Dallas* is built, make her not only a better person in moral terms, but a whole lot more human and hence more sympathetic. Like Hänsel, her tiny strayings beyond the bounds of good sense only mean that she bounces back better in the end. This is not inconsistency – which is unthinkable, save for a clumsy change of writers – but the reinforcement of the stereotype: goodness improved by trial.

There is, of course, a danger in trying to stuff the numerous and diverse characters that people the soaps into the sausage skins on which I have inked the names of various stereotypes. No writer of or about soaps would deny that these types exist: the point at which they would quarrel with me is just where I stuff whom. Of the characters I have mentioned, is David Hunter fairly typed as "decent husband", or wouldn't he fit more easily into the romantic (if ageing) hero? Is Krystle Carrington a devoted wife or an innocent heroine? Is Annie Walker a queen or a bitch? Every viewer will have her or his own opinion: what I hope to do is, not to come up with definitive answers, but to suggest ways of looking at these characters that might help to explain why they are so enormously popular.

First, the decent husband. Usually married when the serial begins, implying that no other state was either possible or desirable for him: a man more troubled by his wife or his parents than by the sirens of his world. He turns to the other ladies, if at all, not so much from lust as desperation. This desperation is born from his failure to live up to his family's expectations of him as a perfect son/husband/father. He is a man with little sense of self, whose chief ambition is honourably to fulfil his obligations. Someone who will never inspire or be inspired, but whose doggedness arouses an answering devotion. A person who breathes in what is right and blows out what is wrong – but who, thank goodness, can occasionally catch something of a cold. Which, being translated, means he may be driven to drink, flirt, fiddle his expenses or even – horrors! – lie, falsify evidence or commit some (minor) crime in order to safeguard or advance the welfare of his loved ones. (A minor crime is one you want the hero to get away with.)

I think I am safe in saying that every single soap opera, day-time, prime-time, daily or weekly, features at least one example of this type. What saves such a character from being tedious beyond belief? What, indeed, makes him attractive to so large a part of the audience?

First, that he appears to like, or at least behave well towards, women, both inside and outside his family. This is an extremely rare quality in men, both real and fictional.

Second, that though he may stagger under the burdens society has laid upon him – which are basically those of the Ten Commandments – he will do his utmost to shoulder the lot, while most of us try surreptitiously to drop the ones we think won't be noticed. He will look after his wife with unrequited tenderness when she is ill or mad, he will continue to offer his children love when they bulldoze their way through adolescence, he will care for his cantankerous father and intolerable mother– and he will resist, most of the time, the advances of glamorous young ladies. In a world where duty is often – is usually – ducked, such devotion is extraordinary.

Third, he is successful at the hardest, dullest and least rewarding (because most familiar) task of all: providing the official goal of the middle classes – security. Not financial security, I hasten to say – any soap fan knows that something as vulgar as poverty rarely darkens their screen (we are dealing with myth – did Oedipus ever worry about who was going to pay the servants?) – but emotional security, of the kind that allows a son to admit he was wrong, a daughter to nuzzle her father's lapels in recognition of his rock-like dependability, a mother to shed a tear of pride, a wife's eyes to shine when she hears his key in the latch. All this after maybe fifteen years of marriage?

Yes, the decent husband is a success all right – and the funny thing is when you're watching him, as opposed to reading about him as you have just done, you *want* him to succeed, you *want* him to win through, you *will* him to triumph. Now I belong, as do my readers, to a viewing public more sophisticated, sceptical, scornful and selective than any yet known. How can I convey to you the willingness with which I suspend disbelief, and demand a happy outcome for someone

I would cross the room to avoid at a cocktail party?

There is the look of the man. Decent husbands are tall, clean, well groomed (even *Coronation Street*'s Bert Tilsley was never grubby), and possess, not so much sexuality as openness, a friendly charm combined with a hint of exhaustion – not of desperation, but an expression (a cloud that crosses the otherwise limpid eyes) that makes one aware of the pressures, and the resolve to resist them. This is very different from the sexual potency or vulnerability that make male characters attractive. The decent husband has the rumpled look of experience, which makes him reliable; the innocence that makes you ready to share his troubles; the suggestion of weariness that makes you want to punch him on the shoulder and say "Keep up the good work". He also has a beautiful wife, a lovely home, the sort of children you wouldn't mind having your daughter marry, and parents who mostly want to crush his balls. It is not hard to understand a man like that.

You also know very little of his history: somehow the decent husband sprang fully formed from the bed of his marriage. He was never a child, never passed through the agonies of adolescence, never fumbled with his first girl, never worried about getting a job, a wife or a mortgage. He has *always* been married, reliable, besieged but secure: you don't see him grow, you watch him squirm. Oddly enough, this personality without shadows, this existence only in the present, this clean-slated past and unwavering future, make him easier to root for – and easier to neglect. One of the astonishing things about watching soap operas is how quickly you accept their conventions. Once you succumb – and that takes time, which is one thing the genre has a-plenty – it is like entrusting yourself to an aeroplane or railway train: their arrangements become yours. While you can choose whom to talk to amongst your fellow passengers, in all other matters you abide by the company rules and schedules.

It is the same for children being told a fairy tale: they know as if by instinct – or is this something we adults consciously or subconsciously shape? – who is to be rewarded and who punished. It takes a perverse child (or viewer) actually to want the wicked witch to triumph, just as it would be a perverse soap fan (perhaps a reviewer) who didn't want the decent husband to win through. Because he is such a simple figure, you can spot him a mile off. You know what he stands for, you are comfortable in his presence, your responses are quite uncomplicated. There he is, poor fellow, standing in the bright sun without a parasol, absorbing the heat for all of us. You rattle by, willing him to stick it out, amused but not involved. He is a small hill in the foreground of a more challenging landscape: you look beyond, but you'd miss him if he weren't there.

People come to the soaps primarily to be entertained, and those who deliver the goods are in the entertainment business: they do not consider themselves to be manipulators of the moral or cultural attitudes of the masses, but are there to give the public what it wants, nothing less, maybe a little more. Does public approval of the decent husband therefore mean that such a character is everyone's ideal? By no means. I suggest that it is the *whole structure* of soap opera that appeals to the public – that it is the conflict and progress of the characters that hold their interest – and that the decent husband appeals because he is an integral part of the whole. Without the decent husband there would be no role for the bitch, the villain, the mixed-up child. He is, in a sense, the pole around which the rest of the tent is arranged – and though he is forced to remain forever upright, there are plenty of occasions on which he bends a little.

Take Bobby Ewing. Although one of *Dallas*'s super-rich, money could not solve any of his most pressing problems. (Money doesn't solve anything in the soaps: if anything, it gets you to hell quicker.) He had, when his father was alive, terrible problems living up to the latter's expectations, and proved incapable of running the family business in the ruthless manner expected of a Ewing. He was closer to his mother, though living in the same house with her and his father's ghost (not to mention the rest of the family) put a permanent furrow in his otherwise unblemished brow. He was the family peace-maker, and none too successful at that – though he never gave up trying, despite provocation from the rest, especially his elder brother J. R., that would have driven any other red-blooded Texan straight to the nearest whorehouse. His worst problem, however, was his wife Pam who, though strong, was as brittle as peanut crunch. Unable to conceive a baby, she had to be institutionalized to prevent her from killing herself. Even the shrink couldn't persuade her that she was a whole woman despite not being a mother. So Bobby went to the heart of the problem (thus revealing the severe limitations of psychotherapy: a brave indictment in a country addicted to such treatment). He knew that no amount of talking was going to compensate for a real, live baby – so he bought one. Pam was cured on the instant, and Bobby's troubles really began.

To obtain the baby he had to pay off a blackmailer (incidentally becoming a murder witness), falsify a birth certificate, lie to his wife and family, perjure himself in court – and (in addition to neglecting his official duties) he stumbled on a secret that almost delivered him, soul and voting shares, to his villainous brother. Why would such an honourable and decent man, someone who had been a State Senator and who was held in high public esteem, involve himself in such sordid goings-on? Why, for the love of his wife, of course, a love that transcends all things, even murder. (There was a moment when it looked as if Bobby might have killed the blackmailer. For another character one would have wanted retribution. But for Bobby one wanted escape – even though one knew he was falsely accused. One of the things soap opera teaches is that evil deeds *never* go unpunished. Therefore Bobby, as a devoted husband, could not have committed such a crime.)

Bobby emerged unsmirched, even triumphant, from this appalling mess. His wife had a baby (which turned out to be an orphan), he confessed his peccadilloes, was forgiven, and their love became stronger as a result. This was the happy ending to that particular story every viewer anticipated and wanted – though of course it was only temporary. The simpler the character, the simpler one's responses to their situation: thumbs up or thumbs down, and on with the next. The decent husband represents the cornerstone of hearth and home that we are all taught to revere. Cornerstones are dull things in themselves – but without them the place would just be a pile of rubble.

The decent husband is not the star of the show, which is proof, in the market economy of soap opera, that he is not the most popular character. Such a role is often reserved for that yin to his yang, his polar opposite, the scheming bitch.

That the audience rates a baddie higher than a goodie ought to be revealing. Does this character – selfish, manipulative, destructive – stand for all the frustrated wickedness that bubbles beneath the surface of our decent and caring culture, a culture personified by the decent husband? Is it arrested childishness in all of us that loves to see the whiskers of virtue tweaked by the imp of devilry, secure in the knowledge that no real harm will be done? (After all, the baddies always get it in the end.) A constant striving to behave honourably is what animates the decent husband, even though he is there principally as a foil for the other, less perfect, characters; his popularity is a measure of his importance to the structure, rather than his intrinsic merits. But rarely are the fans excited by him – whereas the scheming, seductive, immoral, greedy, snobbish activities of the bitch arouse more reaction from the audience – by letter, and in public, where the actress playing the role is often subject to personal abuse – than anything other than the removal of a popular character, or the frustration of a long-standing romance. The public may admire a good guy, but it appears that they really *need* a bitch.

Well of course we all do. Writing as a *viewer*, I am always delighted when the bitch puts her spoke through someone's wheel, and they fall off. The Americans do this kind of thing better than the British: there is not a day-time or a prime-time serial in the US that lacks its bitch-figure, and many of them have boasted two. *All My Children* (day-time) has Phoebe Tyler and Erica Kane, *Another World* (day-time) had Iris Carrington and Carol Lamonte, *Dynasty* (prime-time) has Alexis Carrington, not to mention her daughter Fallon, *Falcon Crest* (prime-time) has that matriarchal bitch Angie Channing. And what have the British to offer? There is Valerie Pollard on *Crossroads*, but she features more in sub-plots than as a central character. There isn't a single bitch worth the name in *Coronation Street* – the woman everybody loved to hate, Ena Sharples, was merely an interfering busybody, not the full-blown manipulator of other people's destinies the epithet implies. *Triangle*'s Marion Terson was not above bitchery: she manipulated, but while her will was done in corporate matters, in personal affairs she was too easily resisted to be a worthy opponent. *Emmerdale Farm*, like its radio counterpart *The Archers*, has gossips and bossyboots, as befits the popular notion of the farming communities with which both serials concern themselves – but none of them could hold a candle to their bitchy American sisters. Yet we in Britain love *Dallas* and *Dynasty* and *Falcon Crest*, at least if the viewing figures are anything to go by. Which implies that we love their bitches – so why don't we produce our own?

When it comes to character, I suggest the British like to think of themselves as subtle. Our serials (despite the excellence of our colour system) are studies in various shades of grey. Nobody is all saint or all sinner (any more, I hasten to say, than they are in American soaps): more important, they behave with a *naturalism* that American characters have never pretended to possess. British serials are less colourful than American ones, less dramatic, less escapist (though equally entertaining, which is what counts). They allow greater depth of characterization, at the expense of fantastic plotting. In all soaps you get to know a few characters well, and their interaction is what keeps the mechanism going. But the dramatic level of British soaps is that of everyday life, and there is little room for someone as outrageous or crude as a bitch. (I must also point out that, since British soaps are at most half an hour, and most of the American serials run to an hour or so, there is much more room, and need, for extra and extraordinary characters in the latter than in the former.)

I would like to be able to say that this lack of a bitch in British soaps is because of our superior attitude to women. Not, however, so. It has to do with our broadcasting tradition, our way of telling a story. Our soap operas have always prided themselves on their naturalism, in character, situation, background and pace. We have avoided, in our serials, the strident, the larger-than-life. This contrast is highlighted particularly when you look at a commercial on both sides of the Atlantic. In America, the ads are shrill, repetitive, crude. In Britain they are (or at least they can be) allusive, and often teasing. Wit – in which I have always thought the Americans superior to us – is not evident in their commercials (the knockabout humour you occasionally see is but a distant and grimacing cousin). In Britain wit is often employed to persuasive effect.

Now I would not argue that, by extension, British soaps are "superior" to their American relations: I find both types equally fascinating. But in making serials, the British go for a small-scale, low-key naturalism that fits in with our culture and even our landscape. The Americans, in a country that is larger, younger, richer and more dramatic, adopt an altogether more expansive approach – an approach that has also proved popular in Britain, as demonstrated by the viewing figures for imported serials like *Dallas* or *Dynasty*. We like other people's bitches, but in the home team such a character might upset the carefully constructed (and of course artificial) naturalism that is the hallmark of our popular dramas.

By definition the bitch is not a lady whose behaviour is in "good taste" – another phrase beloved of the English. The bitch may consider her own tastes superior to everyone else's: indeed the most celebrated American bitches, like Phoebe Tyler or Dorian Lord Callison (*One Life to Live*), are snobs. It has always fascinated me how snobbery is more openly expressed in an avowedly egalitarian country like America than in a consciously class-structured society like Britain. But by far the most satisfying thing about the bitch, from the viewer's point of view, is watching her stir up a storm – putting rocky marriages into the hands of salvage operators, driving good men to despair (and the arms of other women), liquidizing tentative romances, cheating innocent babes out of their rightful property – and knowing that, when the sand settles, those who deserved to stay together will have their links strengthened, those who had it coming to them will have got it, with knobs on, the patrimony of the innocent will miraculously be made safe, and the bitch herself will have found no satisfaction, and so will have to start again from scratch.

It is the cyclical nature of soaps that is one of their chief attractions, the knowledge that evil will continue to challenge good, no matter how often it is defeated. The bitch represents the personal, emotional, devious and unrelenting side of this challenge. As a character she has grown steadily more complicated over the years. No longer is her evil undiluted: now she reveals herself to be vulnerable, frustrated, the victim of an unhappy childhood, a miserable love-affair, a loveless marriage. She has a history, which makes our responses more complicated; her schemes, once animated simply by jealousy (after love and curiosity the most basic of human emotions), now admit a confusion about motive and reaction that can be both sad and touching.

Phoebe Tyler, America's reigning queen bitch, long refused her husband Charles a divorce because she claimed to hold the marriage vows sacred. Despite the fact that she ensured his married life was hell (he sought solace in the arms of his medical secretary Mona, whom he later married), when Phoebe was swayed by the attentions of unscrupulous Langley Wallingford – the bitch bitched – audience sympathy for her increased, since they knew that, however much she deserved it, she was in for a hard time with Mr Wallingford. Just as when Anne Hammond, in the British soap *The Brothers*, finally left her husband, one was sorry, not just to see her go, but for her misery and isolation. We want the good guys to come out on top, but we don't want the bad punished too thoroughly. Endings are not welcome in the continuous serial, and the permanent presence of the bitch ensures that there is more plotting ahead.

However outrageously they behave, the bitches are much more human than the good guys. There is more complexity to them, which allows both writer and actor a richer mulch to work with; and they are also catalysts, creators of action rather than reactors. Bitches are provocative, daring and none too predictable – three good reasons for their popularity. But do people say, as they do of other characters, "that's me" or at least "I know someone like that"? Judging from fans' responses, no, they don't. A few may applaud the bitch's flouting of convention, but most appear to be wanting, and waiting for, her inevitable chastisement. They enjoy being witness to the battle, as long as the result is not in doubt. The bitch that is in all of us must not be allowed to triumph.

Realism is one of those words, like morality or wealth, whose definition is subjective. On the soaps, "reality" is an artificial thing that is always being manipulated for the plot's benefit. I wrote earlier that British soaps work in a naturalistic context which the American soaps do not attempt. Let me qualify this by saying that the Americans employ a heightened reality – characters and setting that are larger than life, but totally consistent and convincing within their own terms of reference – while the British go for what I might call a "flattened" reality, a middle-brow, nuts-and-bolts, everyday sort of reality, on the whole unglamorous, none too adventurous, even mundane (but still absorbing to the viewer).

The milieux in which British soap characters move are not those of banking, oil or even the dappled uplands of law or medicine. Our soaps are still in the "kitchen sink" era, that form of naturalistic drama which sought to dignify the everyday by concentrating on the plumbing rather than the porcelain. Of course this naturalism, like any form of fiction, reflects the selective view of the author, and has no more claim to be objective or authentic than *Seven Brides for Seven Brothers* could claim to give an objective view of marriage practices in tribal America. Nevertheless the British like to claim that their soap – indeed, their drama in general – is "realistic". What they mean is that their characters don't need to have a lot of money in order to be unhappy. As a nation we do not have the wealth we used to enjoy – a situation with which Americans will soon become increasingly familiar – and so we discreetly shunt this subject away from our central concerns. I don't mean that we aren't as obsessed with money as everyone else – I mean that, in popular dramatic terms, we don't like to talk about it much. This is another reason why the bitch figure, being both greedy and larger than life, fits ill with the British form of naturalism.

The long-suffering wife, or Good Woman, is common to all soaps everywhere. If the devoted husband is the tent-pole, she is the groundsheet of the exercise: everyone walks all over her, everything happens on top of her, and yet she stays in place, keeping those who choose to remain so, clean and dry.

We are talking now of a central character, she with whom the largest part of the audience (a majority of whom are women) identifies. For that part of the audience which is, at least, of marriageable age, the long-suffering wife is the heroine, someone actively to admire, a role-model. Unlike the rest of television, women characters predominate on the soaps, and the good ones (and many of the bad) have great strengths. When you watch such a person through daily crises several days a week, every week, you know her better than you know your friends, your neighbours or your family. Part of you *becomes* her. What Freud identified as "transference", the shifting of the burden of unrequited love or guilt from the actual cause of the problem to the therapist trying to cure it, takes place between viewer and heroine. (This is one reason why many therapists use the soaps to reach their patients.)

Let us take two examples of the wife, one British (*Coronation Street*'s forceful Rita Fairclough), one American (Rachel Cory from *Another World*). Rita Fairclough, née Littlewood, was brought into the Street to provide Len Fairclough (now departed) with a woman. She ran their household, providing three cooked meals a day (breakfast, dinner and tea), managed their newsagent's shop, and sustained an interest in her husband's plumbing business. Having no children jointly – they were too old when they married – Rita devoted her considerable energies to being a working wife, although one story-development turned her briefly into a foster-parent. She regarded herself as, and showed herself capable of being, the equal of her husband in most matters except beer-drinking. She was – and remains – unafraid of standing up for herself, has always spoken her mind, and preferred to let her heart rule her head, except in business matters. Without scheming or conniving, she has always contrived to find a way round obstacles so as to get things done without loss of face.

She also had a lot to put up with. There was her husband's stubbornness, for a start: although Len loved her dearly, he could be as obstinate as hell, especially if he felt long-standing arrangements were under threat, whether it was his drinking, his domestic arrangements (he resisted with some bitterness the idea of adopting a child) or the way he ran his business (when the boys who delivered his newspapers went on strike for higher wages, it was Rita who came up with a negotiated settlement). Then there were those twin rivals for his affections, the pub and (hinted at but never consummated) Elsie Tanner, another of the Street's original characters who vanished in the Great Purge of 1983, a woman with more generosity than sense. She and Len were old friends: Rita treated her with that sort of fast-frozen friendliness that made the viewer instantly aware that Rita would fight Elsie to the death if it came to it.

Rita had to deal with the small crises of life, the loose change that is the currency of the British soaps. There was no embezzlement threatening to put their shop into the hands of the receivers, nor was Len to be implicated in fraud, theft or adultery – until after his demise in a car-crash, when the discovery of his affair became a sensational plot device presumably aimed at alienating viewers' affection for him. Rita was never kidnapped, involved in an accident that gave her amnesia, nor did she discover that a youthful indiscretion had grown into a handsome youth with multiple problems for her to solve. Those sort of things don't happen to Rita, or to any of the Good Women who stand for the British Wife and Mother (or foster-mother). Rita had to deal with throwing together an acceptable meal when she'd had an annoying day at the shop, lacked the time to buy food or get to the bank, and was fed up to the back teeth with cooking and cleaning. But she did it, she performed the chores, not because she was any sort of saint – her fuse was far too short for that: you got a fair amount of shouting at the Faircloughs' – but because they were there to be done, and if she didn't do them, no one else would, certainly not Len. He might not have thought of himself as a male chauvinist, but that is what the long-suffering wife has to put up with: keeping the domestic machinery running smoothly and (relatively) silently, with little help and less thanks.

It was – and is – the way she works, and the variety of tasks she is called upon to tackle, that qualify Rita as a heroine. Patience, good humour and common sense: those are the qualities she brings, in varying combinations, to the challenges confronting her. Nothing particularly rare about those, you might say – but you'd be wrong. Patience seems to be the preserve of the old and the simple in a culture where you push a button for instant gratification. Good humour is increasingly uncommon in a wrecked economy. And common sense is something very few believe themselves to possess, with so many "experts" around to undermine self-confidence.

Rita's qualities, therefore, are the stuff of nostalgia – which is itself the stuff of soap opera, at least where old-fashioned morality and traditional values are concerned. Rita, like all heroines, stands for the modern woman who not only possesses, but actually bases her actions on, the virtues of her ancestors. Take one example from a 1982 storyline. After frequent rows Rita persuaded Len that they should try to adopt a child. They were then devastated to be told they were too old to be considered as prospective adoptive parents. Where such a knock both to self-esteem and to the maternal instinct might have put a lesser woman off the whole idea – certainly Len wanted nothing more to do with it – Rita, acting positively (always the sign of a true heroine) discovered there was a need for short-term foster-parents. The next thing Len knew, there was a small boy for him to talk football with. And after that, a teenage girl who was forward enough not only to like boys, but to want to "help" Len in his business by acting the ambitious and flirtatious assistant.

Any parent of an adolescent girl knows, with sinking heart, the traumas that accompany her first sexual forays, not to mention the rivalry for the father's attention. No one, until they have to deal with it, knows how to cope, or even what to do: one reads books, one is above all determined not to repeat one's own parents' mistakes, one hopes to muddle through with a mixture of firmness and understanding. But if anyone's example is to be followed, it will be that of someone one respects. That someone will not be a member of the family (look what a mess they made of it!), and certainly not an "expert" full of theory to disguise the fact that their own children are delinquents. The chosen example must above all be seen to work – as Rita made it work. She was firm about foster-daughter Sharon seeing boys, where Len could only huff and puff: hours were laid down, boundaries set, privacy respected. And as for Sharon throwing herself at Len (not sexually, for that isn't the *Street*'s normal style – which is another reason for its popularity), Rita joked it off, jollying Len into affability and Sharon into accepting the absurdity of it all.

Rita's qualities would not only have made her forefathers (and fore-mothers) proud – they also brought results. Sharon did not become a model teenager overnight, nor did her problems disappear: what happened was that she gave the Faircloughs (even Len) her love and trust, which is what every parent longs for: a longing that if you, the parent, behave with tolerance and understanding, your monster of a child will turn into a rational human being. When this happy state was threatened by Sharon's social worker, who wanted – for the best possible reasons – to place the girl elsewhere, it was of course Rita who saved the situation And not with tears or any display of "feminine" weakness either, but by an extraordinarily effective combination of emotion and common sense. She pointed out that where love was concerned, so was emotion – and that there was nothing so important to a girl like Sharon. The social worker, however improbably, agreed, and at least one happy ending was safely in the can.

Maybe if more viewers followed Rita Fairclough's example, the world would be full of contented teenagers. The important thing about her character, a heroine for many an ageing viewer, is that it draws on qualities with which everyone is born, but which the modern world, in a sense, has bred out of us. You don't have to be clever to be like Rita, you don't have to be rich, you don't even have to be beautiful. What you need is the courage of your convictions, however old-fashioned, and the common sense to bend them to advantage in a crisis. You've got to be sensible, romantic, even passionate, rational and emotional all at once. You've got to have the physical strength to follow two professions – one that of wife-and-mother, the other a salaried job – and excel at both, thus proving yourself to your husband (who'll not acknowledge it) and to your elders, who persist in believing that working women make poor housewives. You've got to prove yourself superior to your man while accepting a position that certainly looks inferior. You've got to blend ancient and modern, to keep faith with tradition while retaining your sense of humour, to show that no amount of ordure can blot out a happy outcome. Anyone who can do all that, as Rita can, deserves to be a heroine.

In America, the long-suffering wife has to cope with ordure of an altogether different kind. Rachel Cory, my chosen example from the day-time serial *Another World*, was for years a bitch, part of a romantic triangle (the soaps' favourite shape) involving Alice Mathews and Steven Frame. The arrival on the show of Harding Lemay as new head writer, however, led to tremendous changes in Rachel's character. Lemay, himself middle-aged when he took on the job, wanted to deepen the characterization of the middle-aged parts, involving his audience with people who were complex instead of one-dimensional, and around whom sympathy, once engaged, would wind itself ever more tightly. (This was in the 1970s, when the majority of the viewers were presumed to be middle-aged themselves. The "discovery" of a young audience, and the steady killing-off of elderly characters, with whom the young are presumed not to identify, is a relatively new phenomenon.)

What Lemay did was to create, or build on, the part of Mac Cory, an extremely rich but caring publisher, with whom Rachel – who came from an impoverished background against which her mother tried to teach her right from wrong, and the virtues of hard work – fell in love. Cinderella entranced, not with the handsome prince, but with the king his father: an ideal plot to quicken the pulses of viewers of "a certain age". Rachel's bitchiness had been caused by her envy of other people's wealth: Lemay's idea was that, once married to money, she would be "cured", and turn into a caring wife and mother (also a stepmother, as it happened).

A creative writer of some renown before coming to soap opera, Lemay was careful to alter Rachel's character in a manner that would leave the viewer thoroughly convinced of her new status as Good Woman. Since she had been married several times, it was important to "trail" her new attitude, not only to the sacred ties of wedlock, but also to those of motherhood. Lemay began by making Rachel helpful, sympathetic and genuinely concerned for the welfare of her mother when the latter, late in life, gave birth to a baby. This proved (at least to those viewers who wrote in support) that Rachel was capable of real affection, whereas previously any such expression on her part would have been dismissed as one of her self-serving schemes.

Next it was necessary to create other lightning rods for the hostility the audience had for so long directed at Rachel. Lemay found one in Iris, Mac Cory's spoiled daughter, and another in the siren Carol Lamonte, who worked in the Cory office. Iris developed especially well as a villainess: she soon became part of a new triangle whose other sides consisted of Rachel and Mac. Making the last two fall in love was something of a risk, since Mac was several years older than Rachel, and in soap opera terms their relationship was doomed. In his book *Eight Years in Another World* Lemay insists that the relationship arose, not because he had carefully planned it, but because of the chemistry between the actor and actress involved. (Whatever the case, this set-up was used some ten years later by *Dynasty*, when the middle-aged Blake Carrington marries his young secretary Krystle, who also has to contend with the jealous manipulations of Blake's daughter Fallon, just as Rachel had to cope with Iris.)

Another aspect of the devoted wife's character is that she does have to deal with situations, rather than – as the bitch does – creating them herself. Rachel thus found herself returning the love that Mac offered her, after a lifetime of being denied emotional security; responding gracefully to his generosity where previously, having had little, she would grab any gift with greed. Encouraged by him, she expressed herself as a sculptress, thus showing herself more creative than destructive; even more important, the strength of her will – essential to the Good Woman – went into reinforcing the love that flowered between them, instead of destroying it as the old Rachel would have done. Like Shakespeare's Shrew (to whom Lemay compares her), she was transformed from harridan into housewife – and the audience, now convinced by her new character, demanded (in their letters and telephone calls) a happy life for her and Mac, where once they had besought the writers to foil the old Rachel's schemes and allow Alice and Steve Frame some peace.

It is interesting to note that, after he resigned as head writer, Lemay's successors forced Rachel slowly to revert to bitchery. Her son Jamie went (temporarily) to the bad, and Rachel hysterically accused Mac – who adored the young man – of driving him to drugs to get at her. She had an affair with a younger man: with this lapse Rachel finally forfeited her title of Good Woman. She and Mac still loved one another, but it was the physical side that brought them together now, no longer the spiritual. Rachel's standards, when she was a heroine, were simply those of fidelity in marriage, an adherence to the vows that in a previous incarnation she had ignored. New writers made her betray them – and in so doing illustrated the difference between the good and the bad. Instead of coping she fell apart; instead of loving, she was grasping; instead of using her common sense, she behaved wilfully and vindictively. The viewers liked her as a bitch, but became positively idolatrous when Lemay turned her into a Good Woman. Maybe her reversion to type – managed over a brief couple of years, where Lemay laboured for eight – left them confused and upset. Perhaps the present absence of a strong heroine is one reason for *Another World*'s low position in the current ratings.

The "king" or "queen", the lynch-pin of all fairy-tales, has never been absent from soap opera. Imbued, like Zeus, with divine power derived from hard work, social position, ruthless destruction of enemies and vast experience, these characters are above mortal judgement, and are worshipped accordingly. Like Zeus again, they are quick to anger and vengeance, fallible, loyal but unpredictable, certain about their motives, awful in their majesty. They rarely explain, and to get them to apologize requires a court appearance. There hovers about their presence an aura that confuses strong women and reduces strong men to babblers. The regal method is not so much to inspire (like the Good Woman), as to lead; to get people to do "not what I do, but what I say". The secret of their appeal is our worship of power, even when arbitrarily used.

In the days of American radio soaps, when power, like money, was somehow suspect, even evil, there was always "Ma", who combined the roles of queen and fairy godmother. She was the head of the clan; her words, and even more her standards, were adhered to at all times (or when they weren't, dreadful consequences ensued); she was the final court of appeal, delivering judgement and sentence with majestic confidence. Hers was a *moral* authority, derived from traditional wisdom which it was her role to inherit, safeguard and pass on.

Such matriarchs still exist: Bert Bauer in *Guiding Light*, Annie Sugden in *Emmerdale Farm*, Miss Ellie in *Dallas*, the departed Meg Mortimer of *Crossroads*. Patriarchs too: Dan Archer of the long-running British radio serial *The Archers*, Chris Hughes of the defunct American day-time soap *As the World Turns*.

These "rulers" are not always rich, at least not in their own right: indeed they mostly share that antique distrust of wealth evinced by their radio predecessors. They are survivors. Like all rulers, they like to preserve a certain distance from lesser mortals (with the notable exception of their own families). They do not interfere in day-to-day affairs, but have to be reverently approached. Once approached, their decisions must be abided by – and of course they always turn out to be right.

The important thing about these traditional matriarchs and patriarchs is that they have *earned* the authority they wield. They are practical people who, in addition to raising a tribe, have proved themselves capable of running a business (whether a lumber yard like Ma Perkins, a farm like Annie Sugden, or a motel like Meg Mortimer). Or they have risen to the top of some highly regarded profession such as medicine (the god as healer was a traditional figure in prehistoric times). As befits tribal rulers, they have taken part in every aspect of tribal life, from child-rearing through the gathering of food to the politicking that affects the tribe's relations with the outside world. The reverence in which they are held comes from their success in all they have turned their hands to, their ability to transform their own experience into a philosophy that is of benefit to all.

But there has grown up in recent years a new type of ruler-figure whose power springs solely from money. Rich people used to be villains, untrustworthy city-slickers, corrupted beyond redemption. On many current soaps, indeed, the villains are the rich: Palmer Cortlandt in *All*

My Children, J. R. in *Dallas*, even *Coronation Street*'s Mike Baldwin, the nearest character on that genial serial to a swine. Yet the new American prime-time soaps seem unanimous in worshipping wealth. Admittedly the matriarchs of these serials are all first-generation wealthy: more is forgiven those who make money than those who have simply inherited it. Some American day-time soaps have long featured rich and beneficent ruler-figures: the late Victor Lord in *One Life to Live* was one, Mac Cory is another. But their concerns were and are rooted in the community they rule. In the prime-time soaps we are now invited to admire – are drawn to admire – the ruthless exercise of power by self-made, self-willed people, whose only motive is profit, whose only lever is cash.

Obviously the creators of the prime-time soaps felt the need to glamorize the background of the form they had borrowed from the day-time serials. Sex is merely foreground glamour: for background there are few things more glamorous than wealth. In a culture that consumes on credit, it is fascinating to watch limitless extravagance; in societies where money is power, it is easy to be drawn to a figure who uses that power masterfully. Just as victims often have a peculiar admiration for those who torment them, so viewers come to admire those who not only have more than they, the audience, can ever aspire to, but who use it grandly, selfishly, even tyrannically. Neither *Dynasty*'s Blake Carrington nor the late Jock Ewing of *Dallas* could be considered *good* men, yet their strength of character, the way they fiercely defend the family interests, the manner in which they rise to a crisis compel admiration – which is all a ruler needs, apart from obedience. With them love is something dazzling, but also destructive, especially of their children. In the older day-time soaps the offspring benefit through the patriarch's inheritance: on the prime-time examples it appears to drive them bananas.

In all the soaps the rulers retain their best qualities until they die. They are sharpened by age and respond firmly to challenge; they are there when needed, and a powerful background presence when not; their authority, and the reverence accorded it, grows with the years rather than diminishes. A young audience may find such a figure unsympathetic, too reminiscent of the authority-figures in their own lives. But a young audience grows older (and once hooked, they can remain addicted for years). The older you grow, the more anxiously you search for approval from a figure of authority. Whether we be royalists or republicans, we most of us retain that childlike awe for kings and queens, and the soaps provide us with a royal flush.

*

The romantic hero, fairy tale's handsome prince, is by the soaps' definition a man unattached. Once he marries his princess he must become a devoted husband, otherwise he wouldn't have been a hero in the first place. Flawed he might be – indeed, should be – but marriage to the right girl must redeem him, and remove him forever from the list of men eligible to be fallen in love with. Naturally this doesn't stop women falling in love with him, but if they are good women they'll resist temptation, and if they're bad, he will resist – most of the time.

Being unattached naturally involves certain risks, but essential to the hero's character is his dangerousness. Sometimes this is taken to the extreme: a highly popular hero, Luke Spencer from the American day-time soap *General Hospital*, actually raped the girl he subsequently married. More usual is the *threat* of explosion when passion is aroused, the sultry (an adjective I maintain applies equally to men and women) brooding that can precede some unpredictable act, the willingness to take risks that no rational family man would contemplate. Such risks include braving frightful dangers for the sake of his love (the knightly quest), fighting for her honour (the chivalric duel), and – most astonishing of all in these supposedly permissive times – not sleeping with her until marriage (romantic purity). If this makes the modern serial hero sound as if he came straight from Arthurian legend, this wouldn't be far off the mark. Romantic heroes carry the impossible burdens of passionate love and personal chastity (most of the time). They may stagger, or even stumble occasionally and do penance, but they do not fall.

What makes the hero work, and why is he so popular? First of all, he is handsome to look at, and proud of it. Contemporary American soaps make a big feature of their good-looking heroes, exposing as much of their bodies as can be done within the limits of decency, as often as possible. Scenes by swimming pools, showers, beaches or places where a sweat can be worked up (such as sports grounds) are mandatory in every story-line. Opportunities for ladies to touch, towel, rub, massage, oil or knead his heroic flesh are plentiful. All this is relatively new in serial terms. What started on radio as pure description, adjectival eroticism, became, when made visible on television, that sort of wholesome attractiveness designed for child-rearing rather than sex. Such loins as you may have glimpsed when the soaps started in the 1950s – and remember we are talking of the heroes – were aimed at arousing, not desire, but the spirit of possession. The only way to get him was to become his wife. The romantic lead was a symbol of virility destined to channel his sexuality into the marital bed. He was not a heart-throb: that description was reserved for the older man whose sex-appeal was safely surrounded by the electrified fence of marriage. In those days sex was the property of those thought old enough to handle it: people of marriageable age. For anyone younger to indulge in it was downright dirty.

That has changed more than somewhat, inside and outside the soaps. In the early 1970s (1973 to be exact, when the "youth kick" of the '60s was becoming almost acceptable to the middle-aged), a day-time serial called *The Young and the Restless* revolutionized (so the critics said: the word was much in vogue at the time) the soaps, by giving them "the Hollywood look". Since this serial was actually made in California, this wasn't altogether surprising: the place is famous for beautiful young flesh, bronzed and unclothed and terribly photogenic. *The Young and the Restless* (a title that makes its terms of reference pretty clear) was not the first soap to be produced in California: both *Days of our Lives* and *General Hospital* preceded it out there ten years before. What Y&R did was to feature beautiful kids, to put their concerns and story-lines at the centre of the show (rather than at the edges, as was more usual elsewhere), and to make them the stars. The result was a different-looking, different-sounding soap. It also pulled in a young audience – which of course had an effect on its rivals. Soon they were all at it too.

Of course the romantic hero has been around forever. The soaps, however, had always assumed that a significant number of their audi-ence – certainly those who went out and bought the products advertised on the shows – were middle-aged, and mainly interested in the problems of their own generation. The '60s saw youth come out of the bathroom and into the limelight. The young were discovered, via endless media coverage, to be active, passionate, articulate, inventive, beautiful – and a great consumer market. Y&R was the first to cash in on this. Its original hero, however, was in the old mould (to talk about "revolution" where the soaps are concerned is rather like talking of a "new" Nixon: the cosmetics may be different but the spirit remains the same). Dr Bill "Snapper" Foster married his Chris while he was still a medical student – after she had been raped (not by him, of course). Her chief concern was whether her dreadful experience would ruin her sex life forever. Snapper soon won her round to the pleasures of wedded flesh, by the gentleness and patience for which all romantics are renowned. The result was a true love match – and ten years on, although they may argue, they are still an example to us all.

The problem with the hero as a continuing character is two-fold. He may be a bit of a tearaway, but if he's the hero he's bound to marry his girl and live happily ever after. Once he's married he turns into the devoted and long-suffering husband. He can't behave too badly before

he's sworn his vows, and he certainly can't behave too badly afterwards. We all want a happy ending for him – but endings are the death
of characters in the serials. Without conflict, without that aura of danger
which distinguishes the appealing hero, the poor fellow is in grave
danger of becoming boring. And while a sexy bachelor is fair game for
any girl (including the audience), once he's wed, unattached girls turn
their attentions elsewhere – unless they're bitches, sirens or worse.

This is why romantic heroes have a relatively short life (in soaps as
in reality). The key to their appeal is their availability, though they are
expected to restrict it to the object of their love. (If they have the
occasional lapse they are expected to pay for it. If they carry on, they
aren't heroes at all.) As married men, they can only become available
again through death of spouse, or through divorce. Now given that a
successful marriage is still the most popular ending for a soap hero and
heroine, as it always has been, a divorce would imply that something
was wrong in the first place. If they can't stick it out, make it work,
allow their love to triumph over the little difficulties that beset a
marriage – jealousy, children, ambition, work, temptation, parents-in-
law – then they weren't really hero and heroine. Though there are
numberless divorces in the serials, they do not happen if the hero has
married the heroine. He could, of course, have married the wrong girl,
which won't alter his heroic status. But if he's done the right thing –
Snapper and Chris managed it in *Y&R*, as did Luke and Laura in *General
Hospital* – then bang goes the interesting part of his life, the quest.
Everyone knows that the search is more fun than living with the
discovery. The romantic hero is living proof of this.

In England we have a totally different attitude to male sexuality. In
fact, we scarcely feature it at all. Beautiful girls, in various stages of
undress, are sometimes glimpsed in our serials; handsome men showing
off their bodies are rare – and when they are exposed, they usually
belong to the sort of unscrupulous scoundrel who is only interested in
getting girls into bed, as quickly and as often as possible. Not heroes at
all. Does this mean we have a more realistic attitude towards romantic
heroism – that, knowing the rarity of such creatures in real life, we
don't accept them on our screens? Or does it mean that we have a more
repressed attitude towards men who declare their love (for women),
who are unafraid of passion and unashamed of their bodies?

I think the latter. We are altogether more tight-lipped about expressing our feelings than are the Americans: the kind of therapy that
encourages you to let it all hang out is not only rare here, it is considered
risible. We are as romantic as any other people – we yearn for the happy
ending no less – but we don't like talking about it. Well, not as much.
It's the kind of thing we watch others do (as with the bitch-figure): if

it's ourselves, we squirm and make a joke, or a cup of tea. We know the serials aren't *really* real, but we require from them a naturalism consonant with our culture. When it comes to sex or sexuality, such as that possessed by the American hero, we prefer to talk round it, rather than about it. We are incapable of the directness that the Americans possess in such abundance. (A brief personal example which illustrates this: emerging from an apartment in New York early one morning, I got into a cab and was immediately asked, "Well, did you get laid?" That would never happen with an English cabbie.). We do not crave, in our serials at any rate, action as much as reflection. The romantic hero, to suit our tastes, would have nothing to do but sup his drink and remain heroically silent while other men boasted of their sexual conquests. By his manners we would know him.

There is also our hypocritical and chauvinistic attitude to sex. We love beautiful women to show their bodies; but for a man to display himself is somehow unmanly. Those unattached men in our soaps capable of attracting the opposite sex – Joe Sugden in *Emmerdale Farm* was one example – are taciturn, solitary, hard-working. They would no more rape a woman than bugger a sheep. If they took off their clothes, it would be to rescue a drowning dog or child. They cover their bodies as closely as their feelings. Beauty is something for men to admire, not possess in themselves. A good-looking man is either a villain or gay. A man who admits he wants a beautiful woman is not a hero. Our heroes are all Sir Galahads, not Lancelots: pure, silent and hard. That is why they are so hard to find in English soaps.

We do, however, share with America a puritan tradition which lies like heartburn over our appetite for pleasure. We go for the nibble rather than the blow-out: in sexual terms, the tease rather than the punch-line. (I am talking, of course, about our attitudes to the soap opera hero: for characters with fewer scruples and smaller parts, going the whole way is a frequent, indeed mandatory, occurrence.) With the hero, any thrill that may be derived from the fact that he's available (and, if you're lucky, gorgeous) is counterbalanced by the fact that he can't be had (except by sirens and bitches). Everyone can admire, but nobody except the object of his love can touch. The pleasurable tension of wanting what is at the same time offered and denied, is dissipated by the knowledge that he who caused this frustration will at least become the property of the right girl. That instinctive desire to see the hero happy may not come from a wish to see his goodness rewarded, as much as from the feeling that someone capable of arousing such guilt-laden longings (guilt-laden because we want what we can't have) is better off safely hitched. This, I think, makes more sense than the views of the religious-minded, which are that the popularity of a virtuous hero rests on the fact that he is ready to proclaim his virtue, thus setting an example to all of us mumblers. My view is, alas, the opposite: that those who find him attractive feel sufficiently bad about it to want him married off. Like the butterfly, the hero's life may be tantalizingly gaudy, but there is relief in the knowledge that at least it is brief.

The fans of the hero are to be found amongst the rather young and rather married. The former are attracted to male beauty until they discover the importance of personality. The latter, chained, perhaps, to bodies less arousing than that of the hero, may see in such beefcake something they might have missed. The majority of women, however – so my extensive researches reveal – do not rate masculine beauty very highly. A list of what men find desirable in women could be written on a single page; what women find desirable in men would fill volumes. (I trust it is clear that I mean this as a compliment to woman's extraordinary complexity.) It follows that beauty or handsomeness is not essential to the hero: his appeal rests, rather, on that peculiar tension between availability and unreachability.

The heroine, by contrast, has to be flawlessly beautiful, and that's only a start. In order to appeal to the young women who identify with her (would it be true to say that women can admire beauty in their own sex, where men on the whole can't?), and to all the men who drool, the heroine also has to be good and kind and vulnerable and innocent and hopeful and honest and devoted and filled with the kind of passion that only needs the Right Man to kindle it. At least she doesn't have to be rich, or able to cook, or capable – except of giving love to him who has earned it.

The appeal of this unfortunate character – unfortunate because more is demanded of her, and more terrible things happen to her, than anyone else – lies in her ability to arouse the protective, nay dominant, masculinity that normally lies dormant in her male fans, whilst retaining, through her sweet innocence, the affections of the ladies. It's the damsel-in-distress, Cinderella syndrome – and the strength of its appeal, in these liberated times, shows just how strong a hold these myths still have on the popular imagination. There are plenty of liberated women in the current soaps, women who live and work and play as they please. But they are not heroines. We are left in no doubt that the most desirable character, in looks and qualities, is she who will one day reap the ultimate reward, and find happiness in love. But not yet.

Unlike the hero, the heroine very rarely gets to marry the Right Person. Probably this has something to do with the fact that the producers, knowing that more women than men watch the serials, feel bound to offer more eligible men as suitors for the heroine, instead of having too much undischarged emotion washing around an unsettled hero. If it is correct to assume that there is a mighty waterfall of unfulfilled love roaring in the breasts of the fans, then it is safer to direct it onto the heads of a succession of men, rather than drown one poor chap altogether, however heroic. Hence the turnover in gents and the relative longevity of heroines. Bearing in mind that, in soaps, the happy ending has to be indefinitely postponed, it's the men who fall victim to the story-line, and the women who survive.

Take Sue Ellen, the heroine of *Dallas*. Her astounding stupidity is an important asset. No viewer could be too jealous of her looks when she is months behind everybody in catching on to what is happening. She may be permanently confused, but she suffers heroically, which brings out the protectors in her audience. Wooed and won, as a young beauty queen, by the villainous J. R., she bore up remarkably well under his slights, infidelities and manipulative manoeuvres. She tried to keep her love as bright as her lip gloss, but when she couldn't take any more she turned, not to other men (though there were plenty who offered themselves), but to booze. This was a lapse, and a heroine should not have succumbed – but then Sue Ellen showed true grit in pulling herself out of it. Besides, she had just cause, what with J. R.'s numerous cruelties – and just causes keep a heroine going as sins do a penitent. Even when driven to leave her husband, and take up with Dusty, the crippled cowboy who truly loved her, her body – what we might call her extra-marital virginity – was not to be sullied. Dusty couldn't get it up, after falling off some bronco. That most important quality of a heroine, her chastity, remained unviolated.

What, you will ask, of those heroines who have suffered rape or other unspeakable assaults from ruffians unfit to lick the hem of their negligees? How can these heroines still be considered pure? Ah, but you forget the healing power of love. And time. If love cannot actually reseal the hymen, it can certainly make flowers bloom in the desert. The limpid stream that brutality may have sullied can be purified. And when the fans have had the pleasure of a heroine's company over several years, they may forget nothing, but they learn to forgive and understand. It is not as if the heroine wanted such a thing to happen. It could happen to anyone, as, on American soaps, it does. (In England, although rape is common in real life, it is extremely rare in the serials. We are still very squeamish about sexual matters.) A girl who consistently tries to be good deserves another chance.

The English heroine has the same qualities as her American sister, except she is not quite so luscious (no doubt a matter of diet and climate). She has long hair, usually fair, large eyes, a lovely complexion and a beautiful back. No doubt she also has long and beautifully formed legs, but we rarely get to see these – our summers are so short and our swimming pools so rare that these ladies undress but seldom. There may be the occasional tennis match, but you're more likely to see a fine set of shoulders in an evening dress than any more intimate part of the anatomy. The first episode of *Triangle* did feature the actress Kate O'Mara, former siren on *The Brothers*, sunning herself in a bikini, but she was not a heroine, and didn't reappear in the second series.

Heroines are slender, fit (though you may see them wet, you scarcely see them exercise), exquisitely dressed, and have only one fault: they wear their make-up in bed. This may just be a failure in imagination on my part: perhaps they leap out of bed and apply the slap before their husbands prise open their eyeballs. Just as you don't see a heroine – or any soap character, for that matter – performing any bodily function (what's wonderful about piles or period pains?), so you don't see them making themselves beautiful. They are *always* beautiful: that is part of the illusion.

The hero's role tends to end when he gets married, but since the heroine is so often teamed to the wrong man, she gets bedded more than the hero ever does. In America you can see the foreplay and its aftermath; in England, not. In the standard set of the English soap, the bedroom simply doesn't feature, not even that of *Coronation Street*'s once most desirable sex-cat Elsie Tanner. We are an economical as well as a reticent lot, and we leave all that to the imagination. That still allows our heroines – Jill Harvey, say, on *Crossroads* – a powerful sexual charge to go with their innocent vulnerability, but we never see this charge earthed, as it were: for us, there is only endless discussion of what a let-down it all was.

Does the characterization of the heroine as someone pure, helpless and foolish-feminine mean that the soaps are anti-feminist? Or that those who accept such women as heroines are reactionaries? To think so is to misunderstand the nature of soaps. They cannot be considered in the vanguard of anything: on the contrary, they place themselves deliberately in the rearguard. One of the valuable functions they fulfil is to act as a refuge, a safe haven for the fantasies of those millions of people alarmed at the size of the gap between fashionable thinking and their own ideas. The greater the gap the greater their alarm – and the greater their gratitude to the soaps for filling the breach (or at least stretching something pretty over it). The soaps simply reflect old-fashioned yearnings – and if they didn't, they'd soon stop being popular. (Even the very naturalistic *Coronation Street* deals with a nostalgic neighbourliness everyone thinks they remember, but which scarcely exists any more.) However much radicals and progressives try to deride such old-fashioned sentiments as the soaps portray, their existence can no more be denied than the sympathy they arouse. Though, as I wrote earlier, there are plenty of liberated females in the serials, the popularity of someone beautiful, desirable, innocent and pure – who gets involved in adventures that only strengthen these admirable qualities – remains high among both sexes. Those who want to tinker with that might just as well start with the fairy tales used to condition our children. The soaps dip their buckets into a well deeper and older and more primitive than anything the so-called "moral majority" would want in their homes. The serials aren't reactionary, any more than their viewers. They're prehistoric, and there's not a lot anyone can do about it.

As viewers we tend to identify less with the characters than with their *roles*. In other words, we do not want Sue Ellen Ewing to find happiness because she is an ex-beauty queen chained to a family who happens to be filthy rich, but because she is the *heroine*, and the heroine's happiness is what everybody wants. If we had Sue Ellen's gifts, never mind her credit cards, no doubt we would make better use of them than she does: she is not a model for the fans: they are behind her because it is her heroine's role to suffer endlessly in the pursuit of happiness.

The immense popularity of the villain, then, does not mean that right-thinking people have secret yearnings to behave like Adam Chance on *Crossroads*, Palmer Cortlandt on *All My Children*, or (the biggest of them all) *Dallas*'s J. R. Ewing. They welcome his presence (or hers: there's no shortage of lady villains) because of his vital role in making things go wrong, which makes seeing them come right all the sweeter. There is also the possibility of being surprised by a good act – though deep down we know this is highly unlikely.

Villains tend to have all the fun, which is another point in their favour. They get to bed all the pretty girls (except the heroine, unless they're into rape) and by the same token, lady villains get to bed the handsomest men. Being for the most part rich, they spend their money extravagantly and selfishly. They're mean to their mothers, kick around small children and animals, and don't give a damn for the social rules and graces that all the good people have to abide by. They get drunk, punch people, insult hostesses and servants, and ruin their rivals (or, failing that, lock them up and threaten them with death). They behave, in sum, as all of us at some time would like to behave, and they only get punished for it when they've finished.

Like the decent husband, the villains are entirely predictable in their actions – but because they get more pleasure out of it, we also enjoy them more. We don't even have to feel guilty about them: everything they do will have an evil motive, which makes life very simple. And of course they will be thwarted in the end. We still hope to be surprised, but to be comforted by the inevitable is very satisfying. Whenever J. R. smiles, we know he is planning to bankrupt, prostrate or eliminate a rival, or obtain control of Ewing Oil by using (or rather abusing) his own flesh and blood, his family, the totem erected at the centre of all the soaps.

Why should J. R. be a hero (I mean a villain) wherever people have access to *Dallas* – which is most of the world, including some chinks in the Iron Curtain? Partly, of course, because of the successful sales-manship of the producers, which has made *Dallas* the most widely seen serial ever. But hype apart, audiences as large and as faithful as those who have followed *Dallas* would not stay loyal unless it were worth watching. People admit their addiction openly – the same people who would hotly deny ever having seen a day-time soap, who rather than watch one would turn off their sets and do something to improve their minds, like mowing the lawn or doing the ironing! *Dallas* is a phenomenon, an idea that found its time, a serial that made soap respectable in the eyes of the unconverted. And the character of J. R. is at the centre of its appeal.

This appeal, this pull of the villain, is, I have to repeat, based on the age-old certainties which are the currency of all soaps; certainties which appear to have gone out of fashion only because they are not often articulated in public. Power corrupts. Money does not bring happiness. Forfeit the love of a good woman and you'll regret it forever. Screw around, and the patter of little consequences is bound to come and haunt you. Mess with your mother and you'll never hear the end of it. Destroy your family and who is there left when you're in trouble?

The glory of J. R. is that he revels in his villainy. Other villains fail to derive from their misdeeds the same pleasure as he does: they tend to look miserable, constipated or fall prey to fits of remorse. Not J. R. He *loves* manipulating people and stocks. He adores surprising Sue Ellen with some new revelation that will appal her even more. When he wakes up in the bed of some lovely lady, he's grinning all over his face (this is the special skill of the actor who plays him, Larry Hagman, but it is part of the character too). He can't wait to twist the knife further into brother Bobby, long-standing rival Cliff or even his poor old Ma (who in his eyes could never appreciate Daddy enough). He exploits all the tensions that grab an audience by the eyeballs: the tension between amazement and envy, righteous horror and guilty delight. Whether he is seen as an example of the decadence of western capitalism or of crass materialism, his, and the serial's, enormous following rests on the glamour of his misdeeds, and the certainty of their being, if not punished, then at least foiled. He is the sinister Black Knight of childhood legend – with the bonus that, beneath his visor, you can see him smile.

I have dealt, I hope, with the chief characters found in every soap (with appropriate qualifications to account for the differences between English and American tastes). There are, it goes without saying, whole battalions of smaller parts who regularly appear, and for whom large numbers of viewers have enormous affection (or loathing). There is the stranger whose appearance in the town causes secrets to be revealed, relationships to fragment, prejudices to resurface, alarm and despair to run riot. There are the children whose rightful parentage is in doubt, who are the victims of divorce, tug-of-love, parental demise, kidnapping, sickness or teenage rebellion. There is the wicked witch, who pops in to put a curse on the heroine; and the fairy godmother, who makes an equally brief appearance to put certain things right.

There is the jester, or holy fool, whose wisdom is imparted through simplicity or (more rarely) wit. Should the ruler have trouble putting his thoughts into words, there is often a sage on hand, a philosopher disguised as a lawyer, doctor, psychiatrist or ancient family friend, who can be relied on to utter Great Truths which – equally reliably – the good will take to heart and the wicked will ignore. There is the child who never grows up, even having borne kids of her own; and the young man or woman with a maturity beyond their years.

The fact that I do not, and cannot, deal with these characters as fully as I have dealt with the others should not belittle their importance to the soap's structure – which is as delicately balanced, as apparently symmetrical, as unashamedly ornate, as a Gothic cathedral. What I have tried to do is to show how the soaps' characters are deliberately created stereotypes in a narrative form with a particular set of purposes. These I would sum up in the phrase Everything You Have Always Wanted To Believe About Life But Have Been Ashamed To Admit. As in Greek tragedy, each character has a role, a destiny and a set of attributes that are familiar and predictable: what is fascinating is watching the destiny played out. We know what will happen; we don't know quite when or how. Like the ancient Greeks, our emotions may be purged by our involvement with these dramas – for in every successful soap there is a set of characters with whom every viewer can identify. Once you've found someone who is there daily, weekly, forever – someone whose beauty you admire or whose problems resemble your own or whose weaknesses you sympathize with – you are hooked. This is the purpose of the form, and also explains why the characters themselves – the seed corn from which the serial grows – are not "original creations", in the sense that they shock you into seeing life differently, but stereotypes who are instantly recognizable.

I would argue that, given the form of the soap opera, there is nothing wrong with stereotypes. When a writer sits down to create a new serial (as we shall see), he or she is not looking to startle, but rather to involve an audience. To startle, to say old things in a dramatically new way, is the purpose of the single play (familiar on British radio, a rare though not yet extinct bird on television). The purpose of the soap is to grab large and increasing numbers of viewers and hold their attention for years at a time. There is of course a limit to the amount of inventiveness that can be invested in a form as uniquely demanding as the soap opera. But what can be done can be done well or badly: the aim remains to entertain an audience with the activities of characters whose problems are not only universal, but timeless. Such characters have been around forever, from myth to pulp serials. The soaps' particular achievement is to give them a life that has every appearance of being eternal. Few of them change, except to age: they may deepen slightly (though this is rare), but you will not know much more about them after ten years than after their first appearance: you will have seen them react to a different set of circumstances, but in the same old way. This is deliberate. They are not there to surprise you: quite the contrary. Their purpose is to reassure.

This, I think, is the explanation for the remarkable absence of minority group characters in the serials. There are few blacks or gays (Steve Carrington in *Dynasty* was rapidly "retrieved" for heterosexuality, and, in case anyone should doubt the machismo of Carrington sons, the villainous foundling Adam was added to the cast). There is a singular dearth of Latinos (except as silent servants), and of Indians (bar a receptionist in *Crossroads* and her tycoon father, who was more British than David Hunter). This is surprising because members of these groups are so much a part of everyday life in the dying quarter of the twentieth century; sharing a common culture, they would do much to enrich a mix that prides itself on absorbing the concerns of our time.

But creed and colour do not intrude into the serials any more than they do into myth. Sex, yes (though not homosexuality): incest is almost as common as adultery in both genres. The absence of creed is easily explained: it distracts the attention from the essential simple morality animating the characters. Besides, it is something that shows itself more in words than in deeds, and the stuff of serial drama is the interplay of action and reaction. Talk, which can be interminable, must be about things that have happened or are about to happen, but theory (which can be boring) is out. Also, no one wants to offend any part of the potential audience. The prejudices that are aired are those that no one can argue with, such as the desirable triumph of Good over Evil. The divisive hatreds aroused by religion or politics have no place in the mouths of soap characters. Anyway, you get enough of that on the news.

The absence of colour – or for that matter gays – seems more mysterious. True, blacks are now beginning to emerge in parts other than domestic servants, but it has taken almost half a century for that to happen. On *Coronation Street*, with its supposed bluff northern naturalism, there have so far been no regular black characters at all. On *Crossroads*, however, there are now some. I venture to suggest this is part of the nostalgia common to all the soaps. Not a fictionalized return to the supposed time when everyone knew their place, and love between men was reserved for monasteries, prisons and private schools, but the recreation of a childlike world where anything that might disturb the assumptions of the majority was simply not mentioned: for that you had to wait until you were "older" and "understood more".

Where politics is concerned, the characters on the soaps are neither courageous nor advanced. As we shall see, they are capable of dealing with certain social issues such as alcoholism and rape. But they confine themselves to problems whose solutions lie within the capabilities of the individuals concerned. *That* is their business: to remind and reassure each member of their audience that there *are* areas of contemporary life over which he or she has control. The problems that the politicians involve themselves in are not their concern (except in so far as they show, as in *Dallas* or *Flamingo Road*, that politicians are as capable of corruption as financiers). This is no comfort to those who believe that all problems are, at bottom, political. But the soaps deal in Destiny, not politics where today's concerns will look so petty tomorrow. They deal in the destiny of individuals, not of classes or creeds, and, at a time when the individual has but a precarious hold on the levers of the machinery of control, certain characters in soapland, individuals though archetypal, can look, to a sympathetic eye, almost, well – progressive.

3

THE PLOTS: ALL FOR LOVE

There are, of course, only seven themes in all drama. These revolve around love (happy and unhappy), ambition, jealousy, revenge, madness and confused identity. To this basic *roux*, on which all playwrights rely to make their confections, the soaps have added one new ingredient – hysterical illness.

Novelty is neither expected nor welcomed in the soaps. The plots are mere vehicles for the characters to ride in: while their destination is known, viewer interest centres on their style of driving. What is extraordinary about the genre is how efficiently the writers provide plots which entertain and satisfy millions day after day, year after year; and which also peal the changes on the familiar themes that keep huge numbers of actors, directors and technicians working at a form of story-telling whose demands and complexity are quite unique.

Supplying the plots is a complicated mechanical process. A large cast of permanent characters has to be provided for, which means juggling at least three and quite often six separate story-lines in the air at any one time. This results, as we shall see, in a fragmentation of narrative which sounds fiendishly complicated when described, but which any viewer can follow with ease, even a newcomer to the genre. The story has to be capable of infinite protraction, in order to fill the endless hours, and it also has to accommodate a certain amount of repetition and recapitulation for the benefit of those viewers who may have missed something.

Most important of all, the plot is the engine for the workings of Destiny, which means the punishment of evil and the rewarding of good. This works dialectically: a crime is committed (by crime you must understand any transgression against the accepted moral code), which leads to reaction and revenge, whose consequences are only resolved by retribution and restitution.

At the centre of every plot there is love. Indeed, most of the basic themes spring from it – it is notorious for arousing every kind of emotion save happiness. Love makes people ambitious, racks them with jealousy, fuels them with revenge and sends them barking mad. Confused identity (where a child does not know its true parent) is the result of love-making out of wedlock; and hysterical illness is caused by the strain of frustrated love (amnesia means never having to say you're sorry).

A year's plotting in American soaps shows the principal story-lines to be rape (sometimes between estranged couples), the problems of motherhood, illegitimacy, the sharp points of the triangular love-affair, divorce, amnesia and/or insanity caused by grief at the apparent loss of a loved one, and death. Themes less obviously connected with love were drug peddling and the foiling of sinister plots, but as the happy outcome to these stories could only be achieved by the irresistible alliance of lovers, these too can surely be counted as love stories. As can the conquest through love of social problems like drug abuse, alcoholism, petty thieving and a little beating-up; and the inter-generational romances between young men and older women (or vice versa).

English soaps are no less love-lorn. Forgotten lovers, presumed dead, turn up unannounced, elderly but eligible. Love threatens to change the balance of an already unstable boardroom. Planned marriages are upset by the appearance of former husbands. Little bastards are revealed. Men offer to leave their wives and businesses for the love of a good woman – who of course turns them down. Faithful wives are temporarily abandoned by their husbands, yet still manage to avoid temptation. Manipulating ladies, frustrated at being given the brush-off, cry rape.

It is obvious from all this that the soaps are essentially romances, with all the sentimental appeal implicit in that term. But they are also a whole lot more. Because they are there week in week out, because they never end, they can have – when they choose – a powerful effect on an audience with a plot or theme that, however thickly coated in romance, is nevertheless both contemporary and provocative. As I showed in the previous section, they don't go in for political contro-versy, only individuals' problems. But whether it be rape, mugging, drugs or obesity, the way the plots handle these delicate, even un-pleasant, subjects is neither cowardly nor condescending. When it comes to dropping in the odd bit of grit, the soaps can produce a pearl. And if you think that such items go unnoticed by the audience, amidst the ceaseless romantic waves the soaps make in passing, you'd be greatly mistaken. One of the most striking things about the fans is the way they remember the tiniest details of past plots, even if they form a small part of stories that have been endlessly repeated, with minor variations, on each and every serial. It is the casual viewer who gets confused: anyone who believes that the regular audience is either unthinking, or incapable of absorbing what they see, could not – judging by viewer response – be more wrong.

It would be going much too far to claim that the soaps are important vehicles for social change. What one can say is that, simply through retaining the attention of an enormous and faithful audience, they can exert an enormous influence, in certain limited areas. These areas are those of the personal problems capable of individual solution – that is, those problems that really might be cured through love, understanding and determination. The very fact that the serials deal sparingly with such problems, spending most of their time on romantic fantasies, means that when they do move into such delicate and personal areas, their incursion is all the more noticeable. Nor are the fans put off by what might appear to be a change of style. Nothing happens suddenly in soap opera: measured deliberation (or, put another way, endless repetition) is the hallmark of the genre. Plotting is done so carefully, and so far ahead, that there is plenty of time for the viewers to prepare themselves for a "shock" – which isn't really a shock at all. If a favourite character is going to display an aberrant trait – take to drink, say, or indulge in a bit of rape – you will see them looking surreptitiously at bottles or bodies, running their tongues over their lips, letting themselves go a little, weeks before the event. Somebody will say something – a secret will be let out – hints will be planted, worries expressed, long before anything happens. The appetite feeds on such anticipation: when the blow falls, the lack of surprise is more than compensated for by the satisfaction of seeing what has been long-awaited finally occur. This process is one of the most successful parts of the mechanics of serial planning.

Crossroads, a programme not normally noted – even amongst its British fans – for its social conscience, is extremely proud of the work that it has done for the handicapped. The paraplegic Sandy, departed son of the motel's former owner, was often, throughout his years on the show, less than stiff-upper-lipped about his condition: he did not always behave with that quiet dignity expected of cripples, and even gave way, occasionally, to self-pity. The response of viewers was warm and sympathetic; and the lesson was not lost on those who considered cripples to be either saintly or sub-human. There was even a Crossroads Care Attendance Scheme, through which volunteers were put in touch with families needing a break from nursing disabled members. Sandy learned how to be independent; the public, more than twelve million of them, learned to look at the wheelchair-bound with more understanding. Similarly when a child suffering from Down's Syndrome (played by such a girl and not by an actress) was featured in a story-line that stretched over several weeks, public appreciation of the difficulties involved in looking after the handicapped increased measurably: donations increased to charities concerned with helping the similarly handicapped.

Meg Mortimer, the redoubtable (and now retired) matriarch of the *Crossroads* motel, actually went to prison, as a result of a motor accident which got her a three-week sentence. Her car had a defective wheel, and she'd had (so she said) one drink: the social message was thus "don't drink and drive, or put too much faith in a garage" (even if you happen to own it, as she did). Another message concerned the prison population. If Meg could survive in jail, the people inside couldn't be all that bad: it stands to reason (as she pointed out) that they're not *all* there because they have committed crimes of unimaginable wickedness. Some must, like her, have got there because of a minor offence (though it was important they learnt their lesson); others because they simply couldn't cope with all the problems of modern living. The moral actually went further than "There, but for the grace of God, go I": it implied that the usual assumptions made about the majesty of the law, the fairness of sentencing, and the deterrent value of prison – never mind the conditions inside – cannot always be taken for granted.

Of course there must be, amongst *Crossroads* viewers, many whose faith in the whole legal system is less than total. Nevertheless the fact that a middle-brow, middle-class serial could put its central character, a star who enjoyed roughly the same status as the Queen Mother, inside a jail, and have her emerge more sympathetic to its inmates, shows how a plot can prick the social conscience, even if it doesn't do so very often.

The American day-time soaps, each with some five hours of story to fill every week of the year, can – indeed must – take their time when airing an issue other dramas can only treat superficially. *The Young and the Restless*, the first show to put youth at the centre of its structure, was also among the first to feature a plot about rape and its consequences. Their story came out at the same time as two movies on the subject, which caused the *New York Times* to compare treatments of this theme, and conclude that *Y&R* did it best, because they had more time to give to it, and more space to examine all sides of the problem. Spreading the material over a period of weeks did not weaken its dramatic impact: hardened though viewers are to prime-time violence, there is something peculiarly shocking about having a violent act invade your screen when you are alone in the quiet of the afternoon.

Violence is so uncommon in the soaps that its impact is all the greater. The serial, unlike the movie, does not leave you to imagine the consequences. Rape is one of those things that tends to happen to other people: when it happens to one of your friends – and friends are what the serial characters become to the faithful viewer – you take the whole thing much more seriously. Certainly more seriously than you would a two-hour movie, however gut-churning.

The "right to die" has also been dealt with on several soaps, including *Ryan's Hope*, when Dr Seneca Beaulac was brought to trial for disconnecting the machine that was keeping his wife alive, even though she was in an irreversible coma. How you define death, and what is the best course of action for a loved one who will never recover, were fully discussed at his trial – at which Dr Beaulac was convicted and barred from practising medicine (though he continued as a hospital administrator). *Y&R* aired a similar plot, in which Snapper's highly moral mother switched off the life-support machine connected to his dying father. California, where *Y&R* is produced, soon afterwards became the first American state to put through legislation about defining death. No one would claim that *Y&R* was responsible for changing the law – but equally no one could deny that a programme that considers itself "unabashedly romantic" was unafraid of tackling something as painful as it was controversial.

Soaps have taken their audiences inside prisons and shown not only the depressing tedium of prison routine, but also the violence and homosexual attacks (*Crossroads* didn't quite get around to that.) A drug addicts' rehabilitation centre was used in a story about addiction in *One Life to Live*. Alcoholics Anonymous, long a favourite in movies, has finally been featured in the serials as a more reliable cure for drinking than sermons on love and understanding. Gamblers Anonymous too has had its moment.

If an important problem can be personalized, the soaps will often try to deal with it. *Crossroads'* resident bigot Arthur Brownlow (now dead) had to come to terms with black neighbours; the Australian soap *No. 96* featured gay neighbours – no easy matter where "bastard" is a term of endearment and "pooftah" one of the worst insults in the language.

Far more common are the illnesses that befall individuals. Agnes Nixon, known as the reigning "queen of the soaps" because she has created so many, brought in a character who was saved from a cancerous death by taking a Pap test. This was a tribute to one of Ms Nixon's friends who had died of the disease. No doubt millions of American women felt themselves for lumps after seeing soap characters do the same. The subject of mastectomies became no longer unmentionable (though this was after celebrities like Mrs Gerald Ford had spoken of their operations). Infertility, and the hopes raised and problems caused by such solutions as surrogate mothers and artificial insemination, have become plot-lines on both sides of the Atlantic.

Then there are the taboos, so common yet so covered up. Wife-beating, prostitution, even incest – the most powerful of all – get a regular airing. The possessive longings between parent and child, or brother and sister, are often featured, though of course the characters concerned are ignorant of their true relationship (unless one of them is *really* wicked). The viewer knows, or suspects, however, and naturally the relationship is doomed. But the very fact that these things are openly discussed, with a delicacy that stops well short of approval, is proof of the soaps' social awareness.

They may parade their conscience, but the soaps' staple remains romance. Love in one form or another will find its way through a maze as complicated as anything in Jacobean drama. For example:

Paul Stewart on *As the World Turns* married Liz Talbot. She gave birth to a child whose father was Paul's brother Dan. Some years later Paul died of a brain tumour. Dan divorced his wife to find happiness with Liz (who was the mother of his child and his brother's widow). But this was not to last: Liz was killed in a freak accident. Dan eventually settled down with one Kim Dixon: when he too died, his daughter Betsy – who had by now survived bastardy, confusion of identity, and the deaths of her supposed father, mother and real father – moved in with Kim. No wonder the poor kid left town to go to college and hasn't yet returned.

This complicated interweaving of characters' plot-lines is an economic device for finding new stories without introducing too many new players. Going through all the permutations of the people you've got under contract is a wonderful way of spinning things out. As Penelope did with the bit of tatting she said she had to finish before she would marry again – Ulysses being missing, presumed dead – the writers keep their suitors dangling by unpicking the threads they have already woven, when they think no one's looking. The thing has to look a little different every day, which it will if the material is successfully rearranged.

Of what does this material consist? Since the main object is to avoid too many happy endings, which spell the death of that conflict which keeps the characters going, a triangle is always preferable to the straight line between two beds. Of course there *are* love affairs that end in marriage, and very popular they are too with the audience. In spite of, or because of, the ever-increasing numbers of divorces, we adore watching girls (preferably in white, however unsuitable) walking up an aisle to promise themselves to a man with a flower in his buttonhole.

No doubt the soaps are simply reflecting the social approval for marriage as an institution. Statistics show that, however high the divorce rate, and the incidence of adultery, belief in the sanctity of marriage remains strong, even among those swearing fidelity for the second or third time. The fans long for their heroes and heroines to get spliced: they swamp the writers with requests to get the wedding bells jingling, and some even go out and buy a new dress for the occasion. Nevertheless the soaps' view of marriage is subversive. The romantic glow fades with remarkable suddenness, even on the best colour sets. The marriage will quickly come under strain, not because of the drudgery involved (that is never shown), but because of boredom, the ambitions of the husband, the temptations of a siren, the chance visit of an old lover. Everyone welcomes a nice wedding, but the serials' close-up of the knot shows it to be roughly tied and temptingly easy to unpick.

This is not a sinister plot by writers to undermine the most sacred of domestic arrangements. It is another flourish of that cocktail of fantasy and realism that is the soaps' specialty. To make a marriage work is hard graft, and the soaps do not flinch from showing the stress involved. While approval of the institution is implicit, and the build-up to it teasingly protracted, the consequences are made quite explicit: argument, suspicion, jealousy, revenge. The plots demand such conflict if the characters are to continue, and contemporary experience of marriage shows that there is plenty of material to draw on. Marriage is thus not a happy ending (unless the actors concerned are leaving the show). It is the beginning of new troubles ahead – which is precisely the view many hold of that most beguiling and exasperating institution.

It is rare to have an encounter between a man and a woman without there being some sexual electricity. In real life, the chores and obligations of everyday living tend to short-circuit any such current. On the soaps, by contrast (especially in America), nobody is bound by anything except the obligation to love. If a girl is chained to the sink, she is probably washing her hair in anticipation of her lover. Characters fall in love over and over again, whether they are married, separated, bereaved or suffering from amnesia. Love – not marriage – is the glue that holds the soaps together.

Yet anyone who watches them knows that sex, to which love is a preamble, is far more talked about than performed (a phenomenon noted by Manuela Soares in her excellent work *The Soap Opera Book*). There are endless discussions about the yearnings, the intensity of a feeling that no other human being has felt till this moment. All that is just warming up. Even lengthier are the exchanges about whether it's right, emotionally and ethically, to do this wondrously terrible thing. If the couple finally do get it together (and even if they don't), they are good for several weeks of deliciously guilt-laden dialogue about the consequences— on the children, on their regular partners or spouses, on their friends and relatives and neighbours and fellow-workers, even on each other. People who just have sex without full-scale debate have no scruples whatever.

Ms Soares maintains that women want to hear words of love from men who, as a sex, are rarely as articulate (about love or anything else) as they are in the serials. To that I would add that men too prefer talk to action, even if they listen rather than give tongue. We live in an age of peculiar sexual insecurity, where promiscuity – despite the happiness it has brought to some fortunate souls – has given rise to a whole industry of experts, whose advice and exhortations few can follow. The result is a miserable frustration, a feeling – not universal, but surprisingly widespread – that if you can't come three times a session you have failed yourself and your partner. The fatuous *machismo* which has thankfully lost its respectability in caring circles still haunts the bedroom, at least where two or three men are gathered together to discuss such matters with a drink in their hands and a gleam in their eyes. Then it's all talk, the imagination spiralling to conjure up performances which in reality would cause heart attacks or hernias. Men will talk (especially to other men) rather than do; and women, I venture to suggest, are much the same.

I do not believe that we are as highly sexed a species as the experts and exploiters would have us be. Why else would romance, whether as high art or low camp, have attracted so many listeners, readers and spectators since time began? Because, surely, it bridges the gap between the rhetoric and the reality. In romance, the man is never inadequate, much less inarticulate, while the woman discovers someone who wants her for more than her body. Their love is more than an act of sexual congress: it is a commingling of minds, spirits, ambitions, aspirations. It is a transfiguration, an alchemical conversion of base metal to gold, – and you don't have to worry about whether or not the sheets are clean. The act itself *always* happens off-camera: the most we get to eavesdrop on is the post-coital banter. More than that, the act itself is not nearly so important as the changed relationships in reality: through a mammoth build-up, and an even more colossal run-down afterwards, the act is put in (romantic) perspective – as something that happened surprisingly quickly when no outsiders were watching.

Romance also glosses over the mechanics of love-making that can be so intrusive, and often downright baffling, in life. You don't get the chatting-up that is usually (I mean in reality) so mawkish and repetitive. The man doesn't worry about his beard, his breath or where to put his hands; the woman has no need to bother about her complexion, her conversation or whether or not she is on the pill. She is as unconcerned about getting pregnant as about catching the dreaded herpes. Once they have decided to go to bed together – and that in itself is a less traumatic decision than whether or not to give vent to their feelings for one another – a shimmering veil descends. No foreplay, no grunting and groaning and hoping you're doing the right thing at the right time, nothing but a fade-out followed by a grateful smile.

And then what happens? As that bible of the American trade, *Soap Opera Digest*, put it, "If two people love each other and they want to have a baby, the pregnancy will end in miscarriage. If the woman doesn't love her husband but wants to stay married to him, she'll get pregnant by another man, *accidentally* (during one adulterous rendezvous), and *claim* it's her husband's baby." In the first situation, you have endless plot possibilities. The lovers will keep trying; if they fail one of them (usually the man) will get drunk and be seduced by a woman who will instantly become pregnant; or they can adopt someone who will turn out to be either the lost child of a dead brother or the real child of the husband's last girl-friend who was killed in an aeroplane. In the second situation, that of the unloving wife, you have a marvellously neat triangle which in many ways mirrors the first. Either way romance magics away the mechanics.

If I am right in believing that most of us – and not only those of us who watch soap operas – spend more time talking about sex, or watching other people talking about it, than engaging in it ourselves (of course we love doing it, but not as often as we boast we do), then this is an example of how words can disarm. When you express yourself about what moves or frightens you, you start to feel better. In the soaps when a character says, "I can't tell you how much I love you", that is invariably a prelude to a Niagara of articulated emotion. I don't believe that romantic dialogue is popular simply because its fantastical contortions are unlike anything heard in real life. I don't think it supplies something for which empty-hearted addicts yearn, but take the view that people find such sentiments therapeutic: their pleasure is in hearing, not what they might want to say themselves, but what they find unsayable. What the lovers in serials are doing, in other words, is to voice sentiments which frighten, or puzzle, or at the least dismay many people. By giving them utterance the characters rob them of their terror and mystery. The relief for the audience is not in finding words that one might store up for use to one's own lover, but in seeing expressed, in intimate surroundings, all the things which, having been said, can then be forgotten. Having soap characters exhaust themselves in love-talk is a wonderful way of clearing the mind for more pressing business.

Children have always been a potent source of plot in the soaps. Usually a source of trouble. Rarely do they ensure their parents a serene old age (what do you think this is, fantasy?): instead, they toddle off, or are despatched, as infants; get kidnapped; are the source of endless litigation, expense, and heartburn in divorce cases; fight with their fathers, mothers, siblings and contemporaries; get into drugs and become the victims of blackmail; or suddenly discover that they are somebody else's kid.

This last is a peculiarly common serial plot. No doubt, as Manuela Soares suggests, this answers a fantasy most children have of being adopted or discovering they are foundlings, whose real parents are of the blood royal or, at the least, immeasurably rich. Not that kids number large among soap viewers (though they appear to be a growing section of the audience) – but it is enough for grown-ups to be reminded of this childish dream/nightmare for it to strike true. Like amnesia, it allows the victim to escape the traumas of an existence that may be unbearable (because of parental squabbles, bereavement, or simply the miserable identity crises of adolescence), and slip into an entirely new personality. In the case of a child who suddenly discovers his or her real parentage, it offers a whole new background and life-style – usually better, and always different, from the one in which they grew up. The woodcutter's child who was raised in a hovel in the middle of the forest, and who then discovers he is really heir to the throne, was old when Oedipus was a lad, and if its modern equivalent is the secretary's daughter who turns out to be the boss's bastard and inherits his shares, not a lot has changed.

Conflict between the generations is the chief spur to progress (as philosophers from Socrates to Freud have pointed out). In serial plotting this conflict is particularly important, and one might imagine that, given the traditional morality underpinning the whole genre, it is always the old who win. Yet the soaps not only give full rein to the role of the young as fighting representatives of new values and styles, they also allow them a few victories or at least to come to some sort of acceptance of traditional wisdom that leaves the door open to change.

We all know the agonies of growing up, of trying to find and express our own truths, of the frustrations and arguments involved in defending these against our elders, of the painful victories and rueful compromises that overshadow acceptance. We have all experienced that – and we hope, we aspire, to behave differently to our own offspring. The soaps hold out the hope that it is possible to make progress, that things get better or at least become different. There is still the chance of happiness between the generations, of joint solutions to common problems, of peace and understanding, of harmony and contentment (whether through the discovery of new identities or the revelation of facts that alter the old). This is the expression of optimism, the reward for holding to the faith through a time of testing and pain, that all myths contain. And if the story-lines concerning children always feature a fairy-tale ending of recognition and reconciliation, that's all right as far as the plot is concerned. Though happy endings may be the death of some characters, once a kid has had a problem, they are going to have it, or bigger problems, as they grow up. After all the traumas of discovering who they really are (which is all adolescence is about, whether you're a frog or a prince), they've got love, ambition, jealousy, revenge and, no doubt, madness to look forward to.

The family in soap opera is not just Mum, Dad, kids and an occasional infestation of in-laws. People become related to one another at such a rate – through adultery, bigamy, amnesia, surrogate motherhood, rape and incest – that a term like "extended family" becomes laughably inadequate.

One observer has detailed the relationships between nineteen people who appeared in a single episode of the US day-time serial *As the World Turns*, every one of whom (as well as two who were discussed but did not appear) either had blood ties or family associations with everyone else. Tom came to visit John, but what every regular viewer would know about them both, and would be able to tick off as each reference occurred, was that John is Margo's father who works with Tom and her Aunt Maggie, who is Tom's former lover. John was also married to Dee, who is having an affair with Tom, who is the son of Bob (Miranda's lover), besides being formerly married to Carol (currently married to Steve), and the father of Amy. In addition Tom is a close friend of Hayden, as well as being her legal adviser with a brief to look into the mysterious death of her guardian Connie, who was once a lover of James, who also had an affair with John's daughter Margo. John was once father-in-law to the split personality (through amnesia) David/Donald, whose lover Cynthia's daughter Karen rooms with Hayden and David/Donald's granddaugher Betsy. Don't bother to try to work it all out: once you've watched the show for a few months it's as easy as solving Rubik's Cube.

Now the point about all this is not simply to confuse the casual viewer. First, as I have already suggested, it is to produce a stew that is as rich and piquant as possible, while being economical with the ingredients. If the plot-lines for a fixed cast of characters all intersect so that the thing looks like some sort of maypole dance, then what need is there of outsiders?

Second, and even more important, the purpose of such convoluted plotting is to turn casual viewers into addicts, by entrapping them in the web from which there is no escape save via the "off" button.

You know how it is with sports fans when you are an outsider. They talk in a language you scarcely recognize, about relationships and tactics and past mistakes and future glories that make no sense unless you know as much as they do. You may think you're familiar with the principles of the game under discussion, but if you try to say anything, and make a mistake over the smallest detail, you are contemptuously ignored – or patiently lectured. The soaps are a spectator sport of a kind. They go further than the theatre of the field, which is about winning and losing, the how and the why. They relentlessly pursue the relationships of each player, until death and often well beyond. The more complicated the story, the better it is to look at (for those who know what's going on), and the greater the viewer's investment in staying to see how it turns out. The genre works, indeed, on the basis of the viewers knowing something that the characters don't. The more the viewers know, the more they will *want* to know, though paradoxically they are ready to suppress their suspicions about, say, a villain or naive heroine, in the hope of being surprised. The viewer is thus both insider and innocent: one of the more fascinating aspects of the genre.

Any plot summary tends to read like a joke. This from *Crossroads*:

> Joe MacDonald told Kevin Banks the garage was to be redecorated, a major job. Percy Dobson tendered for the work. Joe promised Kevin he'd talk to Sharon Metcalfe about getting an estimate from Kevin. Late at night, Paul Ross was trapped by Valerie Pollard in the motel office. She phoned David Hunter, asking him to come at once because she alleged Paul had assaulted her. (Copyright © *TV Times Magazine*, *19-25 June 1982*)

Or this little melodrama from the discontinued US day-time serial *The Doctors*:

> Unable to endure the guilt of murdering her own brother, and with her desperate hope that he is only playing another one of their childhood games crumbling away, Catherine is finally overpowered by Nola, who manages to grab the gun. At that moment, the police arrive and Capt. Sawden jumps to the conclusion that Nola is about to murder yet a third victim. Mona tells the police that it was

Catherine, and Catherine alone, who did it all. As Catherine totally breaks down and confesses, stating that she only did what her father wanted her to do, Mona and Nola look at each other from across the room. Is their bitter warfare over at last? (from *Soap Opera Digest*, 15 Sep. 1981, whose summaries are taken down direct from the screen as the serial is on the air)

What matters, though, is not how the plot reads, but how it looks and plays. Even a first-time viewer would pick up some of the resonances, the codes equivalent to the good-guys-wear-white-hats, bad-guys-wear-black that tell you in a single glance what each character stands for, and his or her likely destiny. In *Crossroads*, Kevin is young, virile, open-faced and – even though married to the plain and bossy Glenda – is clearly an heroic innocent about to be had. Sharon Metcalfe is both fixer and siren – you can see it in her dark, lively, handsome features – while Valerie Pollard, who tries to seduce Paul Ross, is plainly a snobbish bitch. She takes too much care of her appearance (a sign of self-indulgence), wears too much jewellery (flash), and anyway is married to tycoon J. Henry (and so shouldn't be trying to bed head waiters). Even if you only watch one episode, the plot will make some sort of sense in terms of character relationships: and the more you know – such as Kevin's unemployment, money problems and marital difficulties, Sharon's ambitions and love-affairs, Paul Ross's ambiguousness – the more deeply you are involved.

The looks of those characters who animate the plots make up only one element of the pleasure. It is the *way* in which the stories are played, the conventions (which the fans accept) of splitting each plot up into tiny segments, which make the form unique. Let me demonstrate what I mean by going through a single episode of the American day-time soap *The Doctors* (NBC), one that was aired in June 1982. Though this serial – one of the last of the half-hour soaps – has since been axed, it remains a fine example of the complexity of the genre.

There are three separate stories in the weave. Story A centres on Nola, a tough woman, embittered by harsh experience, though loyal to family and friends. She has come to a moment in her life when she believes that the decisions she has to make will affect her forever. She has realized that the way she has done things in the past is not going to work in the future, and that she must re-think her entire position, at whatever personal cost, so as to do the right thing for her children and for treacherous Billy, to whom she is engaged (and whose baby she is apparently carrying, whilst enjoying affairs with other gentlemen too).

Story B concerns patriarch Dr Matt Powers. His old friend and colleague resigns, and Matt begins to doubt his own worth as a doctor. He worries that, by becoming an administrator, he has stayed too long away from surgery. Is he too old or tired to return to the practice he loves?

Story C is Natalie's: she has secretly eloped with Nola's brother Luke, and, in an attempt to prove herself, has arranged (in Luke's absence) a festival in The Medicine Man, the family-owned restaurant. The festival is a disaster, but although Natalie is worried about what Luke will say, she can blame the weather.

Right. These three stories were fragmented as follows. The first scene is of Nola in bed with Tor, a stranger to the town with whom she had fallen in love. Previous viewers would know that she was trying to decide between a gypsy life with him, or a loveless but secure marriage to Billy, the supposed father of her child. By the way Tor treats Nola, stroking her hair and murmuring sweet nothings, it is obvious to viewers they are in love. Nola asks what they are to do that day, Tor replies they're staying where they are. Nola laughs and tells him not to be silly. Tor says life should be silly and fun. Nola, brought back to reality, pulls away from him and gets up. Tor looks confused, as we dissolve to . . .

Matt's office in the hospital, with Matt being followed in by his secretary loaded with papers. She asks if he has time to see Dr Melendez; he says he's terribly busy, there's a directors' meeting that morning. She says Dr Melendez told her it was urgent. Cut to . . .

The Medicine Man, with Natalie vainly trying to clear up the debris from the festival before Luke arrives. He bursts in, and at once demands to know what the hell's going on. Natalie, caught off guard, can't immediately answer, which only enrages Luke more (he has a short fuse, despite declaring his undying love for her). He drags her ungently towards the kitchen, where the staff won't overhear, and insists she explain herself. Natalie tries to tell him about the festival and how much money it would have raised (again, the fans will know that Luke is heavily in debt). Luke says she should have had the sense to know there was not enough time to plan the thing properly. Natalie defends herself, insisting that however much was spent it would have been worth it. She reveals that the bank wants its ten thousand dollars paid at once. We cut back to . . .

Nola and Tor, with Nola explaining why she has to settle down to reality in Madison, instead of pursuing the idyll she and Tor enjoyed before. Tor (not unreasonably) asks what kind of realism it could be that will tie her up in a loveless marriage. Nola says she will learn to care for Billy, that she will make herself happy, and that there's no future for her and Tor. Cut to . . .

Dr Matt's office, with Matt asking his secretary to get hold of Dr Dave Melendez – who then walks in, saying he's hoping Matt has a moment. Matt says he always has a moment if Dave has a problem. Dave says it's not a problem, at least not for him: he's come to hand in his resignation, apologizing that it's at such short notice. Matt, deeply shocked, asks why. (All these obvious questions are to enable those new to the serial, or who have just tuned in, to catch up on what's going on.) Is there a problem in cardiology? Matt asks Dave. He knows they are short of staff and need new equipment, but he assures Dave he will fight for his department in the next budget meeting. Dave explains that that's not it: he's just tired. Matt offers him leave of absence. Dave says no, he really wants to cut down and spend more time with his family. He's missed his son Rick's whole life so far – and Rick's just graduated from university. Dave isn't going to miss any more. Matt says Dave is the finest cardiologist in the hospital, and how is he to replace him? Dave smiles and says Matt was pretty good himself until he started pushing pencils around. Matt offers to lighten his work-load, but Dave says he just doesn't have the energy or the drive any more. Sadly, Matt accepts his resignation. We dissolve back to . . .

The Medicine Man, with Luke arguing with Natalie. He says he doesn't owe the bank ten thousand. Natalie says she received a call saying the bank was calling in the loan. Luke angrily says that he borrowed the money from his sister Nola. Natalie says that's what she thought, but either they're wrong or . . . Or what? says Luke. Natalie replies that perhaps now that Nola is going to marry Billy he has persuaded her to call in the loan. Luke insists that Nola wouldn't do that to him. Of course not, says Natalie, but Billy would. Luke gets into a rage and sets off to ram Billy Aldrich's teeth down his throat. Natalie grabs him and calms him down, as we move to . . .

Nola's living room. She enters briskly, not looking at Tor who is behind her. He again asks why she is going to marry someone else. She says because it's the smart thing to do. He asks if she always listens to her head and not her heart. She says no and it's always meant trouble. Tor embraces her and asks if loving him is trouble. She says he's confusing the issue. They already made one mistake. He asks what it was: she replies that it's obvious (making it also obvious to the viewer that the child is Tor's, not Billy's). Tor demands to know if she thinks their baby is a mistake. Nola hesitates and says yes. Tor gets angry, as well he might, and says that if that's what she thinks he'll pick up the child wherever she has it and raise it in love. Nola says she doesn't want to give up her child; Tor says he doesn't want to give up either his child or its mother. Nola accuses him of not understanding: she can't live like a gypsy on a boat with two little kids. She wants them to have more than she had, more than hand-me-down clothes, everything she never had. Tor says gently that he knows what she didn't have. Then he should understand, Nola says. He says that if they were together their children would have what she never had. Nola replies that that's true, she never had a sailboat, unless Tor counts the plastic one for her bathtub (joke – rare in emotional moments). Tor says she's afraid to love him. After a pause, he says it's been nice knowing her and if she's ever in St Croix, look him up. There's a free boat-ride waiting. He picks up his jacket and leaves. Nola, stricken, watches him go. She knows she must have the strength to let go of him. Dissolve to . . .

The hospital, where Dr Steve Aldrich, our romantic hero (and Billy's stepfather) is going busily about his business when Matt stops him to tell him that Dave has resigned. Steve is shocked, and asks the reason, while keeping an eye on the clock as he has an appointment. Matt says he doesn't understand the reason: Dave and he were resident surgeons together. Steve has to go but suggests he and Matt lunch together. He rushes off, leaving Matt's reverie to be broken by a paging call. Cut to . . .

Nola pacing around her living room. The doorbell rings. She rushes to it, obviously hoping it will be Tor – but it is Billy. He notices her expression change and asks if she was expecting someone else. Nola denies it and pecks him on the cheek. He wants to know why she's been avoiding him. He wants her to be honest. Nola tries to stay calm and composed. She essays a smile as she turns to him and says she has decided on a day. An astonished Billy asks what she means. She says she means a day for their wedding. Cut to . . .

The Medicine Man, where Steve and Matt are ordering their lunch from Natalie. Steve asks about the trees that have been left over from the festival, to which Natalie makes a noncommittal reply and goes off to get their orders. Matt begins to talk about Dave and wonders why he feels tired. Dave is a young man who shouldn't retire this early. Steve gently reminds Matt that he and Dave are the same age. They all feel tired at times – even Matt has seemed so lately. Matt says he doesn't feel the need to retire; Steve replies that everyone has their own inner clock, which ought to be heeded. Matt says that Dave's departure is going to leave a great gap in the surgical staff, which gives Steve the opportunity to pay him a compliment on the fine surgery he used to do himself. Matt looks thoughtful. As they get their food from Natalie, Steve tries to reassure Matt that Dave's departure has nothing to do with him (Matt). Matt wonders if Steve is right. And finally back to . . .

Nola's living room, and Billy's surprise, held over from the previous scene where Nola had set the date. He asks if she means it, to which she quickly replies yes. Billy hugs and kisses her and asks her what the date is to be. She pauses for a long time, then shakes her head and, on the verge of tears, says she can't do this to him. The child she is carrying is not his. She knew that all along, and is sorry to have lied. He is going to be hurt, but the fact is she doesn't love him and can't marry him after all. Billy's reaction, not surprisingly, is first one of confusion, then of anger. He demands to know who she *is* going to marry. She says no one. Billy accuses her of lying: she will marry the father of the child. Nola says that's impossible. The man has gone out of her life: it would have been as much of a mistake to marry him as to marry Billy. Billy, softening a little, tells her he loves her. Nola accepts that, wishes that things could have been different, but repeats that she can't pretend or lie to him any more. She owes him that much at least. Billy, however wounded beneath the surface, stays cool and tells her to forget it: she doesn't owe him anything. He goes out. Nola leans against the door and gives vent to her tears. End of episode.

I have given this breakdown of a single half-hour episode in a five-times-a-week serial in detail (and at such length) because it illustrates a number of points. In the first place, it gets in at least six of the basic themes with which I opened this section: love (happy and unhappy), ambition, jealousy, revenge and confused identity. It goes without saying that the same serial also manages to feature madness and hysterical illness in parallel story-lines, and so complete the grand slam.

In the second place it demonstrates the moral values of soap opera roaring away in full-throated romantic form – and by putting down the story as you would see it happen on the screen, I come as near as I can to giving you in print what you would experience in pictures: the inexorable unfolding of a morality tale.

Thirdly, it shows how characters carry plot, and how plot advances characters without necessarily deepening them. Nola and Billy, Luke and Natalie are behaving just as they always behave in different situations: you have known them longer, you've spent more time in their company and (the producers hope) will want to know what happens to them. But do you know them better? Are they going to surprise you by doing something different? Fat chance.

The story breakdown also shows exactly how the writers snip up a trio of plots to form a sort of Mobius strip of complex illusion. Each story, or set of stories (every episode has at least three), aims to intrigue and entrap the viewer. To an outsider it might feel like being peppered with the small tiles making up the mosaic. When you allow yourself to succumb and watch a run of a few days (and how could you not want to know what Nola will do?), the picture not only becomes clearer, its colours also brighten. Yet the story I have laid out for you also stands on its own, leaving you to wonder what happens next. That shows the peculiar genius of the form.

Each of the plots with which this particular episode deals is not only split up by the progress of the other two, but also intertwines with them. Each assumes viewer acceptance of a set of conventions that are entirely television's own – I might say, entirely soap opera's. These conventions give you a snippet of information, ending in a teaser, which is followed by an entirely different piece of information, also self-contained, followed by a third. Each snippet contains different characters and concerns different plots, though some interaction occurs. For the viewer, however, this is nowhere near as confusing as it sounds. Indeed it is perfectly clear what assumptions one is to make: a combination of what the characters look like, what they do and say, the sets, the clothes (or lack of them) and the lighting against which they are displayed, all add up to a shorthand or code with which even casual viewers can make themselves instantly familiar. Some of the technique is of course borrowed from films, especially the use of cutting between scenes to advance the plot or increase tension. But the advancing of a multi-layered story is something only the soaps do, and after half a century they have become pretty good at it.

One might say that plotting proceeds in bursts of *coitus interruptus* (which some maintain only increases the appetite for more). Just when you think you're getting somewhere, you're forced to break off and consider something else. These breaks are not only for the benefit of the sponsor, to give time for the commercials: they are also a device for giving the illusion of density and of forward movement. You think you're getting a lot of stories, but in fact you're getting tiny droplets which are allowed to spread like oil on water. More time is taken up with recapitulation and establishing of character than with plot progression. It is very rare (though it does happen) for anything to be resolved in a single episode — the whole point, indeed, is to keep you guessing by stretching the thing as thin as possible, and letting it snap back at the start of the next episode. American soaps, the day-time ones, rely on this "elasticating" process, this stretching and relaxing, more than their English or prime-time brethren, because they have more time to fill. But speed of story-telling is not something you see on the soaps. It is against their nature to hurry a good plot – any plot, come to that.

To return to the *Doctors* episode I have quoted, the main characters and their immediate concerns are established within a very few seconds. Nola in bed with Tor, exchanging sweet nothings: you know their relationship at once, as much by the way that they touch and look at each other as by the dialogue they utter. And you learn that all is not well, that Nola is troubled, by her expression and the way she gets out of bed when Tor talks about life being fun. You also know that he is the weaker character by his confusion at what, in other circumstances, was a blameless thing to say. You, the viewer, need no further explanation.

Likewise with Matt's plot-line and with Natalie's. The paraphernalia of Matt's office tells you that you are in the presence of some big wheel, even if you'd never seen him before: his relationship with his secretary, authoritative without being hectoring, tells you he is someone who is not only used to command, but who enjoys the trust of his employees. Therefore you trust him too – as you did from the first because of his benevolent and patriarchal appearance. You also know he's important and busy, even before secretary Suzie has asked him if he's got time to see Dr Melendez, because she's carrying all those papers for him to sign. But what could be so urgent about Dr Melendez? you wonder – as you leave Matt for Natalie, obviously in a panic, trying to tidy things up before Luke appears. You panic too: what's wrong, what has she done, that Luke shouldn't know about? (even if you didn't see the previous episode)? Will she get things cleared up before he arrives? What will he do to her? Why is she so afraid?

All that, as it happens, was the pre-credit sequence, the introduction preceding the title of the show. It is a demonstration of what I have called the shorthand or code that enables the audience to know just where they sit with everybody and everything. It employs a marvellous economy of words and actions that any artist would be proud of: you are thrown into the middle, not just of one set of characters and a story, but of three. You know at once who is good, bad or indifferent; with a minimum of dialogue you pick up most of what's going on, whether or not you've seen the show before; and you're immediately engaged in wanting to know what's going to happen next.

In comes Luke. He and Natalie have a row: by the way he handles her – roughly – you know he's got a nasty temper, so you're at once on her side, even before she's given him her excuses and it turns out she was doing it all to help him. (This is assuming you're not the kind of pervert who likes seeing men rough up women. Judging from the vast correspondence that every serial generates, there are few deviants amongst the fans.) Then you're told Luke is in bad financial trouble. No wonder he's got such a short fuse! Will he get out of it? What will this do to his relationship with Natalie? Before you've a chance to find out, you're back with Nola and Tor. You learn about her romantic yearnings, and her determination to marry someone she doesn't love, out of some peculiar sense of duty, and just as you're digesting that, you're thrown back into Matt's office, and the shock meeting with Dr Melendez. So it goes on, back and forth, or rather one step forward and one-and-a-half back, a slow foxtrot of tease and withdrawal that looks much faster and more intricate than in fact it is.

This method of story-telling is common to all the soaps, whatever their nature. It is what entitles the genre to be considered an art-form as elaborate, as contrived and as recognizable as the musical. It is a form that has been bashed out over years on radio, but which television has refined and to a great extent redesigned. At first TV soaps were simply the radio stories with pictures. But it was quickly recognized that the new medium could exploit film technique and conventions to do something entirely special and new: engage the eye and entrap the attention with a never-ending story that had loops of tension like lassoes. Television has a unique ability to capture the attention, and the serial is the most powerful way of working on it. One can talk or work through the box's chatter, just as one always can with radio, but it only needs the eye to catch a glimpse of something familiar, and one is absorbed.

The key is the familiar. Consider how often you sit down and allow yourself to watch something – a film, a rerun comedy show, a (rare treat) repeated play – even though you may have seen it before, not once but several times (in the case of old movies especially). One complains, "Oh God, not again!" but if the set is on, one sits in front of it nevertheless. I could say, though without much conviction, that our need to be comforted by the familiar comes from our bruising exposure to the unfamiliar in an age of constant change. Children love the familiar: being told the same story over and over is as much a pleasure to them as it is torture for the parent. It represents the reassurance of much-loved characters in situations whose outcome is known in advance. So of course do the soaps. In a way you're being told the same story, with variations, five days a week every week of the year (or once, twice, or thrice a week for a season: the principle is the same). Nothing can get more familiar than that.

This familiarity is maintained even though what the viewer gets (and the listener to, for instance, *The Archers*) is subject to fragmentation and delay. The splitting-up of the three story-lines of the quoted episode of *The Doctors* is only part of the picture: a week's viewing will include perhaps three *other* plots, which means that, if Nola's declaration of the truth to Billy ended, say, Tuesday's episode, anxious viewers might have to wait until Thursday, or even later, to witness the next stage in her particular drama, since the intervening period was devoted to an important operation on another character, to someone else's problems and to a chance meeting between Tor and Billy. The viewer is expected to retain in his or her mind all these characters, with all their peculiarities and past confusions, and become involved in at least six plots, all spinning in the air at the same time. Written down, it sounds like a demanding intellectual exercise. Yet anybody can do it, and millions do.

What makes it easy to understand what's going on, what makes these conventions acceptable, is the pace of the story-telling, the repetition of past snatches of plot, the reliance on television shorthand for instant recognition by viewers, and the way television itself convinces us to believe what it shows us.

The pace is the slowest that will fill the time available while still keeping the viewer wanting to know what will happen.

The repetition is not only necessary for new viewers, it is also important for those called away in the middle of a show, or who miss the odd episode (it appears that a majority of viewers only watch a half of each week's offerings; which argues that the huge and constant viewing figures are topped up by new viewers).

The shorthand or code I have already dealt with. Radio used a similar code – only bad ladies smoked, for example, and you could tell exactly who was good or villainous from vocal delivery – but television has developed this into an instrument of extreme subtlety that is universally accepted.

Television makes us believe what it shows us because it has broken down our resistance by being on so often for so long. We may not accept it as Gospel Truth, although, for example, more people are convinced of the truth of television news than believe what they read in the papers. Most of us can tell fact from fiction when we see it on the screen (though the soap fans blur these lines in a fascinating manner when it comes to identifying actors with the characters they play). What I'm trying to say is that we accept what television tells us, and even more the *way* in which we are told, simply because it *is* on television.

You may argue that, as a captive audience with that set winking at us from its corner in our living rooms or wherever, we have no choice. They give us what they want in the way they want to give it to us. In one sense that is of course true. But it would be ridiculous to say we have nothing to choose from. We've had mass-market television for a good thirty years now, and in that time a huge variety of things has been tried. If producers have returned time and again to the serial form,

and its intertwining plots, that is because a large section of the audience
has chosen to support them. There is the argument that people take
what they're offered because that is all they're offered. As I am here
concerned with soaps, I can safely say that, although they have a
near-monopoly over the day-time hours, at least in America, they still
make up only a small proportion of the network output, albeit a
proportion which generates more imitation, and more profit, than any
other. If market forces are a safe guide, soap opera works. Approve of
them or not, the customers like them. The form in which they have
evolved is part of their popularity. The soaps show us pictures in a way
that is entirely their own.

There is a theory that the soaps' method of proceeding in a series of
constant interruptions mirrors the routine that is the fate of housewives
and viewer-mothers with young children. Nothing ever gets quite
finished: just as you're doing one thing, the kid demands attention and
you have to stop and attend to its wants. The serials are the first, indeed
the only form of entertainment which caters for this kind of frustrating
and distracted viewing. Although neither characters nor plots deal with
the chores with which a woman has to deal, they offer her an escape,
into fantasy or whatever, that is packaged according to her needs, and
where her own frustrations are reflected. The fact that the woman is
also a big consumer of the products advertised – and a powerful voice
in deciding what the family will view later – has not escaped the
producers.

But it would be a mistake to think that the form has been cynically
– I mean commercially – tailored to the needs of a particularly lucrative
section of the audience. Mothers are only part of the fan-club. Most of
us lead lives of quiet distraction: we all have plenty of chores to perform
– a feature of unemployment is the invention of routines to keep one
from going mad – but rarely do we actually finish anything before
starting something new. Our lives do not resemble those we see on the
soaps, but the form in which we watch those lives unravel – the
interrupted climaxes, the bombardment with other people's problems
– parallels our own. Soap-watching is a lifelike occupation, even if the
lives which provide such a welcome diversion are utterly fantastic
(which they're not, at least not all the time).

The form also caters for viewers with a limited attention span. Some
would say it panders to them, breaking the story up into little bits so
that the most simple-minded will have no difficulty in following the
thread. Those who regard this as patronizing or worse (even corrupting,
or tending to mindlessness) will also have noted that some of the
interruptions are an excuse for a commercial (some of course are simply
scene changes). I would not for a moment deny that the soaps' chief

purpose is to pin an audience down for the delivery of advertising messages – or, where a public service organization like the BBC is concerned, to keep as large a number of viewers as possible from the alternative commercial programmes. The manner in which the serials tell their stories has proved its efficiency both in holding viewers and in following the lives of a large number of diverse characters. In a sense it is the visual equivalent of that most intellectually respectable pastime, reading a book. No one except proof-readers (and sometimes not even they) reads every word: we skip and flip and reread some bits and miss out others. The soaps offer a similar method of proceeding, skipping at one moment and going over and over the background at another. Of course we do not have quite the same control as we do over the pages, but the effect is similar. It is the only form which proceeds at the pace of its audience.

All this is part of the way television convinces us of its truths. The glittering box is a reliable presence and a constant companion, a source of distraction for ourselves and our families. It keeps children quiet, and it fills the silences that occur between the most loving couples. If you want it to or allow it to, it will stop you talking, thinking or working – although it needn't do any of these things. It offers a continual procession of oddly matched items – news, comedy, drama, music, sport – which the soaps themselves offer in their own miniature parade. Television has become a necessary, indeed an essential, service. Therefore, because we rely on it to such an extent, we accept what it tells us. Grumble as we might – grumble as we do – it has come to mean as much as the telephone: once you have it installed, you cannot imagine life without it. And, as with the telephone, also supplied by a vast commercial organization, we may grumble in private at the quality of the service, but we are only moved to grumble in public when something goes wrong, when the thing breaks down, when supply is interrupted. We accept the service, and the mysterious manner in which it is supplied, as a right.

Actually grumbles are taken more seriously in the production offices of the soaps than anywhere else. I shall have more to offer on this in the section on the public, but it is enough to say here that these grumbles are either at inconsistencies in character or – more frequently – at the progress of the plots. Those who take the trouble to write in accept the framework as they accept the conventions of the serial. There are remarkably few complaints at what the critics, with some justification, point to: ham acting, poor writing, dull direction. The fans are interested in the *story* and if the mechanics that keep it trundling along suddenly show a fault, then they are quick to voice their concern. There are a lot of holes to be picked in the quality of the fabric out of which the serials are manufactured. What cannot be denied is that their pattern and cut are acceptable to millions whose intelligence and critical faculties cannot be airily dismissed.

There are many fans who can tell you in enormous detail the background of their favourite characters – what they were wearing at the wedding, who it was insulted them, how they reacted and the dreadful consequences. Their memory goes back years: these are the people who write in indignantly when a writer gets something wrong. Such feats of memory, which are by no means the prerogative of those exclusively devoted to one serial, are made possible by the form in which the plot is retailed. The slow pace and steady repetition etches details on the mind. Why are all the plots so similar? Surely it is possible to offer something new that will find acceptance?

The reason why novelty is so rare on the soaps has to do with the mechanics of the form and the expectations of the audience. The demands that are made on the writers prohibit them from stepping outside the formula, as I shall show. It would be easy to say that they and the producers content themselves merely with giving the public what it wants. They do; but why does the public want it so much? My answer is that the soaps alone provide the reassurance that we all need, through plots that fuse fantasy and familiarity into a formula capable of an infinite variety of applications. And if that sounds like a spiel for a patent medicine, a nostrum to apply to all known ills, the parallel holds.

The Greeks, from whom so much of our dramatic heritage derives, were accustomed to theatre being both competitive and cathartic. That is, new playwrights competed with one another at the festivals, just as as they do on the networks, with dramas whose purpose was to purge the audience of their unworthy fears and strengthen their moral fibre, by showing a serious action whose consequences arouse terror and pity. I could go even further and compare the multiple plotting of the soaps with the trilogy of linked yet independent plays (followed by a satyr-play, or mockery of what had gone before) that each dramatist was asked to present at the Athens festival. Certainly the dialectical principle on which Greek tragedy was constructed – an offence against moral principles, followed by a counter-offence and a final resolution – holds good for the plotting of serial drama. And if we accept the classical definition of tragedy as a play dealing in an elevated poetic style with events which depict people as the victims of destiny yet superior to it, then – leaving aside the poetic style – we have a description that applies equally to *General Hospital* and to *Medea*.

So it is not the *plots* that matter as much as the purpose of the play. The purpose is a moral one: to strengthen the audience's belief in their place in the accepted order of things. But this does not mean that the soaps are the tool of the self-styled "moral majority". If the soaps are anyone's tool, they are the sponsors'. Their moral foundation, however, is that of a classical tradition which is over two thousand years old. Of course theatre has been used, then and since, to try to arouse the citizenry to action over the evils of their time. Even the soaps have made one or two attempts at this, as we have seen. But by and large the plots that sustain them concern the consequences of an offence against the "natural order" which reigns supreme in the end. You can be as rude as you like about the politics of the serials, but the inescapable (or unpalatable) fact is that the audience laps them up.

All this may sound like a long way of saying that the majority is conservative in its tastes. But the cathartic element in the serials goes deeper than politics. My comparison with Greek drama may seem far-fetched – the quality of the language is one area where it falls down – but the purpose of their theatre and the purpose of the soaps is much the same. Not only are there startling similarities in plot-detail (the Oedipus myth is alive and well, as are mayhem, adultery, bigamy, gate motherhood and bastardy in every shape and form), but the expectations of the audience are identical: they want to see evil punished and good triumphant. They want to be entertained, frightened, made happy, uplifted. The plots that do this most effectively are those that have been around forever. The two themes governing the rest are the relationship between the sexes, and that between humanity and destiny. What veins could be richer than those?

There is much comfort to be derived from the thought of destiny, of circumstances beyond our control. From murderous passion to ungovernable lust, it is good to watch others give way where we are forced to rein ourselves in – and to see them suffer for it. This, surely, is the very basis of catharsis (to call it the purgative effect demeans it to the status of laxative). Being involved, a silent partner, in something one has often wanted to do but has never dared – seeing it done in an explosive relief of tension – being appalled, punished by proxy, at the consequences: it bolsters the certainty that if one does do the forbidden, one is not going to get away with it. And yet one wants to see it done. To bed the beauty (of either sex), to abandon the children, to steal, cheat, lie, rob, even to murder: these are the things marking one's defiance of the accepted order. Not to defy it, not to identify with the defier, is to be a passive personality incapable of romance or ambition. Those who defy destiny, or common morality, are the ones whose challenge, although doomed, is a demonstration of humanity's right to protest. Their punishment is a reaffirmation of the values which themselves demand constant challenge to keep them sharp and bright.

Sometimes the plots seem *not* to be delivering the ending we all wish for. When, on *Dallas*, Miss Ellie (a good woman as well as a Ruler) challenged Jock's will, and the judge ruled against her, that was a violation of the soap opera canon. But of course this was a clever way of shocking us into watching all the more intently. We all knew what would happen – certainly J. R. wouldn't have things all his way – but there was a delicious thrill in the possibility that he might. Certain, deep down, of the outcome, but teased by the thought that it might all go wrong, that we might be cheated of our expectations: it is such possibilities that make the genre so addictive.

The soaps' exploitation of hysterical illness – and specifically of amnesia – is a further example of fantasy fulfilled and punished. It brings alive the dream of leaving behind a life that is dull or beset with with problems, and taking up a new existence without guilt or remorse (because if you've lost your memory you can't be expected to remember what you've abandoned).

If the plots all resemble one another, not to mention their classical predecessors, does this mean that our concerns are just what they have always been? Have we not learned, in two thousand years, to take our minds off sex, power and frustration at our impotence? Of course we haven't. The rate of change in human nature makes a glacier seem swift in comparison, and this against a moving diorama of surface change, of altered conditions, that is constantly accelerating. The soaps can and do deal, as the Greeks also dealt, with changing contemporary issues, but the relationships between the central characters, and the attitudes which govern the progress of the plots, have not altered at all.

You may get a story in which a son is goaded into running away by the revelation that the man living with his mother is not his real father. The boy turns to drugs, and sets up with a mistress who either turns out to be his sister, or is acting as surrogate mother to the child of his real father. This theme, which Sophocles handled rather more starkly than *Another World*, may sound – indeed is – full of contemporary references. Teenage rebellion, illegitimacy, drugs, unmarried mothers, a touch of incest: we read about those all the time. Yet you may be sure, as Athenian audiences were sure, that the son will return chastened to his mother (assuming she hasn't gone berserk meanwhile); that his mistress will either miscarry or die in giving birth to a child who will grow up to haunt him (but turn out not to be his child after all, being, in effect, his brother). The boy will submit, in penance, to being bound by the ties of family, and live miserably ever after. The issues are peripheral to the resolution of the consequences of our hero's rebellion, and the way in which this resolution comes about is a foregone conclusion, an affirmation of the known and accepted.

When I started work on this book, I thought a detailed study of the plots would provide me with a fascinating history of popular concerns. Why were the fantasies of marrying beyond your station (*Our Gal Sunday*, *Backstage Wife*, etc) so popular during the Depression? What did the enormous following behind the medical soaps in the '30s and '40s imply about relations between doctors and patients? Was the progressive softening of the centre of *Mrs Dale's Diary* a commentary on post-war disillusionment with the British Labour government? Were the romantic bubbles of the first TV soaps a covert comment on the Cold War, or a yearning for an innocence apparently lost to the rock 'n' roll generation? Does a rash of plots concerning surrogate motherhood (where a woman begs or agrees to carry a child for another set of parents) herald a change in attitudes towards maternity? Is the world-wide interest in programmes like *Dallas* a reflection of capitalist greed? Have the great social changes of the last half-century – technology, urbanization, unemployment, working mothers, mobility, the nuclear family – found an echo in the soaps?

I was forced to the conclusion that if there was an honest answer to all these questions, it was "God knows." The plots are immemorial: contemporary issues are dropped in – often to great effect – simply to remind you which generation you belong to. This does not mean that the writers, now or at any time in the half-century of serial history, ignore contemporary attitudes. They could not do so without sacrificing the recognizable nature of their creations. Their subjects and settings are contemporary, after all: in style, fashion, speech, in everything other than moral rectitude (or turpitude), the characters they invent plots for are larger-than-life versions of people you come across in the street. Anything else would be costume drama, which by my definition isn't soap opera.

All the plots do is to provide an excuse for the characters to dice with destiny, and with each other. The audience knows what the consequences of any major action will be: they want the plot to surprise them with the "how" and the "when". The Greeks waited to be stunned with poetry and the spectacle of the "god" descending in his machine to put everything to rights. Modern audiences do without the poetry, but are compensated with stories that interbreed, large numbers of characters and sets, and – in recent years – exotic locations and exciting visual effects. Even these developments have not altered the bases or the mechanics of the plots that have served writers from Aeschylus to Harding Lemay. Deceit always leads to trouble. A secret will always out. Abuse of wealth or power will always result in unhappiness. Transgressing the moral code will always end in tears. If lovers go through hell to find a happy ending, there will always be somebody or something waiting to steal the bubbles from the celebration champagne.

Of course there should be room here for a plot exposing the horrors of racial discrimination or paraplegic frustration or corporate corruption or the sinister possibilities of plastic surgery, few of which Euripides would have been able to use. But that doesn't alter the fact that the soaps are heir to a dramatic tradition of morality drama whose plots and characters are timeless, no matter how the actors are bedecked. (Is our yearning for a happy ending a sign of our good nature, or of our innate puritanism that allows happiness only to those who really deserve it?) What the soaps have added to tradition is a narrative method of extraordinary fragmentation, a method that has become theirs alone. It is with this that they have created something unique, even on television, from the oldest stories in the world.

THE WRITERS: SMILING
ON THE TREADMILL

Forget the struggling artist sitting in her or his lonely room sucking inspiration from the end of a pencil. The soap opera writer is a cog – more than a cog, a flywheel – in a corporate enterprise.

The production of a soap opera is organized along the lines of a small and highly competitive industry. The writer, that creative spirit without whose words there would be no product, is nowhere near the top of the hierarchy. He or she comes below the script editor or the continuity department, who answer to the associate producer, who is junior to the producer, whose boss is the executive producer, who is employed by the production company, which is owned or controlled or funded by the network or sponsor. The writers are thus a sort of middling executive, the type who has his or her own office with no carpet and who probably has to share a secretary. They are part of a writing team whose work flares briefly into importance before being taken over by others.

Writers even have their *own* hierarchy, headed by the serial's creator (who may or may not play a continuing role in production). There is a head-writer or story-liner, who presides over a gaggle of sub-writers or dialoguers, all under short-term contracts. These typewriter serfs provide the scripts from the outlines prepared by their overlords. It may not be art, but it's very well paid – and very hard work.

Many soap writers carry about with them a certain sense of shame. Are they not artists, who should be producing the odd masterpiece of original and challenging literature? Instead they are expending their creative energies – for ample reward – on what most of their peers consider a piece of junk. Their coinage is cliché, they are stuck with an invariable formula, they labour on an assembly line of whose product they are not always proud.

Even the fans, though they revere the product, often revile the writer.

That is when they (the writers) get things wrong: when a character who for years was a gynaecologist suddenly appears as a paediatrician, or a girl claims the wrong man as her father, or a quarrel is referred to which the fans remember as taking place between two different people. The writer is blamed for preposterous plotting, for putting characters in situations that exist neither in reality nor in context, for dialogue that is incredible and, worse, dull. That is the negative part of public reaction.

The positive part is the reverence accorded to someone not only close to favourite actors and actresses, but who has some control over their destinies (and who is highly paid). Soap writers testify that, when their identity is discovered, the commonest reaction is, "Of course I never watch it, but my wife/husband/mother/child does, and what the hell *is* going to happen to X?" To be seen with a script, that visible manifestation of the writer's contribution, is to arouse interest and awe, especially among school children, for whom anything on television is still somehow magical. A public which, on the whole, does not rate literature very highly, may accord the soap writer the nearest thing to the glamour of stardom he or she is likely to get.

Is soap writing an art, a craft or a trade? It is like factory work. The hours are long, the labour routine, and the product highly visible. No doubt that explains why the public accepts the serial writer as a pro, whereas most other forms of writing are somehow arty-farty. You can *see* what the serial writer turns out daily, weekly, or whatever: even if you don't remember the credits (and endless repetition helps), you know that here is a writer at work. There are a small number of people who believe that the actors make it up as they go along. It may look like that sometimes, but it's absolutely not true. Actors can play hell with what the author has written for them – and they do – but they start with the script before chewing it up.

An art involves the individual product of an original mind. There is not much of that in soap opera, not least because it is so much of a team effort. To produce art also takes time, of which there is precious little in a production schedule; and it involves the pursuit of excellence, revising and refining until the artist is satisfied the thing cannot be further improved. There is little time for *that* in soap opera.

This is not to say that there are no artists working in the soaps. There are sub-writers who knock off a script in a few days, and having thus assured their security (artists don't *have* to be hungry to produce good work), turn to more original and more demanding writing. For such people, and I too have tried to be one of them, the serials act as a sort of patron, offering good money for part-time work that frees them for other things. A few, who have gone on to produce great and original work – Jack Rosenthal and Jim Allen, for example, who both served apprenticeships on *Coronation Street* – regard the soaps as useful training in producing economical and pointed dialogue to a tight deadline.

There is of course the danger that, for less determined and creative writers, both the security and the rigid discipline of the soaps smother the ability to do anything else. The number of soap writers who have broken successfully into other spheres is small (it is greater among soap actors, many of whom burst into print with impunity). Few writers are able to earn a living just by writing: for all those who take up what they hope will be part-time jobs – teaching, delivering mail, refuse collecting, publishing – the names of those who have the energy to write, and write well, when they have finished can be scribbled down on the back of a wage-slip.

There might be a case for describing the people who created the soaps, the Hummerts, Irna Phillips, Agnes Nixon, Tony Warren of *Coronation Street*, Peter Ling (who with Hazel Adair invented *Crossroads*), Kevin Laffan of *Emmerdale Farm*, as artists. Frank Hummert, as we saw, rejected the idea of being the inventor of the form, claiming instead that he took it from the pulp serials – but nevertheless the soaps have evolved something that is special enough to merit the description of art form. And those who invent the basic situation, the small community peopled by characters to whom other writers give shape and personality, can fairly be credited with using an original mind to produce something individual.

Yet they are not artists, unless the designer of, say, the "T" model Ford is an artist. A work of art cannot be endlessly reproduced without loss of quality, and however hard the production team of a serial strives to maintain standards, the writing, acting and direction are not of that quality – cannot, given the restrictions of the form, be of that quality – which art requires. The serial is a commercial product, churned out to precise specifications of timing, style and budget. A commercial product may contain all kinds of artistic flair, but it cannot be art, which is refined to individual standards of excellence. I myself don't think its creators care that much whether or not they are called artists: that they work in a rewarding art form is sufficient. An art form is something less than a work of art: it has the shape, but lacks the substance. That's art enough for soap opera.

But a craft, certainly. You have to be trained to be a craftsman, you have to serve an apprenticeship and attain high standards, you have to have flair. You are in the business of making something special, involved in work that not everyone can do. Whether or not you feel, or are, part of a production line, you can put your own mark on the product, the stamp of individuality. It is an honourable calling, one with its own guilds and mysteries. A craftsman has status and security: he or she is well thought of by those who need their skills, and there is no shortage of employment for those who have shown themselves capable of producing quality work on time. Soap opera writers would be proud to call themselves craftsmen. Why then are they ashamed – or why do some of them affect a sense of shame – at their calling?

Presumably because it is also a trade, and between artists and tradespeople there is a tradition of mistrust and scorn that is hard to eradicate. Even craftsmen can be pretty snobby about trade. The worth that artists or craftsmen put on their own work is reckoned in more than cash: there is artistic merit, for one thing, and the investment of individual effort for another. They resent the treatment of their work simply as product, with a resale value inflated as high as the market will bear. They resent even more the profit taken by the trader, who makes money – usually a good deal more than the artist or craftsman – through no other skill than wheeling and dealing.

That is what many writers *think* about trade. They know, of course, that without it they wouldn't survive, that without entrepreneurs and money men they'd get no advances on their books and scripts. But the trading process treats everything as a commodity, to be bargained for in terms of cash, and this can be bruising to the susceptibilities of artists and craftsmen. They like to think they are offering something nobody else is capable of offering, and instead find themselves priced according to strictly commercial criteria, usually below what they reckon they're worth. Thus slighted, they limit themselves to giving what they've been paid to give, and what's more they add to their resentment a certain contempt for paymasters who are so easily satisfied.

All this, you may think, is the sort of snobbery that should not be shared by people with any sense of artistic integrity. But writers are as status-conscious as any other profession. And soap writers are particularly sensitive about the scorn of their colleagues, especially since they – the serial writers – are higher paid and enjoy larger audiences than anyone except the big best-sellers. Why should the writer of some crummy book or a play, which managed to limp off-off-Broadway, get respectful notices in all the papers, with all the esteem that goes with that, when someone who turns out a script that is watched by fifteen million people, and what is more is widely discussed by its fans, gets dumped on, not only by reviewers (if they deign to notice it at all), but by the writer's peers?

The soap writer would say the detractors are jealous (which is probably true) and that they don't understand the nature of the work involved. To an outsider, a soap might be written by a computer, so restrictive, so unchallenging to the imagination, appears the formula that must be followed. Who could take pride in dialogue that rises from the banal to the fatuous? What satisfaction, apart from the money, can there be in working to such a punishing schedule in a medium that is strictly commercial, that is simple-minded, transitory and so greedy for material that it appears to lack all discrimination?

It is questions like these that make the soap writers bow their heads. I am appearing for their defence – or rather, to enter a plea in mitigation. The treatment received by the writer of the most popular programmes in the most popular medium on earth, is a reflection of attitudes to the art – I mean craft – of popular writing.

The soap writer gives the audience what it wants, over and over again. What it wants is something entertaining, stimulating without being demanding, ordinary without being banal. The writer has to produce work that meets these demands within a short time. The dialogue – although, as we shall see later, it must perform a number of complex tasks – must sound like ordinary, everyday speech, the sort of talk you can hear anywhere. But as far as public esteem goes, what sounds ordinary could be written by anyone. And if anyone can do it, who's going to respect those who do?

The essence of my plea in mitigation is this. It is not possible, in serial writing or anything else, to guarantee quality when quantity is what is demanded. The writer is required to produce dialogue to a certain standard, and this standard is maintained by head-writers and producers who reject work and demand rewriting all the time. But the standard is set according to the constraints of time, budget and serial formula. That is what is involved in giving the public what it wants. In a genre as responsive as the serials are to public demands and criticism – where, in a sense, it is the viewers and not the writers who own the characters – the audience gets what it asks for. The defence rests.

The way in which American serial writers work has altered little from the days of the Hummerts, who based their procedure on the methods of their advertising agency. Broadly, once the idea has been sold to the network or sponsor, the story-lines for the months ahead are worked out by the head-writer (or head-writers) in consultation with the producer (or producers) and a representative from the network (or sponsor or production company).

Once the outlines of future plot have been agreed, the head-writer breaks down each episode in great detail. These detailed plots are then parcelled out amongst the sub-writers, who flesh them out with dialogue. These are then passed back to the head-writer, who edits them before passing them onto the producer for comments. The sub-writer may then have to rewrite, but once the producer has given the final OK, the episode is handed on to the director for casting and recording. The sub-writer has nothing (or remarkably little) more to do with it; as one episode or batch of episodes is in production, the whole process is grinding on with future stories.

English serials, although less bogged down by committee decisions, proceed on much the same lines: story conferences lead to detailed story-lines which are passed to the writers whose labours have to be approved by the producer. Not every soap follows this pattern exactly – *Emmerdale Farm* (Yorkshire) allows its writers more latitude than most – but the hierarchical process is always the same. It is a working method arrived at independently in England and America, and it appears to be the only one capable of dealing with the demands of the form.

One constraint which limits the writer's freedom is what the producer will or will not accept. Now it is fair to say that, within the limit of the serial's own formula, the producer will take quite a lot. It would be wrong to cast the producer and cohorts as the enemy of new ideas, as the brutal, rapacious, commercially minded stamper-out of integrity and originality. The producer is as desperate for new thinking as everyone else connected with the show. Anything that will keep it popular and on the air is welcome. The number of themes that cannot be treated is very small: what is much more restrictive is the way in which they can be treated. That is a limitation of the genre, rather than the producer's lack of imagination.

This is tacitly accepted by serial writers. They express themselves as best they can within their brief, which is to please their public. If they fail, they are not good soap writers. Good soap writers adapt to what the public wants: that way they please the fans, the producers and their bank managers. Bad soap writers may, or may not, be better *writers* than good soap writers, but if they don't manage to hold the viewers' attention, they're working in the wrong genre. That has to be the worst of all possible worlds: doing a job for which you feel a certain contempt, and not even doing it successfully.

Writers are usually hired on thirteen-week contracts that can be renewed, or terminated without compensation, according to performance. Job security amongst serial writers is, however, good, as few writers are capable of producing what is required within the constraints of the form. To outsiders trying to break in the whole thing seems like a guild or freemasonry. In fact those who do get in and accept the limitations and, what is more, enjoy the work, will always find employment. Because they are well paid, because they have to be highly trained, there is enough invested in them to produce dividends for somebody. The more they are fired, in fact, the more they are re-hired, especially if they are head-writers. This is the same corporate principle operating in commercial enterprises: if somebody has been trained to do a job that is difficult and demanding, that ability is going to be useful, regardless of the quality of the work produced. The quality, anyway, is a subjective matter: what is wrong for one company and market may well be right for another. Although all soaps are similar, they are all in competition with one another: a writer who was getting stale with one set of characters may well fizz with inspiration when confronted with another.

In the constant battle – the one that must never be lost – against being boring, when dealing with characters who have been public property for years, the serial writer has a limited choice of weapons. Deployment of these weapons is the real test of professional skill. The character can only be altered over a period of months, if not years, during which compensating factors have to be grafted onto the other characters with whom the original comes into contact. To kill off a main character is to rob the audience of an old friend, and the grief and outrage at such a bereavement is loud and genuine. This, then, is only done by a writer as a last resort. In fact it is rarely done for reasons of plot: rather it is to do with corporate or production demands, such as the breakdown of negotiations with the actor or actress involved over the renewal of their contract. This was the real reason behind the departure of the matriarch of the *Crossroads* motel, Meg Mortimer – and it was given so much publicity (especially in view of the vociferous protests of the fans) that viewing figures shot up, much to everyone's satisfaction except that of Noele Gordon, the actress who had played the part for seventeen years.

Of course the head-writer can always introduce new characters as long as (a) budgetary restrictions are not exceeded (that is, the character does not require too many expensive locations); and (b) the character behaves according to familiar stereotype. When the American soaps all expanded beyond their original 15 minutes, hundreds of new characters had to be introduced to fill the time. Nevertheless the writers had to observe these two constraints. They mean that there is little room in serial writing for the unexpected, which is one of the things that makes the job of writing an exciting one.

Another weapon in the fight against being boring is to invent outlandish plots, in which familiar characters are stretched in different directions. For years soaps were made entirely in the studio, for speed and economy. But in the last five years it has become increasingly common to have one story-line – one only, mind you – set in some exotic locale which involves film cameras and outdoor shooting, the transport of actors and technicians to some foreign country, and the building of an extra studio set for the exotic interiors the story requires.

This applies mainly to American soaps. The long-established British soaps – *Crossroads, Coronation Street* and, in particular *Emmerdale Farm* (which does not run continuously like the other two) – have always used the occasional location or outside shots to add variety and relieve pressure on studio time. *Triangle*, the BBC's recent (1982) twice-weekly soap, differed from all its competitors by being shot entirely on videotape, and was set almost exclusively on a ferry that sailed between one British and two Continental ports. Even the interiors were largely shot on location – but for all that the characters and plots were those familiar to soap watchers everywhere. So even an exotic setting does not allow the writer that much freedom of invention.

What the America soap writers have been doing of late is to plagiarize the sort of plot that made 007 or *The Man from UNCLE* popular in their time (nearly two decades ago). A secret formula to hold the world to ransom is hidden in some object which is buried by the villains on a remote island. Our hero and heroine find their way to the island, but separately and unknown to one another, since they've had a quarrel and never want to see one another again. They are engaged on the quest in order to forget, to get away from their home towns and the families and memories which are now too painful to bear. Each is accompanied by a trusted friend who gets captured (or the heroine does, or the hero, or both). Hero and heroine discover one another, their love is rekindled, and together they overcome the villains, rescue their friends and save Civilization As We Know It. Well, at least it gets them out of the studio.

The trouble with introducing this kind of thing, from the writers' point of view, is that if it works on one show, the producers of every other show want it copied. Imitation is another of the cages the writer is forced to enter. If *General Hospital* rises to the top of the charts with an absurd story about an Ice Princess, *Guiding Light* counters with a melodrama in the Canary Islands and *Search for Tomorrow* with a B-movie plot centring on Chinese jade. No use arguing with the pro-producer that it is the *relationships* between the characters, and not the settings, that get the audience going. If a top-rated show makes publicity out of sending actors and crew abroad regardless of expense, then everyone else wants to be seen to be spending, to keep up with them. The writers have little choice in the matter. Anyway, they won't get to go on the trip.

*

What, you may wonder, about the creators of a new soap? Don't they enjoy the divine power of starting from primeval chaos? Well no, actually, they don't. Entering the genre is like falling into a leopard trap: you can feel the net folding itself around you. First of all a new idea (and how many of those are there?) is pretty hard to sell. I heard a marvellous remark reportedly made by an American network executive explaining his rejection of an outline for a new show. "It sounds," he said "too like something we haven't tried before." That sums up the corporate conservatism by no means confined to television.

An idea for a new serial has got to sound like all the others, while containing some miracle ingredient which makes it do what the rest do, only better. The characters have to be drawn from the stock types discussed earlier, and the plots, as we have seen, must fulfil the basic aims of the genre. No soap will even get to the pilot stage if it doesn't have as its backbone the struggles and tensions of a family, and its relationships with the community. (The exception is *Coronation Street*.) All of which is somewhat limiting to the creator: in fact, it leaves them with only the setting to play with.

Channel 4, British commercial television's "alternative" network, commissioned an initial 104 episodes of a soap opera from Phil Redmond, who had written a phenomenally successful BBC children's serial about a comprehensive school, *Grange Hill* (so naturalistic it drew protests that things couldn't be that rough). The new soap, to be screened twice weekly in peak time, with a weekend omnibus edition, was called *Brookside*, and set in a private housing estate in Liverpool (a sort of recessionary version of *Knot's Landing*). Redmond was keen to emphasize his serial's realism: it was not to be a "romanticized interpretation of life but . . . a reflection of contemporary Britain with a sharp edge, tackling issues of unemployment, feminism, motivation and divorce". He aimed to grasp the opportunity afforded by the unending narrative to examine such problems as the destructive effect of being on the dole. "Realism" was to be provided by filming the whole thing on an actual housing estate, part of which had been bought by his production company.

Brookside early proved one of Channel 4's more popular programmes – though its viewing figures came nowhere near its soap sisters'. But its relative audience success, I would maintain, is due more to the soap opera form – the desire built up in the viewer to know what will happen – than to the content of the narrative. And its failure to observe some of the vital tenets of the genre may explain why it falls between the stools of soap and TV drama. Few of the stereotypes so necessary to the former appear and there is no common meeting ground where its characters can mingle. Moreover, the vaunted "realism" of its location cannot disguise the fact that the people inhabiting it are actors and actresses. And as for the social message that Redmond hoped to put across, this did not have a tenth of the dramatic power of Alan Bleasdale's 1982 drama series, *Boys from the Blackstuff* (BBC), also set in Liverpool.

It is impossible to keep social issues in sharp focus in a long-running soap opera: the need to fill the hours dictates increasing reliance on the personal dramas of the characters, their loves and losses. Soap opera dilutes what plays (like Bleasdale's) can concentrate: whatever Redmond's ambitions for *Brookside*, it has to keep afloat on "personalities" rather than "issues". Moreover there has to be a balance (which plays aren't bound to provide) between happiness and misery, success and failure, hope and despair, goodness and villainy, romance and frustration – if, that is, it is a soap built to last.

Redmond complained that in his previous series *Grange Hill* "everything had to be crammed in only nine weeks". But the open-endedness of the soap is like a black hole which causes the best intentions to disappear without trace. If *Brookside* succeeds as a long-running serial, it will have to succumb to the conventions of the genre. If not, it will have been just a minor drama series. Either way, it is an example of the limitations and challenges of the soap opera form.

Even in the earliest days of radio soaps, the form very quickly became fixed. Irna Phillips may have put more emphasis on the psychological dramas of her characters, but her plots were the same as those of the Hummerts and the others – who took them, of course, from the magazine serials of old. Even Miss Phillips' invention of the medical soap was merely (and this is not to belittle it) a change of setting. And those were the days when experiment was relatively cheap. If something didn't work, you took it off and tried something else. In television the expense of putting on even a pilot show – a test to see if the thing is workable – is such that no producer will take a risk unless he or she is at least 80% certain of success. Now it must be said that soaps are given longer to prove themselves than any other genre. Comedy and drama series get axed at the first chill of public disapproval, but soaps – being far cheaper as well as far more profitable – are kept going for several months, while the writers tinker with their creation in an attempt to improve it. But what they are tinkering with must still look and sound pretty much like all the rest.

Dallas was not the first soap to glamorize the activities of the very rich, but it was the first to present them glamorously, shot on 35mm film so that they looked like a Hollywood product. Naturally a number of very similar looking fish suddenly appeared in *Dallas*'s wake. First there was *Knots Landing*, from the same stable, followed by the rival

Flamingo Road, then the move to the Californian wine belt in *Falcon Crest*, to oil-rich Denver in *Dynasty*. All these were once-a-week prime-time shows, though they stole plot, characters, treatment, theme and style from their older and dowdier sisters. What they added was money, and the setting – neither of which a writer can do much about.

This is not to say that a new setting cannot be the launching pad for a refreshingly different look at the old soap plots and people. It is just that originality is so quickly put on a diet of familiarity that the writer's satisfaction is soon limited to royalty cheques. Tony Warren created the idea and characters of a serial he called *Florizel Street*, set in a Lancashire town. It was original not only in its setting, but in its approach: instead of being what I might call a "vertical" serial, with the plots revolving around a family hierarchy, it was a "horizontal" soap, with no single family at its core, where the plots grew out of the relationships between a whole range of equal characters. Gritty, witty and true to the sort of neighbourliness that high-rise cities had killed stone dead, it was an original creation that has never been bettered, let alone copied in style, and which has never lost its large and faithful audience. Yet Tony Warren's contribution to what became *Coronation Street* is limited to the credit "based on an idea by". H. V. Kershaw, who should know, says that Mr Warren, "although one of the best creators of character in the business . . . lacked the stamina to turn out the endless stream of dialogue which television demanded". Or possibly – and this is my surmise – he preferred to let others exhaust themselves inventing new situations for his characters that had to end, well, predictably.

Kevin Laffan, a playwright, came up with the idea of a serial based on a farming family in the Yorkshire Dales, *Emmerdale Farm*. *The Archers* had been going for some twenty years on radio before Mr Laffan's serial hit the air: whether or not anyone had tried the idea in the interim (and I bet they had), he was the one who made it work. To make it keep on working requires a team of story-editors and writers just like the rest. Mr Laffan plays only occasionally for this team. I am not saying that he or Mr Warren has become disillusioned at how their ideas have been exploited. On the contrary, the serials provide their originators with bread and butter, and as much jam as they can manage. They may act as consultants, like Agnes Nixon, but why should they submit themselves to the punishing routine of the soap writer when they make enough in royalties as creators? All I am suggesting is that their creative contribution is limited once the machinery is set in motion. The chief freedom the creator has – bearing in mind that every writer has to earn a living – is to stand back from his or her creation and laugh all the way to the bank.

Kevin Laffan still keeps his hand in at *Emmerdale Farm* but the only creator amongst those I talked to who is still happily and *totally* involved in his serial is Peter Ling, who with Hazel Adair came up with *Crossroads*. Since its beginning in 1964 Mr Ling has been writing the story-lines that are parcelled out between the scripting team, and he hopes to go on doing so for another twenty years at least. He has a genuine enthusiasm – rare in veterans of the genre – for the form itself, which he sees as the nearest thing to a novel that television can produce. It alone can trace the actions and reactions of a character, or group of characters, over a period of years, as these actually occur, day by day. In fact *Crossroads* differs from all other soaps in that it allocates writers to particular story-lines, instead of commissioning them to write an entire episode or run of episodes. Mr Ling, who worked on other serials before he and Miss Adair were invited to come up with their own, never thought this way of doing things would work, and indeed for its first five years *Crossroads* treated its writers like everybody else, giving each a number of episodes for which they were to provide the dialogue. But then the producer had the idea of dividing the writing according to story-lines: they tried it, and it seemed to work.

Or up to a point. When each writer is attached to a group of characters and their story, he or she is liable to fight hard, in story conferences, for the biggest slice of each episode; and even when agreement has been hammered out, the writer, according to Mr Ling, will still go home and allow her or his attachment to overrun the length allotted. Then there is the problem of weaving the plots together. When it is done by a single writer – aided by story editor, continuity department and producer – at least there should be a consistency in style and tone. This is much more difficult to achieve when three writers have contributed to each episode. Stylistic differences show. Mr Ling doesn't mind. He and his colleagues never run out of plot invention. If asked how he can go on doing the same job day after day, he turns the question on the inquisitor. How can a journalist work for the same old paper for year after year? Or a television reporter or even a critic? He sees his job as no less challenging than theirs. To him the limitations that the form imposes on a writer's ability to work creatively are unimportant. He and his team are writing and producing an entertaining show that is proud of its social relevance. That the script writers are changed every six months to prevent them from getting stale is the producer's decision, not Mr Ling's. He says he never gets stale, and he is very convincing.

Good story-tellers, like Mr Ling, are rare, which is why they are much prized in the profession. Peggy O'Shea, one of two head-writers on the highly rated American day-time soap *One Life To Live*, has worked with the biggest (e.g. *Peyton Place*) and the best (Agnes Nixon created *OLTL* – known irreverently as "One Leg to Lift"). Ms O'Shea too is proud of the product, and rejects the idea that her imagination could be ossified by the pressures of pumping out so much so quickly. Believing that it is the busiest people who get the most done, she worked her way up to become head-writer – a job she justifiably regards as an insurance against old age – and is now, she feels, in a position to be as creative as she is capable of being. She can alter, deepen or extend characters, and colour them any way she wants – within the limits of what the plot, the producers and the public will bear.

But this kind of creativity, she told me, is dangerous in a sub-writer, whose job is limited to interpreting the head-writer's instructions as faithfully as possible. Creative writers would feel unable to accept such discipline: they would want to tamper with things, to try to improve the "rocks" – the chief characters and role-models on which the entire serial is built. Such messing around is not allowed in sub-writers, and anyone who tried it would be fired.

Of course the head-writer has to allow her or his juniors a certain amount of space in which to be inventive. Whatever the limitations, even the humblest sub-writer is still something more than a word processor. Some head-writers, according to Ms O'Shea, supply breakdowns that can drive the dialoguer (for such is the ugly name by which some of them are known) crazy, putting in everything, even the words they are to speak, so that the recipients feel they are being paid merely to be someone else's typewriter. But those who have faith in their team give them room to express themselves. As an example, let me quote part of one of Ms O'Shea's own story breakdowns, and then what the writer made of it. This is from an episode of *One Life to Live* that was aired in June 1982.

> The River Shack Bar, where Jenny is alone with Marco. Establish Larry and Karen have gone to see Astrid aboard and also try and arrange for some kind of transportation to take them to the next village where they might make faster transportation arrangements than waiting for the crop duster to return for them. Jenny is acutely aware of Marco's pain and gently suggests his feelings for Karen are apparently not quite so brother-sister as he tried to make himself believe they were. Marco himself is amazed at his feelings. Everything he told Jenny earlier today about his relationship with Karen he thought was the truth. The words came easy. But those words are sticking in his throat after seeing Karen in Larry's arms, so obviously head over heels in love again.

And now the actual scene, as written by Lanie Bertram:

The River Shack Bar, where MARCO *and* JENNY *are alone –* LARRY KAREN, ASTRID, PAUL *O.C. At the Plane.*

JENNY: Well, if the darned phone would get fixed so I can call my daughter, I might be the happiest person in the world right now! You, however, have turned glum ... *(She sits next to him and takes his hand)* I know why.

MARCO: Good. You can explain it to me. Because I don't know why I suddenly crashed.

JENNY: Sure you do. After the elation of seeing Karen, knowing she and Larry had survived – you also noticed their romance had survived, too.

MARCO: The fact she couldn't keep her eyes off him – you think that bothered me?!

(In response JENNY *just looks at* MARCO)

MARCO: Remember earlier today that guy who made a speech about a certain relationship being the brother-sister kind? *(She nods)* – It might have been a snow-job.

JENNY: I know. It's easy to convince ourselves something is true if we want it that way.

MARCO: Not me – I don't usually do that. Guess it was a defensive reflex. Because in my guts I knew the love between Larry and Karen wasn't just a product of the implant. It's always been there.

JENNY: And it always will.

MARCO: I really deserve the award for Sap of the Year!

JENNY: Marco, you're not a sap. You just have feelings that run much deeper than you usually let people see.

MARCO: I wonder why I let you see them? *(From this warm moment, cut to: Mountain Location, Scene 6, Mountain Top, as* PAT *leans over* TONY.)

Now plainly this is one of those scenes where the characters, in trying to explain their inner turmoil to the viewer, assault the ears with language used only in soap opera. That real people don't talk that way is not necessarily a criticism of the writer. People never spoke the way Shakespeare made them talk, and nobody thinks any the less of him for that. Without going into the relationship between Art and Truth, I quote this scene as an example of the job the soap writer has to do. Information has to be got across, in an atmosphere of heightened emotion demanded by the plot and the head-writer. In a film, or a TV play with more production time, this emotion might have been conveyed by the glances and expressions of the players involved. But serial viewers watch television differently from the way in which they deliver themselves up to a movie or become absorbed in the nuances of a play. Though they may watch with attention, they are always liable to be distracted – by 'phone, stove, or doorbell. And the form in which soap is served up to them often encourages this distraction.

You don't have to watch every frame of every scene, because you know you'll be able to pick up on things later. In a continuing story that must attract new viewers, repetition and explanation are obviously necessary – and perhaps it gives already addicted viewers the chance to make a cup of coffee, to feel easy and relaxed, as comfortable with their serial as with a friend or neighbour. This is obviously part of the attraction of the form. It is therefore something writers have to cope with: they have to provide the television equivalent of gossip, which, as everyone knows, is an invented story, bearing a faint ring of truth, which is magnified and repeated and elaborated upon until everyone is so familiar with it that it becomes universally believed.

The writer of the scene I have quoted had several jobs to do. First, to establish the background of and relationship between the characters, and to provide a commentary on something traumatic that happened to Marco in an earlier scene. Second, to open out a new relationship between Jenny and Marco, to compensate for Marco's loss of Karen to Larry. Third, to provide a moment of calm amidst the tension of not knowing who is going to get home safely, which viewers will be nervous about from a previous scene. Fourth, to offer a love scene – or the beginnings of one – between two subsidiary characters, in a manner that leaves the way open for the head-writer to build on this relationship if necessary. Fifth, to know the head-writer's mind well enough to decide whether the Jenny-Marco relationship is going to be important enough to be worth a lingering scene here, or to get it over as economically as possible. Sixth, to make all these decisions quickly and efficiently, so as not to hold or mess up the business of providing a 90-page script in a week.

The scene fulfils these several purposes in a workmanlike manner. It is not an artistic gem, and the prosaic nature of its dialogue inhibits the actors from turning it into a romantic classic. Analysed aesthetically, it would not emerge with too much credit. But analysed functionally – that is, how well it does what it is supposed to do – it becomes a winner.

You learn from the first sentence that Jenny is a caring mother about to be rescued, and from the second that she cares about Marco too. From his first speech you know Marco is disappointed, puzzled and hurt – but also trying to keep up a front. When Jenny obligingly explains, for our benefit rather than his, the reasons for his mood, Marco turns briefly macho before collapsing in face of Jenny's look. We get a snatch of homely wisdom from Jenny ("It's easy to convince ourselves something is true if we want it that way"), which is precisely the kind of familiar truth beloved of gossips and soap fans. Marco, in response, admits the failure of his hopes for Karen – and in so doing becomes a nobler and more sympathetic character. Jenny makes sure he accepts that Karen loves somebody else, thus provoking Marco into berating his own naivety, which Jenny then denies. She lets him, and us, know that he is really a deeply caring person too – and that she cares for him. In his last line Marco realizes that Jenny means more to him than he had thought.

The viewer is thus made aware, in a scene that lasts less than two minutes, that a new relationship is about to be born. Though the ear has been given more of a bashing than the eye, the latter would have been drawn to the scene by the pause when Jenny just looks at Marco, and by the tone of his voice at the end. (Silence from the screen will get the viewer's visual attention, if only to check that the television is still working.) The audience will know, when the scene is over, that something important has happened – which is the purpose of the whole thing.

I mentioned earlier the writer's use of language in a way peculiar to soaps. Some of the vocabulary employed is of the same vintage as the moral sentiments expressed. No one that I know uses words like "sap" or "snow-job" any more: "sap" is something from war-time movies, and "snow-job" is at least ten years out of date. It is like saying "Crikey" or "Gosh" in those moments of emotional stress when Anglo-Saxon expletives well up irresistibly in the mouth. People do it, with amazing self-restraint, in front of children, in a mistaken effort to protect their innocence; or because they are amazingly genteel. And the soaps *are* amazingly genteel, in their attitudes and language. You get rape, but without the brutal expressions usually associated with the act; you see gangland murder ordered and discussed in phrases of a quaint courtliness that would not disgrace a nunnery.

This quaintness is of course deliberate. There is a certain literary skill in making characters appear contemporary while speaking dialogue that is both artificial and old-fashioned. The expressions used cannot be so dated that the characters sound as if they are stuck in a time-warp: they must convey an innocence of attitude (if not of intention) that sets up echoes of a fantasy world free from the ugliness of modernity, a world complicated only by the difficulties of romance.

This would not be an easy thing to achieve if the writers started with nothing to guide them. But usually they are dealing with a character whose way of talking has been set for many years past – indeed, the actor or actress will change dialogue that is not to their liking, on the pretext that "it is not how I would speak". This is just another aggravation the writers have to bear with, consonant with their lowly status. In an enterprise designed to attract maximum public approval, who knows better, who is in closer touch with the public taste, writer or star? So forceful is the player's answer (in their own favour, naturally) that the writer can only give in.

Yet dealing with an established character and situation may provide a sub-writer hard pressed for time with useful short cuts. Not every writer burns to be original all the time: provided the required standards are met, it is perfectly professional to treat serial writing as a job, or a chore, to be got out of the way as efficiently as possible. Writing to the correct length – making sure each scene does not overrun the time allowed – and delivering punctually is of almost greater importance than the content (which has anyway been worked out beforehand). Besides, the head-writer and producer will do the main work of revising: all the writer has to do is to churn out what the machine demands.

It is still possible for sub-writers to put their individual mark on a script. Difficult, but possible: all writers have their own way with a phrase, a rhythm and cadence that is theirs alone. The process may be mechanical, but it is not machine-tooled, where each constituent is identical to its fellows. Within the constraints of consistency, different lines, different points, different jokes can be made.

It is nevertheless almost impossible to recognize a particular script as coming from a particular author – if, that is, you are an ordinary viewer. If something stands out too much, it has to be flattened, for consistency's sake. Head-writers may put their stamp on the story, for they are responsible for its development over a long period. They can make changes and pursue their personal interests to an extent no one else connected with the product can (except the producer). A sub-writer, having infinitely less responsibility, has infinitely less opportunity to display individuality. But then the viewers do not approach soap opera as they do a book, for the pleasure of meeting an individual author, mind to mind. The soap fans immerse themselves in an experience that is the product of a team effort. Every sport demands that players contribute to the best of their individual ability – but each must subordinate that effort to the victory of the group.

Although television is widely spoken of as a "writer's medium", where the Word is sacred – unlike film, where what the director does is nobody's business but his own (assuming he doesn't go over budget) – the serial writer is rarely seen at the studio at least in America: in England they may attend a run-through with the producer. So streamlined is the machinery that there seems little reason for them to be there: by the time the scripts have been revised by the head-writer and dozens of copies run off for the cast, the main reason for changing things is if a scene is over-length. It is tacitly accepted in the serial world that an actor or actress is allowed to make minor changes, though these are supposed to be small and subtle. Major stars may sometimes make major changes, which do crude violence to the writer's intentions, but such warfare between writer and actor is not allowed to continue long: sooner or later one of them will be fired.

If the writers are part of the team – indeed, the most important players, for without their words there would be nothing to play – how come they are usually absent from the game itself, when the words are made flesh? In single plays, as in stage dramas, the writer is on hand during rehearsal and recording, to polish phrases that could be more subtly expressed, to explain, revise, and even cut if necessary. This right to attend has been fought for by writers, individually and through their unions, for many years, since resentment grew at the high-handed manner in which directors and actors slashed their dialogue to tatters.

The organization of serial production destroys, in fact if not in spirit, the paramountcy of the writer's contribution. Mainly this is due to the time factor. The writer is allotted an episode and given, say, a week or more in which to produce it. Once this is edited and accepted it will be copied, cast, a director assigned, rehearsals arranged and studio time allotted for the recording, which will be transmitted within about four weeks of delivery by the writer. There is enormous satisfaction in seeing your work aired so quickly: the delay that is normal in other forms and other media between finishing something, having it accepted, being paid, seeing it produced, and it finally appearing before the public is one of the worst of a writer's frustrations. But the gratifying speed with which serial writers see their work appear carries its own drawbacks.

The production largely proceeds without them – and anyway they might be busy with their next set of scripts. They are effectively kept away – not deliberately, but that is what it amounts to – from the hatching of the eggs they have laid. This belittles their contribution to the process to which they have bound themselves.

A producer might claim that the energy and efficiency with which the machinery operates in fact relieves the writer of unnecessary strain and labour. But absence, in television, makes the heart grow less fond. There is a camaraderie in the medium which grows naturally between people who work together for months and years. Actors and crew frequently know one another; and since they arrive early in the morning and put in long hours (five days a week for the American day-time soaps, three or four for the rest), they enjoy a bond of common suffering that outsiders cannot share. And if the writers are not there, they will become, in the eyes and mouths of the workers on the floor, a target of jokes or abuse, a scapegoat for most complaints. (Nor is this just writer's paranoia: Harding Lemay testified that on the rare occasions he met the cast, they were either extremely hostile to the changes he was trying to introduce, or fawned on him to give them bigger parts.) The writer is supposed to be a member of the team, but is denied the pleasures of the locker-room.

This isolation is hurtful to people who enjoy mixing with those who produce their work, as a change from the solitary slog on the typewriter. One of the chief pleasures of writing plays, indeed, is the feeling of being part of a group effort, after what seems like months in isolation. Even the supposed advantages of working at home, in hours of your own choosing, surrounded by a loving and caring family, are more apparent than real: Harding Lemay relates that, as head-writer of *Another World* (and one of the few to publish his confessions, which is why I rely on him so much), he had to get up at five every morning, seven days a week including holidays, to write his story-lines and scripts, and edit those of others, in time. If he wanted to go on holiday – and I know this is true of other soap writers – he had to work even harder, till two and three in the morning, to get sufficiently ahead of himself to be able to take time off. Now maybe he wasn't as efficient as some, or maybe he took more trouble – the English writers I talked to did not punish themselves in this way, but then their serials aren't on five days a week for fifty-two weeks a year. Yet Lemay scarcely saw his wife and friends, missed out on his children growing up, and had hardly any social life at all. He could afford a fine house and other luxuries, so you don't have to weep for him, but he really didn't, during his bondage, have the time to enjoy them.

The last of my list of items separating the writers from the production of their work – a classic case of alienation – is the treadmill effect. If you have ever done a series of boring exercises in an attempt to keep yourself fit, you know that there is a perverse satisfaction, however short-lived, in increasing the number of knee-bends or whatever in the time you have allowed yourself. The more you keep at it the easier it becomes, at least in theory. If you have the sort of puritan conscience most writers are cursed with, you carry on, numbed with the tedium, because you tell yourself it's good for you, and if you stop you'll become a flabby wreck. This is what I mean by the treadmill effect, and it works for routine (and well paid) writing much as it does for exercising. Producing the work gets easier the more you get into it: it becomes a routine which, as with all routines, you become

superstitiously afraid of abandoning. Only with soap writing you become richer instead of fitter. After a while you don't want to give up,
partly because of the spectre of poverty, partly because you become so
used to it that you're frightened of change, of bellying out into the
unknown. On a treadmill at least you know where you are, and writers
need that kind of security occasionally, like everyone else. This is not
to deny those powers of imagination and courage which mark them as
a breed apart – but the shadow of the treadmill looms as large over the
serial writer as that of the taxman and is equally enervating.

There are, of course, many satisfactions to be gained from writing for
the soaps. The head-writer can deal with the great moral issues of
our time, the issues that have always exercised the imagination of
dramatists: the corruption of power, the ravages of jealousy, the con-
suming flames of love. More,they are able to present dramas on subjects
no other medium touches (or at least, not at such length or in such
detail). Where else, but on the soaps, would you be able to write about
the pros and cons of surrogate motherhood, of having children late in
life, of adoption or euthanasia? Where else can controversial items like
incest and rape be discussed in front of an audience of millions? The
themes employed by Ibsen, and Tennessee Williams, are at the service
of the soap writer – who can take months of air-time to develop them.

   It is also satisfying to create characters who become known to more
people than Falstaff or Mr Micawber, and to be able to age them as
naturally as if they were real. To live with your creations and see their
good qualities intensify and their bad ones fade. To manipulate them
through a huge and complex canvas of other characters and situations,
to make them interrelate without too much outrageous coincidence,
to enjoy such flexibility as the form allows to bend them in the direction
you want. There is also a professional's satisfaction in producing a
script that manages to control and advance a massive amount of
information, to length and on time.

   Then there is the pleasure of being paid, regularly and well, for
producing something for a large and loyal audience – larger and more
loyal than that reached by any other kind of writer. If one of the
purposes of authorship is to reach people with your ideas, you're never
going to reach them in larger numbers than in soap opera. And you may
tell yourself, on the evidence of the fan mail, that you are performing a
sort of public service. People are entertained, entranced and reassured
by what you say. Some even claim to learn something from it. Those
who suffer from the sort of problems you deal with – and there are
millions of them – write in to say how comforted they are to know

they are not alone. The soap writer may enjoy the sort of heady power that prophets and pundits and playwrights enjoy – from time to time. Even a whiff of it is more than most people get.

On being paid: in a profession that neither insists on proper training nor operates a closed shop – anyone can call themselves a writer, and why not? – being paid (and even better, being well paid) is at least a sign of being taken seriously as a wordsmith. In a society where merit is based on your credit-rating, few will scoff at a person who earns enough to finance a couple of houses, just by sitting at home in front of a typewriter. If rubbish sells, you can bet your life a lot of people will be in the market peddling the stuff. Those who succeed will be few, and will be accorded all the respect due to success. Harold Robbins has become an institution and, no doubt, the subject of academic theses. The soaps have been going longer than he has: why should their writers not enjoy a similar standing?

There is also the perverse and arcane pleasure, shared by most artists, in going against fashionable thinking. Usually this is taken to apply to the avant-garde, who preach now what the rest of the world should believe tomorrow. But those who get a kick from outraging trendy taste can do so by being behind as well as ahead of the mushy middle. The prevailing consensus on issues of private morality like adultery, or public morality like welfare, is (for the moment) liberal – but the soaps tend to be reactionary. As we know, adultery is as common as queuing for benefits is uncommon on the serials. But soapy adultery always ends in tears (and unemployment is rarely mentioned): this hard-line moralizing is the cause of much anguish amongst the liberal critics, who neither appreciate nor understand the form. Mind you, the soaps are currently enjoying a certain chic, thanks to the media. That being so, I wouldn't be surprised if the writers introduced plots outrageous enough to cause a sharp intake of breath amongst those who have come just for the ride, so that they all drop off and leave the genre to the fans who have loved and understood it since long before it became fashionable. To be popular with a coterie – though the soap audience is far too large to be called that – to be popular with huge numbers of people who have no truck with the trendies, that too can be a pleasure for a serial writer, of a certain kind.

In theory, if the production company hired enough soap writers, each would have enough time to produce a masterpiece. (Does the public, though, want a steady succession of masterpieces? Doesn't it rather demand the occasional bit of clunking, repetitive drama to nod or knit to?) But the producers don't hire in large numbers: that would be expensive, it would dilute the essence of the product, and anyway there aren't that many good writers around. Thus those who get the work are forced to repeat it, which prevents them from producing quality goods each and every time.

I owe it to my fellow-writers to say that every so often they do write a serial scene of the highest quality, one that is moving, compassionate, dramatic and true. Such scenes, of which any artist would be proud, do not occur frequently, for all the reasons already discussed. But when they do, they give the lie to the slur that the soaps are incapable of producing anything of artistic value. They are just incapable of producing it often.

Self-censorship is, to my mind, the most dangerous of the several constraints under which the serial writer has to labour. You can live, as a newspaperman lives, with dashing things off against a deadline: once it has gone out, that's the end of it, nothing being deader than yesterday's news or soap opera (until it is old enough to be nostalgia). You can live with a set of characters, and situations, created by others: that is a challenge to the ingenuity. What *I* would find hardest to live with is the need, ordained by the form, to come to a certain fixed conclusion about every character and every story. I realize that the demands of the serial make it impossible for its writers to indulge in the luxury of seeing where their characters lead them. I accept that nothing can be left to chance, that ends cannot be left flapping where so much and so many are at stake. But if, every time I had thought up a promising situation, I knew I was going to have to end it in a certain way – a reassuring way, an upbeat way – I think that would slowly and surely stifle my own sense of dramatic truth.

Self-censorship is worse than that practised by others. It is more powerful, and more deadly. I can, of course, point to certain plots and characters whose end is not reassuring, or at all up-beat. But the need always to tip the balance in favour of the good, to find the happy ending – both of which I accept as necessary to the serial – is like starting with the last line, and working backwards. It's one way of proceeding, of course, and it obviously works very well for some. But it means you must blinker your imagination – and after a while you might find it hard to do away with the blinkers, you might shy at the noise and sight of the rest of the world. You might start to doubt your own ability to say what you mean – an ability soap writing, for all its advantages, severely restricts. That would imply your creativity has been crippled. I'm not saying this is what has happened to the many honourable writers who find employment on the serials. All I'm saying is that, for me, such self-censorship would be the greatest danger of the trade.

5

THE PLAYERS: SECURITY
OR LIFE-SENTENCE?

"An actor," Marlon Brando is reputed to have said, "is someone who, if you're not talking about him, isn't listening." The point about soap actors and actresses is that they're continually talked about – not, however, because of the brilliance of their performance, but because of the characters they portray.

There are players whose physical charms recommend them to some producer who catapults them to stardom. There are those whose natural but untutored talent takes them straight to the top. As in every profession, there is nowhere that flair, determination, pull, and a huge amount of luck can't take you. But none of it prepares you for the peculiar pressure of acting in a long-running soap opera. Some of my best friends are actors, and I venture to say that none of them, when starting out to refine and perfect a technique that must carry them from Shakespeare through the modern classics, ever wanted to end up playing the same part in the same serial for years on end. The money is good, it is wonderful to be in work, but that is not what they had their sights on when they began.

My readers will know by now that I am not here to knock the soaps. On the contrary, I shall show how the punishing schedule under which soap players operate – a schedule more demanding than the heaviest repertory burden, the costliest movie epic – is an enormous challenge to which most of them rise magnificently. Many are the big stars from stage and film who are happy to appear in cameo parts in popular soaps. To be permanently exposed, week in week out, on the little screen can stand an actor or actress in excellent stead when it comes to getting other work – indeed there has long been a trend to feature TV stars in stage productions, since their familiarity attracts an audience who would not otherwise pay good money to put their bottoms on theatre seats. Acting is very much an ego trip, and there is nothing so satisfying to the ego as to see oneself regularly paraded in front of a huge public.

However, no one launches themselves on an acting career without the starriest illusions of somehow, sometime, using their talents to the full. You couldn't take all the rubbish that is thrown at you without believing that there is a part, many parts, in which you can, as an actor or actress, express all that you feel and know and imagine. And the brutal truth is that working in soap opera does not offer you this opportunity. It is good experience: some would even claim it is TV's equivalent of the repertory theatre. But, unlike in rep, you only get to play one part per soap (though with luck you can afterwards work on other soaps). And most of the time the work will be routine and repetitive, more a case of *reacting* than the creative acting you hoped for when you began.

Soap opera roles – the stereotypes we have already discussed – are created according to the demands of the character rather than the player who may act the part. This is how it should be: to write for a particular actor or actress is like creating a voice without knowing what it has to say. The character has to be able to stand on its own, not only because players, like machines, break down or become unavailable, but also because of the demands of the plot and the entire serial itself. The players are mere functionaries – at least in the eyes of the writers and producers: their job is to bring to life a part that has been written, not just for them, but to fulfil some great purpose in the story. Like lighting men and camera operators, the players bring their special skills to the creation of whatever effect is called for by the director. That is the theory.

In practice soap opera acting is different from every other branch of the profession. Playing a part for years and years, in the company of equally weathered colleagues, involves surviving changes of writers, directors, producers, and technicians, all of whom have their own ideas of how a character should look and behave. The players will listen to these new ideas, but if the part has become second nature to them, they will defend it against any notions of radical change. Consistency is what they and their public have grown up with, and they will refuse to make alterations to a character with whom they are totally identified, unless very good reasons are shown. Their survival has given them a certain power: they have a greater say in the development of their characters than players enjoy elsewhere. Add to that the lack of time available for a new writer or director to rehearse and refine any attempt at novelty, which invariably means that the short cut has to be preferred to a route that is winding or unexplored, and you extend the actor's or actress's sway even more. They know their parts as well as they know their own noses, and can fend off interference under the flag of experience. They have earned, or have seized by stealth, the right to do things their way, where even the starriest actors in other fields have been forced (usually but not always) to do the director's bidding.

This situation has its good and bad sides. Where talented players have endeared themselves to a faithful public, the serial will prosper, and everyone will be happy as long as they don't become bored or boring. Where a less talented performer digs in his or her heels, and refuses to make any changes in performance or characterization, the resulting staleness and predictability mean that audiences turn away and the entire serial is jeopardized. And, it must be said, the players are not always the best judges of their own performance. They need a critical and constructive eye from a fresh and objective director if their acting is not to become routine. But the longer they have played a part successfully, the more they feel they know better than anyone else how it should be done. It is a circle peculiar in its viciousness.

The problem facing the soap actor and actress is that they thrive on variety and are reduced to monotony. They have been professionally trained to interpret different parts in such a way that their own personality is both submerged in the character being portrayed, and yet discernible through it. Actors and actresses devote all their efforts to impressing the public with the breadth of their range, a range that shows they are capable of bringing something new to a part that has been played a million times, and that they can create an original role in a way uniquely theirs. They want to be remembered, as great stars are remembered, for some special quality that comes across no matter what they are playing: and remembered by their own names, correctly spelled, not those of the characters they play. Yet in soap opera, the focus is shut right down to a single role. And, worst of all, the raucous voice of public attention, while mostly welcome (not all actresses behave like Garbo), is directed not at the player, but at the part. Individual identities are lost, swallowed up, and taken over by the characters they bring to life.

Of course the players get used to it. Some might even take it as a compliment to their professional skill: after all, Stanislavski believed that his actors should become, during their performance, whoever it was they were playing. But his players were not confined to a single part. If they had portrayed, say, a woman with a wooden leg, Russians didn't go up to them in the streets and kick them to see if it was real. This was not because Russian audiences were more sophisticated than American ones in detecting the difference between illusion and reality. Some confusion is inevitable when a player acts the same character for what seems like forever.

Soap actors and actresses become more intimately familiar to their audience than any movie star, however famous. They are there every day, every week, consistent, reliable, reassuring. Small wonder that the audience identifies them with the person they're playing and refers to them by that name rather than the one by which their agents know them. It seems somehow – natural.

Steady work in a high-risk profession is something to be grateful for. And, just as many bit-players earned a name for themselves by turning in a reliable performance time after time, so many soap actors and actresses bring a lifetime's professionalism to their parts, however often they have to repeat themselves. Actors have this in common with lawyers and cab-drivers: if they need the money they have to work for whoever hires them. Of course they can refuse a role that they consider demeaning – but soap opera roles are not demeaning. They are well paid, they can be fun, and they may lead to better things. (Better things in this case mean more money, more choice and/or more critical acclaim.) Soap opera roles are even demanding, not only in terms of the work schedule, but in the stimulus of bringing something fresh to a character you come to live with daily. I doubt, though, that such pressure is good for a player if it goes on too long. That is because the players whom I know – the most subjective test of judgement – do not relish the thought of playing the same part for all eternity. They believe there would be no challenge in so doing – that they would lose all freshness, become type-cast, and ultimately incapable of extending their range. To which the veteran professional soap star might retort that until you have spent part of your working life building up a character – the innumerable lines, moves, nuances of behaviour and tone that make the audience believe in you – you have no idea just what a challenge it is.

Most actors and actresses – that is, the majority who are out of work for long and unimaginably depressing periods – would be ecstatic at getting a part in a soap, at least for a spell. Big parts are fixed up between the producers and the actors' agents: actors and actresses advertise their faces in fat and glossy albums of photos, such as *Spotlight*, and these are flipped through in the producer's office until someone says, "That's just the face I had in mind for this part." Since the soaps prefer for the important roles actors and actresses who are not too well known – they are cheaper, for one thing, and a new part usually demands a "new" face – an audition is often called for which, if successful, will lead to a short-term contract, usually for thirteen weeks (the same goes for writers), which is renewable (and of course can equally well be cancelled). For the big roles the contract usually specifies that the character will feature in a certain number of episodes over the contractual period.

Chance, as you might expect, plays the biggest part in casting. The right face and voice, available at the right time, and a willingness to be committed to a job that may last a few days or a few years: these count for more than anything. But once you are in a soap, there *is* the opportunity to make yourself virtually indispensable, through the quality of your acting. Bringing out a character's strengths, or making the weaknesses poignant, is one way of ensuring a longer contract than the producer may originally have envisaged. The soap machine is always hungry, and if a part that may have been written to fill out a single narrative thread is shown by the player concerned to have a rich life of its own, writer and producer will seize on this with gratitude.

Once actors or actresses have made a part unmistakably theirs, bringing to their dialogue some quality – it may be anger, it may be tenderness – that was not evident in the speeches as written, that the writer may not even have thought of until the player brought it out, then the writer will go on using that quality and will go on relying on the player to produce it. All of which is wonderful as long as the players have the stamina and skill to keep renewing themselves in their parts. It is only when player or writer starts taking the character for granted that rigor mortis sets in.

Even more unpredictable than what a player will bring to a part is the chemistry between two actors, or an actor and an actress, that can turn a matzo into a soufflé. Think of any soap, and you think of the relationship between its characters – and not just the lovers, but the rivals, the families and the friends. It is these relationships which are the core of every story, but as often as not they have evolved into something quite different from what their original writers imagined, simply because of the way the actors have played them.

One example is the Ogdens of *Coronation Street*. Stan, the whining work-shy slob who would happily live on beer and chips if somebody else was buying, and Hilda, his sparrow of a wife, who has had her hair so long in curlers they have affected her brain, could not have been anyone's idea of an indispensable pair when they lay cold on the page of the script. No one imagined they would last for long. But when Stan lumbered to life in the person of Bernard Youens, and was chivvied along by Jean Alexander's Hilda – a national hero and heroine were created, unlikely, unglamorous, but raucous and real.

At the opposite end of the scale, there is the example of J. R. and Sue Ellen in *Dallas*. Larry Hagman had been a bit-player for years, but nothing in his background suggested that his leer would become as celebrated as the Cheshire Cat's. And Linda Gray, who brought to Sue Ellen such a waterproof glamour, said that she made something of what was a nothing part by giving J. R. a killer look when the camera closed in. Her eyes had such an effect on the producer and director that they forthwith gave orders that the four lines originally allotted to Sue Ellen were to be expanded. The rest, one might say, is lather.

To appear on an American soap you have to be good-looking and – on the whole – conventionally good-looking at that. It is a rare player who makes it to the top without fitting the "white bread" image of all-American glamour. Tony Geary, glamour-boy of *General Hospital*, became a pin-up for millions of teeny-boppers when he played Luke Spencer, the rapist who married his victim, despite, or because of, having long curly hair that was also thinning. But then there was an electricity between him and Genie Francis, who played his love Laura, which had nothing to do with looks. For those bit-players who scarcely feature in the credits, who certainly aren't going to get to play a love-scene, glamour is all. A gorgeous person is going to get hired for a small part rather than a less gorgeous person who may be a better actor or actress – and in New York, where many of the day-time serials are made, there is no shortage of gorgeousness. Anyone who isn't gorgeous and who wants to get into soaps has either got to be crazy or very determined. This is also true in England, though to a lesser extent, since our soaps do not feature glamour so prominently. Talent doesn't do any harm, but unless it has been demonstrated in a successful production elsewhere, one that casting directors and agents have been able to see, there isn't going to be much chance to show it off.

Even if a player lands a small part, the chances of building this into a permanent role are extremely small. There is an opportunity for those who play domestics – waitresses, housemaids, cleaners, bartenders – since their place of service is often a permanent set, and they might well be called back to reappear if they were sufficiently pleasing or interesting. But then who remembers the face or the name of the housemaid in almost every episode of *Dallas*, the one standing on their patio in a permanent gale, guarding the coffee-pot? She has scarcely been given a line to say in all those years: an Awful Warning if ever there was one.

A friend of mine got a small part on an American day-time serial which shall remain nameless to protect the guilty. She was advised by an old hand to "Do it *mean*, and they'll have you back. They like villains." But this was difficult as her character was that of a PTA mother who was insipid to the point of boredom. My friend found it extremely difficult to get involved with her character, and had no sense of understanding her or her supposed relationship with other players. Thanks to a mistake in the production office she got her script only on the morning of her date in the studio. When she arrived at 7.30 a.m., she quickly discovered that her real role was to feed lines to the star.

There was an added complication in the shape of a new director, who kept advising her not to look at the person she was supposed to be talking to. But the director had placed this other person directly behind my friend, whose natural instinct was to turn round to see whom she was addressing. To say that the result did not look natural is to put it kindly.

Add to that the fact that my friend had only one rehearsal without props before being pushed into a quick run-through with cameras — when she found that she was expected to eat a sandwich while delivering her lines — and you get some idea of the difficulties under which soap players might have to operate. In a major role the player can work up some rhythm, some familiarity both with fellow-members of the cast and the character he or she is playing. The bit-player is dropped into hot water and expected to react without a splutter. There cannot be many other professions where high standards are expected to be maintained in such appalling working conditions.

The players in *Crossroads*, the British serial which goes out three times a week, are given their scripts before the weekend, the theory being that they will use their leisure to study them. At Monday's rehearsal they "block", that is, are told where and when to move in each scene of the week's episodes. They also go over the lines, without props, but on a floor marked with tape to show where the scenery will fit. During these early rehearsals, cuts and changes are made if a scene looks like running over time, or if a line doesn't make sense (which occasionally happens despite the best efforts of writer and script editor); or if a player finds they simply can't say something the way it's been written. These changes mean that it's scarcely worth the player's while learning the lines before the Monday night, by which time the dialogue should be more or less fixed. I say "more or less" because it often happens that a player is asked to make changes in the script just before going on to record it. This may be because the length of other scenes, or the slow delivery of other players, or trouble with props or cameras has meant that the episode is over-running. Since the overriding consideration in all soaps is to get each episode recorded in the studio time allotted, last minute changes are inevitable if everything is to be fitted in. For the novice, the idea of being faced with changes to lines already committed to memory, changes which he or she may have only a few minutes to absorb, is nothing short of terrifying. But it is all part of the job to the practised hand, who may equally well be asked to put in some extra "business", or gaze meaningfully into the camera for several seconds, if the scene is running short.

The Crossroads team have three days to rehearse three twenty-minute episodes, and two days to record them (in practice, with commercial breaks on screen, a half-hour show occupies about twenty-five minutes). In America, an hour-long show (reduced by some ten minutes because of commercials) is rehearsed and recorded in a *single* studio day, five times a week. This means getting into the studio around 7.30 in the morning, reading through the script and blocking it, then rehearsing it as it will be recorded. Usually this is done in sequence, that is in the order in which the scenes will appear on the screen. This at least allows the rhythm of the episode to establish itself: actors and actresses need rhythm and momentum like any other workers, since it helps them to see where they are going. Rehearsing and recording in sequence is of some assistance here – but sometimes the rhythm is broken by a location scene, one filmed separately outside the studio. These scenes, which are becoming more common in the soaps, are treated like film (although usually shot on video tape), with all the hanging around waiting for the right light and the right shot that drove the movie pioneers to take refuge in studios.

Soap players (like all members of their profession) spend a lot of time waiting, especially – in American studios – during the morning rehearsals. They pass the hours by going over lines, either alone or with the person they will be acting with, and trying costumes and make-up – of which there may be several changes, so the actor or actress has to know exactly what they are expected to look and feel like in each successive scene. The rest of the time is spent in drinking coffee, playing cards, knitting or making 'phone calls, perhaps in the hope or expectation of other work. This working day, familiar to any actor, involves being cut off from the outside world as completely as if you were in a factory. There is scarcely time to leave the building, in case you are suddenly called for a scene: you exist for twelve or more hours in a totally artificial world where you are lucky even to see daylight.

Personally I find this whole process intoxicatingly magical, and can understand what it is that makes players put up with the frustrations to which they must submit. No doubt the magic wears off if you have to show up every day, every week, every year. But for all the difficulties, the players are able to become someone else, to play to a camera, and to see themselves, in the company of millions of viewers, a couple of weeks after recording. That, in a profession where being seen is all, makes up for almost everything.

After a short break for lunch, taken in the company of other members of the cast in the commissary or canteen – actors and actresses, however artistic, are as cliquey as factory workers in their leisure moments – the recording begins. There has already been a technical run-through, with the cameras, but the atmosphere becomes increasingly tense when playing for real. People get lines wrong, or forget them altogether, or make the wrong move or appear in the wrong costume. Each scene is run through while director and producer watch from the gallery surrounded by monitors. The director will descend to give "notes", that is instructions on how to get things as he or she wants them. The players are given a final polish by the make-up people; the cue-cards or autocues, an American speciality, on which the dialogue is written in case anyone gets lost, are adjusted; and the magic word "Action" is heard on the set.

If mistakes occur in a short scene, it can be re-taken – "fluffs" in longer scenes can be corrected by re-shooting a part of the scene and splicing it into the final tape, but this is expensive and time-consuming and there are few of the post-production facilities available to television drama or films. The director cannot record a scene several times and choose the best version: he or she doesn't have the time or the space. Soap acting is the nearest thing there is to live television, which is how it all used to be.

In the beginning the players were rehearsed, and then gave their performances "live" – what the cameras shot was being shown as they did it. Any mistakes were seen by the entire audience. There are those – mostly the older players, who do not have as much to do as they once did – who regard this punishing process with nostalgic affection: some even maintain that the tension improved their performances. All I can say, having watched a few typical studio days in America and the UK, is that there was enough tension to snap a hawser. Besides, in those early days, the soaps were usually only fifteen minutes long. The idea of preparing an hour's show in a single day, knowing that there was absolutely no possibility of correcting your mistakes, would be enough to kill most players. Putting in a twelve- to fourteen-hour day several times a week is hard enough. (No player could appear in every single episode: that would be physically impossible.)

What does this kind of pressure do to the acting? Obviously, as with soap writing, the lack of time means that quality suffers. A stage or movie player, or indeed one who appears in that rare creation, the single television play, usually has several weeks to read and learn the part, and at least three weeks, often more, to rehearse with the director before the first night, recording, or whatever. A stage player has the added benefit of being able to alter his or her performance every night, according to personal feelings, director's instructions or audience reaction. A film actor or actress can offer several versions of a performance for the camera, knowing that the best – or at least the one the director prefers – will be chosen.

Soap players have only one or two opportunities to make the best of their parts; so pressed is the director that if the lines and moves are right, the quality of performance passable, that will have to do. Interpretation of character, the player's special trade, is allowed minimal space to flower. This in turn can mean that soap players will give, not always of their best, but what will pass, what will get them through. Which in turn explains why so much soap acting appears to the casual viewer inferior in quality.

In its defence I would have to say that (a) on occasion soap players turn in a performance that can move one to tears, especially in tragedy; and (b) there are plenty of Equity members on the stage and elsewhere who cannot act their way out of a paper bag, and who make even the most cringe-worthy soap player look good.

But, if compared with the best acting on offer, soap playing does not often come very high up the table. Television is chiefly a reactive medium – by which I mean it copes better with the reaction of the players, through close-ups, than with action, to which the small screen does scant justice. Soap actors and actresses often react in ways that are less than subtle. There is a lot of "mugging", that is, exaggerated facial grimaces, to go with the "hamming" (exaggerated gestures) that is also too common. Lines that are less than polished are delivered not only flatly, but in a peculiar kind of isolation, as if the player were listening to some heavenly voice (no doubt that of the director) rather than the person to whom the dialogue is addressed. One of the signs of good acting, indeed, is to look as if what was being said to you was entirely new, and to react accordingly. This is all too rare on the soaps, as are the kind of physical movements, subtly executed, that make sense of a character even when silent.

But let us consider what the players are up against. If it were not hard enough to react with freshness to people and situations that have become achingly familiar, there are the visual conventions that have become so standardized no serial can escape them.

To handle several plots at a time, each scene has to be broken up into segments, ending on a "teaser" which is supposed to create tension in the mind of the viewer that will last until the next part of the scene is picked up later. This segmentation makes it extremely difficult for the actors to get into the swing of a scene, to create that rhythm on which dramatic writing no less than acting depends. Now intercutting between scenes in movies is a common method of tightening the screw of tension – when the characters in each scene are going to meet, with explosive effect. But often the characters of each scene in the serials do not meet, or not for a long time. The intercutting is merely a lengthy delaying tactic, infinitely protracted.

The commonest method of providing the "teaser" at the end of each little scene is the lingering close-up that is supposed to convey surprise, alarm or despair. This has become a convention as rigid and stultifying as any: because it is a way of filling, or killing, time, the player's expression too often degenerates into a stylized grimace. Asked to hold a particular look for an artificial length of time for no other reason than the mechanical demands of the genre, the player has little choice but to exaggerate. Practise a pout for six seconds in a mirror and you'll see what I mean.

Do the fans care about the quality of the acting? The reviewers, of course, who stumble across the soaps every so often and always seem surprised, take delight in saying how rotten the acting is. This hurts – all artists are hurt by all criticism – but soaps are not made for reviewers. It is the audience that counts, and what they care most about is that their favourite characters continue in believable stories. The fans will object if a character behaves inconsistently (for which the writer is to blame), or is killed off (the producer's decision, usually), or is replaced by another player. But if an actor fumbles a cue or drops a prop or goes over the top (a useful theatrical expression, OTT, meaning exaggerating the acting without restraint), no one seems to care too much. Such things are even the cause of private mirth, and become cherished experiences to be watched for and shared, like outbursts of temperament on the sports field.

The older actors and actresses suffer from those twin neuroses that beset every long-serving member of a company, regardless of profession: that they will be sacked, and that they will never work again. Job insecurity is familiar to everyone in these days of growing, and permanent, unemployment, but for an actor, especially one who is middle-aged, it amounts to paranoia.

There are no standards to reach, no qualifications that will guarantee work. All depends on the subjective judgement of the producer or casting director, whose verdicts are handed down without reasons. A player can have had years of experience, can have been garlanded with laurels, even making it to stardom, and still not find work later. So when he or she is "rediscovered" and given a part in a soap, it may be something of a come-down after appearing in London's West End or Hollywood, but it is work, and is usually grabbed.

An actor like *All My Children*'s Hugh Franklin had worked with all the great names of American theatre in the 1930s and '40s but, finding them all "miserable people", he left to run a country store and raise children in peace and quiet. Returning after nine years, bored with making the same small talk morning and night, he found that, despite his past, he had to begin again as an understudy. Ruth Warrick, who played his wife on the same show for many years (both of them are still going strong at the time of writing), first came to public attention as Kane's wife in Orson Welles's *Citizen Kane*. Her career went up and down thereafter – with a fair amount of down – and when she got into soap opera, it was only as Nurse Janet in *The Guiding Light* (though she did play a small part in the radio soap *Joyce Jordan, Girl Interne* – and when this was revived for TV, Warrick played the lead and the radio Joyce took a supporting role. There's up and down for you).

But the longer you serve in a soap, the less your chances of doing other parts (save for the occasional stage play, which rarely pays a living wage, especially if you're used to regular and substantial TV pay cheques). For one thing, the working schedule, as I have shown, scarcely allows much time off for outside rehearsal, let alone appearances. For those in smaller parts, the production office is sometimes prepared to schedule their rehearsal and recording sessions to fit in with other things. But working in soap in a full-time occupation, physically and contractually. Outside work is often forbidden except under special circumstances. And, unlike the old radio days, appearing simultaneously in several soaps is definitely out.

So those who play the bigger and permanent parts are usually denied the opportunity of doing anything else. They are thus firmly identified in the public mind with the character they portray. Even more important, they are identified in the minds of producers and directors with a particular role. And once you are type-cast, whether the part be big or little, you have the devil's own job to break out.

The more they hold on to the same part, the more terrifying is the thought of losing it. (Unless, of course, they're not in it for the money, which is unheard of.) But the more entrenched they become, the harder it is to change. And producers change, like directors, writers, and even – though at tortoise pace – the taste of the public. It is always tempting for a new broom to sweep, if not clean, then under the carpet those who refuse to bend to the new regime. New regimes are always brought in if the ratings fall. The ratings may fall because – it is felt – the actors, their characters, and the plots they animate have become stale. Change one, change all, so new producers might be tempted to think. Thus the dreadful paradox: the longer a character has been around, the higher the risk.

Of course drastic changes are rarely made at the top of the soaps, unless the ratings have become really bad. But public outcry is no defence even when, at the merest whisper of an execution, the letters pour in by the hundred thousand protesting at the threatened loss of a dear friend. Such is the cynicism of producers, that all publicity is good publicity. Nobody is safe (not even producers). Is it any wonder paranoia rules?

A particular bugbear of the permanent players is the odour of worthlessness that persists in clinging to the soaps. There are, as E. M. Forster said of writing, two reasons for acting: one is for the money, the other for the respect of the people you respect. One can live without the second, but one is impoverished by the deprivation. If one works as hard as soap actors do, one deserves something more than contemptuous dismissal, even from those who are ignorant of the difficulties involved.

This hostility from outsiders, coupled with the uncritical acceptance of the fans, tends to isolate soap actors and actresses. I am talking of those who have long contracts and long memories for the slights they have received. The younger players usually prefer to move into another field after a year or two: it is the long-serving members, many with distinguished careers on stage or screen, who tend either to take themselves extremely seriously, or to mock their work, off screen, in that self-deprecatory way old pros have brought to a fine art. Hardened by steady employment in a form few except the fans take seriously, they resist both criticism and praise, dismissing them as, respectively, misinformed or undeserved. Thus soap acting becomes a sort of self-fulfilling prophecy: if players give of their best, no one will appreciate it, while if they give less than their best, no one cares, or understands. It is another of the artistic dilemmas peculiar to the genre.

It is tempting for the players to blame others for the low esteem in which the soaps are held by those who do not work in them. Producers may be brought in at what looks like the end of a long – a too-long – career, as if the soaps were a sort of pasture in which spavined work-horses may safely graze. I exaggerate a little, of course: some soaps, especially the successful ones, have young and vigorous producers, or even old and vigorous producers, who regard the job as a challenge and respond to it with enthusiasm. But there are many soaps and producers who look on them either as a stepping-stone or as a pension. They do not inspire confidence in their cast.

As in every assembly line, each group of workers is keen to blame someone else for failures. The players criticize the writers for sloppy dialogue, crude characterization, unbelievable plotting. They may also consider the directors to be untried children put on the soaps to cut their teeth, or sucked-dry failures with no hope of other employment. These bring to the job either ignorance fatally combined with ambition, or a tired professionalism from which all inspiration and imagination have long been squeezed. If and when these other people, on whom the player is totally dependent, don't give of their best, is it surprising the show doesn't look as good as it should?

All players are nevertheless loyal to their shows (until they are fired).

They take a professional pride in turning out a characterization which is popular, in spite of long hours and (perhaps) dud scripts and cardboard sets and insipid direction. But what if they are not popular with the public? What if that final court of appeal, the verdict of the masses, goes against them?

This most often happens when a new player takes over an existing role – an American rather than a British practice. The fans are used to someone else, and they complain at having their routine, their sense of involvement disrupted. A new face means breaking in a new identity, which involves straining that suspension of disbelief on which much of the magic depends. A new player is an intruder in a familiar world. While a new character is perfectly acceptable for the sake of the plot, a different face in an old part means that the player becomes more noticeable than the character he or she is supposed to be playing. The fantasy is broken, and comparisons are made with his or her predecessor, usually to the disadvantage of the newcomer. The public complains that the replacement doesn't look, move, or sound like the original, that they can't believe in him or her, which in turn threatens their faith in the serial itself. They are usually won round in the end – thirteen weeks, a common contractual term, is long enough to get used to almost anything. But why risk public wrath in this way? Why isn't the character concerned merely killed off, and a fresh one introduced, which should make everyone happy?

Because the death of a favourite character is the most traumatic thing that can happen to a serial. And just because a player may want a move – to a different field of activity, or place – there is no reason for the writers to give up perfectly good plot-lines for that player's character. That would be a terrible waste.

Many soap players have successfully made the move from one show to another over the years. Sometimes their own part was written out, sometimes the show was cancelled. But good or familiar soap players are as much in demand in the business as head-writers: their stamina and expertise, not to mention their skill and audience-appeal, mean that, if fired, they will usually stand a good chance of being re-hired. I know I said earlier that soaps prefer "new" faces for their bigger parts, but there are large exceptions to this rule. Arthur Pentelow, who is *Emmerdale Farm*'s Henry Wilks, and Kathy Staff, *Crossroads*' Doris Luke, have worked their way through all the major British serials. Ronald Allen starred in two British soaps, *Compact* and *United*, both of which died. But up he popped as the suave director of the *Crossroads* motel, a part he has played for several years with a mechanical charm that obviously appeals to many women, since he gets umpteen proposals by post.

Robin Strasser appeared in *All My Children* and *Another World* before starring as *One Life to Live*'s resident bitch, Dorian Cramer Lord, a part she took over from Claire Malis, who had herself taken over from Nancy Pinkerton. There is also the occasional cosmopolitan soap player, like Tristan Rogers, an Australian who retains his native accent and who appeared in an Australian soap, *Bellbird*, and in the English *Crossroads*, before ending up as the rich, tough Robert Scorpio on *General Hospital*. Of these, only Ms Strasser has had to step into an already existing part and make it her own. This she managed, as all professionals would, by playing it her way, rather than trying to repeat the mannerisms of her predecessor. And because the part was a very strong one, the public accepted her. Indeed, the ratings rose.

The producers always maintain that the players are not as important as the serial. And public reaction backs them up. When the part of Meg Mortimer was written out of *Crossroads*, all the threats received from viewers that they would never again watch the programme failed to materialize: the figures stayed where they always had been. For many people, *Dallas* without Larry Hagman as J. R. would be unthinkable – yet one of the show's producers is on record as saying that if Hagman or any other player suddenly thought that they were bigger than anybody else, they would be replaced regardless of the fuss. "We can always find somebody to take over J. R.'s place," Lee Rich maintained. "You cannot allow the inmates to take over the asylum." I hasten to say that as far as I know there is no threat to the excellent Mr Hagman, who enjoys his job and has also directed several episodes. Nevertheless what his producer was saying is true: the programme is more important than any single individual. It is a mistake to think that soaps depend entirely for their popularity on the players who appear in them. Soap appeal is based mainly on the lure of the continuing narrative – as the post-Meg-Mortimer *Crossroads* audience proved – and for that it doesn't matter who plays the role, as long as the plot itself is sufficiently attractive.

The players are nevertheless stars in the true Hollywood tradition. When Noele Gordon was playing Meg Mortimer, she was treated wherever she appeared with the same affectionate reverence as that accorded to royalty. Harold Wilson, when Prime Minister, entertained the stars of *Coronation Street* at 10 Downing Street, his official residence. Leading players in *Emmerdale Farm* are issued by their employers with autographed pictures of themselves to hand out to passing fans. American day-time stars have had their own individual fan-clubs for years, and there are regular gatherings during which worshippers are permitted to see, hear, talk to and even touch their heroes and heroines.

All of this offers continuing proof of what the old moguls knew all along, that a star is made more by repeated appearances (never mind what vehicle), and judicious publicity, than by any particular talent. Soap stars appear with more regularity than even the most over-exposed movie person. They remain stars as long as they are visible. Their own special skills, however formidable, count for less than their prolonged exposure. The players are important because they are the form made flesh. But there's no particular security in being a star, nor has there ever been. That's not an easy fact for a player to live with either.

Though the form may have changed little over the years, there have been great changes in the machinery. I have already mentioned how the soaps used to go out live, like their radio cousins, when they were some fifteen minutes long. Stories of disaster are innumerable. "Drying" or forgetting lines was the most common. This got some actors into a terrible state: I was told of one who had to come in and say, "All right, fellers, this is a raid," but who for some unknown reason stuck after "fellers". This happened throughout rehearsal, but there at least the unfortunate actor could be prompted. When it came to the transmission, he entered in fine style, and got as far as "All right, fellers . . ." then dried. There was a long pause. Then the actor threw up his hands, said, "Jesus Christ," in tones of genuine anguish, and rushed off. What the viewers thought is not recorded, but the other members of the cast were delighted.

These early soaps also followed radio's pattern of giving information in a lengthy, and totally artificial, recitation of facts. Here is an example from the American TV version of *Young Dr Malone*, in which a neurological surgeon – played by Hugh Franklin – was called in for an emergency. Dressed in white tie and tails, he joined a group huddled round the operating table, and was required to deliver the following in one gulp: "Jerry, I'm sorry to be late, but my daughter was married this afternoon, and since my wife is dead, the reception was held at the boy's parents' home out beyond Charleton, and I had to drive back in all of this rain. I'd've made better time in a submarine!"

Since then, improvements in camera mobility and studio technique have given actors, directors, and of course writers the freedom to convey important information by gesture, expression and nuance, without the need for so much dialogue. The use of recording tape means that the worst mistakes can now be prevented from reaching the screen. And the increase, in America, of screen time from fifteen to thirty minutes (the standard English length) has brought increased capital investment from the production companies (especially when the episodes stretched through forty-five minutes to an hour, and even an hour and a half –

though it was soon realized that the strain of producing ninety minutes of drama five days a week was intolerable, and an hour was accepted as the soap maximum). More money was spent on more and better sets, which in turn lessened the players' anxieties about knocking down the scenery, or moving out of camera range merely by leaning forward on their chairs. All of which has allowed them to appear more natural, even in the most unnatural of circumstances. This, I am sure, has been an important factor in making acting in soaps a lot more respectable than it once was.

In the old days, a job on the soaps was accepted only out of desperation: any player with ambition would appear in them for the shortest possible time, and with scant respect for the product. This was because there was so little scope to display individual talent: not only were moves limited and direction rudimentary, but dialogue like the quote from *Young Dr Malone* was the norm, and moreover had to be followed to the letter. When one player dared to complain about having his private life invaded by 'phone calls from Irna Phillips demanding total fidelity to her sacred script, he was fired the following day. Modern actors and actresses take – or have earned the right to take – far greater liberties.

Younger players have become more and more common in soaps in the last few years. In America this has been caused by the sponsors' conviction that young people – all of them potentially big spenders – watch soaps, and will do so all the more avidly if they see themselves and their problems on the shows. Also the expansion to an hour or more meant that many more story-lines had to be introduced to fill the time available, and this inevitably involved more and younger characters.

In England, where the hand of commerce takes the pulse rather than applies the tourniquet, it has also been realized that there is a young audience for serials, who appreciate seeing their generation getting some screen time. No English serial is without its young couples, either having marital problems or trying to bed one another. Indeed, in the eyes of the veteran players – especially the Americans – youth is so prominently featured that an imbalance has been created. They bemoan that absence of breadth that they seem to remember, when the age range covered everything from infancy to senility. In fact, in American serials the young were rarely seen and almost never heard until the 1970s: a commercial decision by the sponsors and networks who believed that the standard soap audience consisted exclusively of mothers, widows, and housewives. The English soaps, by contrast, included youthful players and story-lines from the start, and have never practised age discrimination. But then they are aimed at an early-evening, family audience – and are less bound by marketing considerations (English advertisers have no say in the making of pro-grammes).

If acting style, especially amongst the long established players, has altered only slowly, this is obviously part of the appeal of the soaps – an oasis of consistency and conservatism in a whirligig world. There is no other genre in which players can age with their character, at the same pace as they age in reality. Some regard this as a challenge, others as professional suicide: another of the contradictions thrown up by the soaps (like any elegant formula, their seeming simplicity is nothing but a deception). There is no doubt that there *can* be Life after Soap: Noele Gordon was booked to appear in a revival of *Gypsy* following her removal from *Crossroads* after serving seventeen years; Christopher Reeve extricated himself from *Love of Life* (CBS) after eight years, and was soon after discovered to be Superman (the soap itself finished a twenty-eight-year run in 1980). At least this proves that long service in one part doesn't necessarily kill you as an actor or actress (and the fans' readiness to accept you in another role is further evidence of their their ability to distinguish illusion from reality). But what of an actor like William Roache, who has played Ken Barlow from the first episode of *Coronation Street* in 1960 to the present, taking him from college student to middle age? That he continues to find the role interesting, and make it seem so to the audience, is as much of a tribute to his acting as to the quality of the *Street*'s writing. This has always leavened with wit what might otherwise become boringly predictable, especially since the serial has never indulged in melodrama, preferring its own brand of nostalgic naturalism. If an actor of Mr Roache's calibre is happy doing nothing else, content to go down in history simply as Ken Barlow, then there must be something compelling about the job.

Ageing is something that comes to all of us, but continuing to play the same part convincingly on television is no pushover. Actors are not like writers, who so often express themselves through the mouths of their creations (conversely, there are many writers who prefer not to, or who cannot, write about themselves at all, and have to immerse themselves in other people's lives before their fictive kindling begins to crackle). Acting means bringing to life other people's creations: however much Mr Roache is Ken Barlow to his fans, however much the part is his property, he is still delivering someone else's lines in situations invented by someone else, to direction by yet another. He is not, then, playing himself: the challenge is to keep separate his private and public selves, to allow just as much of Roache to seep into Barlow as will bring the latter convincingly to life. That is obviously enough to keep him on his toes.

It seems strange that there are not more story-lines dealing with the problems of age itself: slowing down, failing memory, deafness, stiffness and those ailments that make growing old seem like the hardest work of all. Though there are few breeds tougher than the working actor or actress – their stamina is legendary – they could illuminate these problems with conviction. What irks them most is having too little, not too much to do, though they accept, with as much grace as anybody who reaches pensionable age, that they have to step aside, at least a little, so that their juniors can have a go. Yet infirmity, though both inevitable and irreversible, seems not yet a fit subject for the soaps, although it would not be hard to be positive about it. Perhaps this will change now that cancer and kindred horrors have been aired: if so, the old stagers may enjoy a whole new lease of life.

Since soap opera is currently fashionable – that is to say, it is undergoing one of its periodic splashes in the news – it is as good a shop-window as any (and better than most) for players to display their talents. Look what happened, in an earlier period of soap trendiness, to some of the cast of *Peyton Place*, which played in the middle and late 1960s: Mia Farrow and Ryan O'Neal, the romantic leads, have since become superstars, a course every actor and actress has charted for themselves. Such, indeed, is the glamour of the soaps that superstars from elsewhere have dropped by to bathe in it. In England, in the early days of *Crossroads*, well known faces called at the motel to chat to Meg Mortimer. That was soon stopped, as the producers felt that it destroyed the illusion that the rest of the cast strove to create: stars from other media are known as themselves, not as the characters they portray. But there appears to have been another change of mind, if one is to judge by the 1983 appearance of the celebrated comic actor Max Wall in a character part in *Crossroads*. And in America the modern trend seems to be to feature more and more big names in cameo roles (thus demonstrating they don't give a damn about "realism"). Elizabeth Taylor made a guest appearance in *General Hospital*, Sammy Davis Jr has made several in *One Life to Live* – both claiming that they did it because they loved the show and always watched it. (Ms Taylor, however, cannot have been unimpressed by the fantastic media attention *General Hospital* was receiving – it even got the cover of *Newsweek*.)

A few years ago such stars would not have been seen dead on the soaps: no one who mattered watched them, and it was too much like hard work (for little money, compared to what they might receive elsewhere). Now some regard it as a bonus, others as a way of reviving their careers – like Jane Wyman on *Falcon Crest* or Robert Morse, whose brief exposure on *All My Children* at least made people say, "Where have you been?", or Joan Fontaine, who started all over again after appearing on *Ryan's Hope*. And of course there are some who may not have needed the work, but who found soaping congenial – like Joan Collins, the super-bitch in *Dynasty*. Howard Keel made the change from singing beefcake to rugged and reliable Clayton Farlow in *Dallas*; Lana Turner, once billed as "The Sweater Girl", appeared in *Falcon Crest* as the mother of both hero and villain. These stars are not slumming: their reputations matter too much for that. Their appearances are not only a sign of the soaps' attraction – they are also a demonstration of the professionalism of most soap acting. Superstars have been known to appear with inferior players so that they themselves will shine all the brighter. But this doesn't happen on the soaps: the playing of the humbler roles does not suffer by the comparison.

The players are perhaps the most vulnerable, or anyway the least protected, people in the soap opera process. There is not a lot they can do about the writing, and even less about the direction. If they give a bad performance – because of a hangover or a domestic row or a fight with the director or the threat of being removed from the cast – there is little chance to put it right. If they turn in a masterpiece, the most that can be expected is a pat on the back or a few words of praise from producer or director. Players know when they are bad and are sickened by it; they thrive on praise, but in a soap being good is all part of the job, which goes on regardless.

Yet if one puts the question, is it worth being good, or trying to be good, in a genre where the pressures are such you can pretty well get away with being mediocre, every actor and actress would almost certainly answer, yes, it is worth trying. They are proud, and they may be defensive, but they know they are doing a job few can do well. They are all determined to prove they are one of those few – especially when there are some twenty million people out there ready and waiting to give them hell.

6

THE DIRECTORS AND PRODUCERS:
CAMERAS AND COMMITTEES

The director brings you the pictures, the producer brings you the show. Or, to put it another way, directors are part of the artistic and technical team, while producers are executives. In theatre, neither interferes with the other's sphere of influence: the director lets the producer worry about the money, the producer lets the director decide how the play should look. In television, as in films, the two roles are intertwined, like creeper and rose. First we'll deal with the flower.

The director has, in theory, control over casting, costume, make-up, lighting, camera work, pace and editing. I say "in theory" because the producer has the final vote over all of these – as she or he has over the story-line, writing, contracts, budgets and everything else connected with the show, including the hiring of the director. To use a nautical metaphor, the producer is the Admiral in charge of the fleet, while the director is the Captain of one of the ships. But only Captain for a quick trip round the bay: a director may do only one show out of three or five in one week, and maybe two the next. Or one week on and two weeks off. Like the writers, they are part of a team who divide the work between them. Unlike the writers, they are all equal – except, of course, in the eyes of their crew, who know their strengths, and even more their weaknesses, and air their mutinous feelings accordingly.

Perhaps the one person in the whole soap opera set-up on whom the producers are prepared to take a risk is the director. If someone has directed in the theatre, or a movie, and wants to try her or his hand at television; if an actor or actress wants a go at pointing the cameras; if an old pro wants some quick cash or a talented newcomer needs some practice – each may be let loose on an episode of a soap. They may do some good, and the harm they can do is minimal. The momentum of the juggernaut is great enough to carry a weak or inexperienced captain, at least on a short outing: the crew know their roles and places, and the producer is there to ensure conformity. Of course the director is colossally important – the show wouldn't work without them. But unlike the writers, whose story-lines are planned months in advance, and the actors, whose appearances or disappearances are meticulously plotted, the directors can be changed at whim. They enjoy a lot of responsibility, but very little power.

Directors under contract to do a regular number of episodes have maybe ten days to study the script and write their camera script. They do not meet the writer and discuss changes that may improve the plot or dialogue: all that, as we have seen, is a separate process carried out in the writing department. This means that the directors have none of that creative contact or responsibility that allows them to make their mark in other genres. They are handed the script and expected to confine themselves to making it work within the limitations of time and budget. So the first thing to say about soap opera directing is that it is more mechanical than creative.

But the mechanics are daunting enough. A score of actors to man-oeuvre through as many scenes in a few hours requires incredibly thorough preparation. Dealing with the actors is the easy part: under-standing and explaining characterization, telling them where and how to move, persuading them to look and sound convincing, soothing and cajoling – these are minor problems compared with the technical ones. There are the cameras, each with its own crew and long, snaking cables: the director has to know in advance exactly where they are to go, not only to get the required shots of the actors, but also to avoid them colliding with each other. There are the sound men with their micro-phones on long rods or booms, whose positions have to be plotted so that the smallest sigh from a disappearing actress will be picked up without the shadow of the boom getting into the picture (a frequent cause of retakes). There is the lighting to discuss with the lighting director, deciding between the hundreds of lamps slung from the studio ceiling, whose shutters are banged open, shut, or anywhere in between, by men armed with nothing more sophisticated than long poles. The sets have to be minutely studied and laid out exactly to plan, so that neither actors nor cameras will knock over the furniture. Time has to be included for the players to change their clothes and make-up, which involves discussions with designer and wardrobe department. But above all the advance planning has to include the mix of shots available, so that the director will have a good idea of how each scene will look on the screen.

A camera script carries, by the side of the dialogue, the director's instructions to the camera crews and technicians, using a code everyone in the profession understands. Say you have a simple scene set in an office where a man is talking on the telephone and a woman comes in. Obviously you do not simply keep the camera in one spot and shoot the whole scene from a distance – that would bore the audience. Mixing types of camera shot is the accepted way of keeping up the tension. So the director might start with the man in mid-close-up (that is, the top third of his body) talking on the 'phone, and close in as his conversation continues till his face fills the screen and the viewer is aware from the merest flicker of his eyebrow what he is thinking. Such a shot would mean the camera tracking in on its dolly, or it might involve having one camera close to the man all the time, and cutting to it from the one which is more distant.

If the viewer were also to see the person the man was talking to, by splitting the screen in half (a very common device for 'phone conversations), the permutation of shots is thereby doubled.

Enter the other woman. Is the viewer to see her before the man does, in which case you need a third camera to cover the door, or should the director pull the second camera back and take in the whole set in a wide angle shot? Is she entering stealthily, which can be shown with a close-up of the door handle slowly turning, followed by a shot of the man engrossed in his conversation, or is she to sail straight in and stop, which would mean a full-length shot of her, a cut to him, then perhaps a two-shot view of the pair of them? (A two-shot mid-close-up is perhaps the most common in soap, and requires skilful blocking by the director to show the faces of both artists in reasonable detail.) If stop she does, at what point in the man's conversation on the 'phone should this be for maximum effect? What reaction will each of them show – guilt? alarm? horror? Is it better to show these reactions by cutting from one close-up to another, or to go from wide-angle two-shot to mid-close-ups and then cut to a shot of something significant – say her hand twisting her wedding ring?

The script is not much help in these matters, and the actors need guidance. All the writer is likely to put in by way of directions is "Woman enters. Man is on 'phone . . . He hangs up and turns to see her standing there." Most writers learn not to litter the script with too many directions, since this encroaches on the professional territory of the other artists. Actors take unkindly to being told how to react, at least by a mere writer, and if the latter presumes to suggest a shot in a script, other than those essential to convey meaning (as for example "We see her smile fade"), the director will simply ignore it.

I must admit that when I first went to a television studio, it seemed to me the directors cared much more about their machines than they did about the actors. Large, gleaming, powerful, silent, efficient and expensive cameras; microphones on their booms, twitching like fish at the end of a rod; banks of monitors in the gallery that overlooks the studio telling the director and technical staff exactly what each camera is shooting; even the personal walkie-talkie – enabling the director to communicate with the floor or studio manager – these marvellous gadgets that are finally responsible for bringing the pictures to the viewer, seemed to offer the director a more satisfying sense of power than moving actors from A to B and ensuring they say their lines correctly.

But of course a good director cares as much about actors and script as about the show. It is just that in soap opera, the pressures that we have noted as operating on everybody with equal effect, limit the scope the directors have to practise their craft. They cannot mould a character to their liking, in case this goes against the demands of future story-lines (the responsibility of writer and producer). The choice of shots is limited by time, budget and convention. Given a few days rather than weeks to prepare a camera script, the director will take the short cut and go for the obvious and familiar, rather than the novel or difficult. The set is either standard, and has been used over and over again, or, if it is new, it will be the cheapest possible. Either way there won't be that much choice of camera angles. Even the various methods of ending a scene – cutting, fading, mixing, dissolving, wiping, going to black – are dictated by precedent. The director, too, is in the business of giving the audience what it expects. Yet directing is the one area where a little novelty – not too much, but a little – might be expected to show.

The arrival of a new serial, or a new producer for an old one, every so often does change the look of the genre. The appointment of Jacqueline Babbin as producer of the American day-time soap *All My Children* brought several alterations in the appearance of the show: the lighting was made brighter, the costumes less glamorous, the hairstyles more contemporary. More music – so important in signalling changes of mood – was called for, and the pace of the show speeded up: where each episode had been 80 pages long, whipping the players through more quickly meant that 87 pages became necessary. But all these changes – small enough not to alienate the show's fans, and different enough to improve its ratings – were binding on each of the contract directors. They were imposed from the top, and the individual directors could not argue with them. Of course it is the producer's job to enforce consistency and continuity. But the visual style and content of a show is usually the director's responsibility. Soaps once more demonstrate how different they are.

It is almost impossible to detect an individual director's style from one particular episode. Sometimes attentive addicts will be able to identify different writers' contributions, because of their way with language, but with directors this rarely happens. They are like assembly line foremen, ensuring that the product rolls off smoothly and up to standard. As a result, they are often judged more harshly by their fellow directors than are other artists in the genre. No doubt this is something to do with that pride which comes of having a technical as well as an artistic expertise. Anybody can write or act (which is not the same thing as saying that anybody can earn a living at it), but to learn how to get the best out of cameras, let alone actors, requires special training and knowledge. Exploiting the machinery to achieve an effect which is individual confers an esteem on directors which stands them in good stead when it comes to dealing with writers and actors. The director is the person who brings everything and everybody together. His or her signature should be on the piece, on a par with the writer's. But in soap opera this signature has to look ‚the same as every other director's: a bit of artistic forgery which arouses professional criticism.

Writers, actors, and everybody else can blame the director for short-comings. The director can only blame the limitations of time and budget which made high standards impossible to maintain – abstractions rather than human factors. If the director was any good, people say, he or she wouldn't be in soap. But then, as one of them told Dorothy Hobson in her book on *Crossroads*, if they work in soap they are never at the top of their profession: they are either on the way up, or on the way down.

A soap can be instantly identified by the way it looks. Leaving aside the prime-time serials (*Dallas* and its like) which brought prime-time budgets to day-time romances, most soaps are still largely studio-bound, using sets whose economy shows. There is little of that solid feel or attention to detail that you get in more lavishly funded dramas: rather, the soap's sets *suggest* a place with the minimum of furniture and props, using a kind of shorthand which, because it is employed over and over again, the viewers come to recognize and accept.

Although the sets are the responsibility of the designer, who has to build them as cheaply as possible and ensure they fit into the limited space available on the studio floor, the way they are used is the director's responsibility. He or she can ask for what furniture there is to be lit in such a way as to make it look less tacky. But different directors have different views, and it's no good having things shrouded in shadow one week and harshly lit the next. So the directors settle for a compromise that eschews subtlety and variety.

Since the sets are built to accommodate actors and cameras, it might be thought that, when director meets designer to discuss a particular episode, the director's wishes can easily be carried out. In theatre or film or single TV play, the sets are an integral part of the drama, and an aid to understanding character. But in the soaps they are merely a backdrop, a flimsy framework for theatrical gesture, even though particular sets, such as bedrooms, living rooms or offices may occasionally suggest the tastes of particular characters. A director may want something altered for the sake of a particular situation, or to allow a different camera angle – but the designer has to work with three or more directors, all using the same sets. Things cannot be altered every time: that would be too expensive. Thus set changes are limited, which in turn limits the angles the director can employ. Despite the improvement in production budgets and values, the scenery – though it no longer falls down the way it used to – is allowed to age to the point of infirmity. Characters and sets rarely interrelate the way they do in other genres, which helps to give the soaps that look of unreality. The director is denied a further means of suggesting depth, where little may exist. All of this helps to make the soap instantly recognizable to its audience – but routine to its director.

What happens when a director *does*, despite everything, make a particular effort to make a scene look a little special? When he or she insists on altering the mood through different lighting and camera work and pace, or makes a great fuss about something that has been imported especially for a certain scene (I am thinking, say, of a kidney machine brought in to save a character's life)? Either this special effort will leave too little time to devote proper attention to the rest of the episode, or someone (probably the producer) will complain that the "special" scene sticks out too much. Consistency of tone is all-important, even if the tone has to be low.

Those who try to make their individual mark in soaps are usually the young directors who hope to be noticed and go on to greater things. Unfairly, the road to steady employment, if not to promotion within television, is paved with the cobbles of imitation. If a new director shows that he or she is capable of turning out a product that looks like its predecessors, that will at least be taken as a sign of professional adequacy. And, paradoxically, if they knock themselves – and everybody else – out to produce something completely different, they will be regarded with suspicion for having spent so much effort on a product which didn't need, let alone deserve, such treatment.

The one area where a soap director enjoys real authority is over the technical crew – although they, like orchestral players accustomed to several conductors, have their own ideas of how to do things. The soap opera set-up consists of a series of interlocking groups, each with its own distinct hierarchy. Under the director there is the production assistant or associate director, whose chief function it is to call the shots and tell the cameramen what their next shot is to be. He or more usually she sits in the gallery with a copy of the camera script, shouting out things like "25 on 3, camera 1 next", which means that camera 3 will be "live", transmitting pictures, for shot 25 while warning the camera-man on 1 that his turn is coming. Meanwhile the director is beaming out instructions to other members of the team – to the cameraman, getting him to move in for a nice tight shot; to the sound man, telling him to get his boom out of the way; to the floor manager, demanding quiet on the set; to the lighting crew, requesting more or less light on the scene. And of course the actors get told a thing or two, either by the director if he or she is on the studio floor, or via the floor manager, who censors or generally cleans up the director's instructions before passing them on. These may be to the effect that the player should remember the lines and the moves that had been worked out in rehearsal, get the pauses right to enhance dramatic effect and allow the cameras to cut to somebody else, and not lean so far towards another character that they go out of shot. The director, in the excitement of actual recording and under pressure of time, does not put things so politely.

Once a scene has been taken more or less to the director's satisfaction, he or she relies on other members of the technical staff to check on the quality of what has been recorded. Tests are run to ensure that the tape was recording properly and that the sound levels are adequate. Machines can and do go wrong, and retakes of at least parts of certain scenes are sometimes necessary, for mechanical as well as human reasons. The most critical decision for the director and his or her editor to take is where to start again. Editing – the assembly of shots from various takes and sources into the final form dictated by the script – is a luxury for which there is little time on the soaps (the Americans allow more use of this facility than the English). Video tape cannot be spliced like film or audio tape. The director has to start recording again from a suitable point to avoid jumps or inconsistencies – and all this takes up valuable time. Often a director has to allow a scene to pass which is less than satisfactory, simply because to retake part of it will eat into the remaining studio time. It is thus that soaps get the reputation for "fluffs" (actors getting the lines wrong) and mistakes that productions with more time and access to post-production facilities (that is, the proper use of editing) would not allow to pass. Old hands among actors, however, will frequently ensure a re-take after what they consider an unacceptable mistake by the deliberate use of an unscripted expletive.

Why should directors work in such conditions? Because if they didn't, someone else would. Because it is a challenge, and something of an opportunity to display their professionalism. And because the viewers, millions of them, lap up the product, or at least remain faithful to it without much complaint.

Naturally this can give the directors a somewhat jaundiced view of public taste. But even more jaundiced is their view of those who control their budgets. Most directors would be glad of more time and more money to spend, not on themselves, but on the show. What is hardest to understand is why serials which are so profitable – because they are popular and cheap to produce – should be so niggardly with resources. The increased expenditure that has been available to soaps on both sides of the Atlantic in the past few years has altered the look of shows greatly for the better. Why not allow a bit more cash and a bit longer in the studio, to produce a show that will look really good, of which all participants can be proud?

The answers, as might be expected, are that the nature of the soaps does not allow more studio time, that they have been produced in the same way for a very long time without anyone complaining, that improving them will swallow up the profits without increasing the audience. Nor are the producers held responsible for this state of affairs by those who work under them. The purse strings are controlled by persons out of the reach of those on the soap's payroll. The producers, if they command the respect and affection of their colleagues, are generally agreed to be working to get the best possible show under the circumstances.

So the final responsibility for the quality of the soaps rests with the sponsors (I use the term in its widest sense). And they in turn pass the buck on to the public. As long as the viewers are happy, the word goes, just carry on as you are, and make the most of it.

What can be criticized is the cynicism – or, put more sympathetically, the commercial sagacity – of the sponsors. By them I mean not just the American advertisers who used to own the shows, although ownership has now passed in the main to the networks. I mean those in the offices of the TV companies who are responsible for allocating funds to their various departments. Except in the BBC – who have not had a truly continuous serial, that is, one that runs every week throughout the year, since 1969 – soaps are infinitely cheaper, in costs per transmitted hour, than prime-time shows. *Crossroads, Coronation Street, Emmerdale Farm* (which, like *Dallas*, is done in batches), and the English day-time serials like *Taff Acre* and *Take the High Road*, or Australia's *The Young Doctors*, cost far less to produce than evening dramas, and in America this difference is even more marked: an hour of prime-time drama there can cost more than an entire week of a soap opera.

But if the costs are low, the profits are high. In commercial television, advertising rates are calculated according to audience ratings: the bigger the audience, the higher the advertising rates. In day-time, there are obviously fewer people watching, which may be offered by the sponsors as an excuse for keeping the serial's budgets low. But even so the costs of five episodes of an American soap are covered by the advertising revenue from one, or at most two, days. That means there are three days of revenue which are pure gravy. In England the cost differential between soap and other drama is less marked, but it exists all the same. *Crossroads*, for example, figures regularly in the top ten programmes watched by the nation, and thus generates massive advertising revenue. Yet its costs, as can be plainly seen, are kept as low as possible. Even the BBC, which pays less than the commercial companies in all fields, but which spends more on drama, does not splash out on soap. There are no stars' salaries (save for super-star cameos) – these are forgone in exchange for a contract offering job security – and little location shooting (with the exception of *Emmerdale Farm* and the BBC's *Triangle*). You can tell that a British soap is as starved of funds as its American relatives, and yet its profitability, in terms of viewing figures, is greater than that of any other genre.

It would and should be possible to give the soaps the improved conditions and better finish that their prime-time colleagues enjoy. To do so would mean allowing more rehearsal and recording time, to ease the pressure on actors, directors and studio crews; it would mean more money spent on design, and more access to post-production facilities; it might even mean hiring more writers, giving each of them longer to produce their scripts. Small improvements along these lines have been made piecemeal over the years, and no one could deny that the quality of the serials has improved along with them. But equally no one can prove that the audience has increased in numbers as a result. It would be going against the commercial grain to spend more without convincing evidence of necessity or increased profit.

In America there have been two major strikes in the television industry, one by the writers, another by the technicians. Both were over wages rather than conditions, and in neither case did the soaps stop being screened. Blackleg writers – often from the cast of the soaps – were brought in, and apparently the only people who noticed were the original writers, who were furious at what was being done to "their" characters. As for the technicians, non-union people – production secretaries and the like – were given a crash course in working cameras, lighting, and sound equipment, and let loose on the floor (only, let it be said, with the soaps: a sign of the networks' desperation to keep hold of their day-time audience, never mind the quality of the product). After a couple of days, according to some actors, the blackleg crew were as proficient as the regular technicians. And the audience never complained, either at the new writers or the new look.

Only once has a change been ordered in the production schedules of a soap with the stated aim of improving its quality. This was when the regulatory body of British commercial television, the Independent Broadcasting Authority (IBA), insisted that *Crossroads* reduce its weekly output from four episodes to three. The IBA's reasons were that the programme's production standards were not high enough. They ascribed this to the pressure of putting out four shows a week (all other British soaps limit themselves to two). Their idea was that by giving more time to each episode, there would be room for a bit more polish.

In fact no one noticed a qualitative difference, not even the people working on the show. What the enforced reduction did cause was an enormous amount of resentment amongst viewers, and amongst those who worked on *Crossroads*. The fans were intensely angry at having their dosage cut down, and the workers felt they were being rubbished by their own industry. The timing and reasoning behind the IBA's edict were both suspect. It came during the run-up to the allocation of the new franchises, and some felt it was a flashing of the IBA's tooth to warn potential programmers that popularity wasn't everything – a little nip at a target few in the industry would defend, to prove that the IBA was a worthy guardian of the nation's viewing standards. Others felt it was a swipe at ATV, who produced *Crossroads*, and whose franchise for commercial television in the Midlands was later broken up by the Authority. The IBA's stated desire to set some limit to each type of programme that occupied network time – that is, just as they limited imported programmes and feature films, so they wanted to limit the amount of soap opera – was considered specious by those involved. If the extra half-hour vacated by *Crossroads* had been occupied by something new, wonderful or even different, the excuse of bringing more variety to the early evening schedules might have had some force. But what was screened in *Crossroads'* place? Situation comedy. As if there wasn't enough of that.

If the IBA's idea was to improve quality, it didn't work. The resources that had been stretched over four episodes were applied to three, but the difference wasn't enough to affect the look of the production (which had been improving anyway, albeit imperceptibly). Nor was there much easing of the pressure on the writers, actors, and directors: for one thing, a single episode only involves each set of writers and players in some ten minutes' worth of screen-time (remember that in *Crossroads* writers are responsible for a particular set of characters, not an entire episode, and each set of characters will only appear once or twice per show); and for another, work expands to fill the time available (according to Parkinson's law). The message seems clear: the mechanics of the genre operate best at a level of botching competence that is immune to external pressure for improvement (save for the spur of the competition).

The chief pressure on any soap is to be popular, and in the name of popularity are many sins committed. I say "sins" half jestingly, for I am not about to launch into a sermon on the evils of capitalist greed. Yet "sin" covers a multitude of shortcomings, including acts of moral cowardice. And I would argue that many of soap's failings are due to a lack of innovative courage on the part of the producers, who hide behind the shield of popularity.

The prime failing is the same self-censorship that I have said writers are endangered by. Those subjects which the soaps will not deal with are proscribed because "the public does not want to see that sort of thing". All problems on the soaps have to be personalized, and the personalities involved must conform to stereotypes whose views reflect majority thinking. There is a different notion of "balance" on the soaps from that which is understood elsewhere. There is a strong presumption in favour of good triumphing over evil, and since casting a particular religious or political viewpoint as "good" would mean its opposing view being seen as "bad" – which would cause offence to a substantial number of people – all such topics are avoided. For some of the right reasons, no doubt, the simplest being that the soaps are mere entertainment, which the public look to in order to escape the gory complexities of the real world – "goodness knows there's enough politics on TV without the soaps getting involved".

And yet what is missing from the soaps is precisely that sense of genuine challenge to prevailing evils that made the myths and folk-tales that preceded them such exciting, indeed radical, crowd pullers. The soaps certainly attack selfishness, wickedness and greed, but only in the domestic sphere. As they themselves boast of being contemporary, it should surely be possible to see some current dragons – racism, unemployment, warmongering, to name but three – hammered, if not slain. Folk myths may appear to be reactionary because they deal with a time long gone when everyone except a deviant few believed in the same things. And yet in times of national stress and revolutionary upheaval it is the radicals, of left and right, who most often claim to be acting in the name of the mythical heroes. I cannot imagine anyone claiming to be inspired by a soap character in any other than the most private battles. Indeed, what politics there is on the soaps is usually the politics of apathy. I am not suggesting that the soaps should become vehicles for political (or any other) propaganda: all I am saying is that they lack a political (in its broadest sense) dimension, which is one that affects all their viewers.

The reason is of course that the soaps are, in a very real sense, selling not just a product, but a culture. Unlike folk myth (which has often been perverted for propaganda purposes), the soaps are directly under the control of the producers, who answer to their sponsors or network chiefs. Far from being the spontaneous product of creative minds, they are, as we know, precisely crafted and tightly controlled cultural artefacts. Now I'm not saying they are part of a commercial conspiracy to brainwash the public into accepting capitalism and all its goods (or evils). What I am saying is that they are a commercial product competing in a free market by retailing the views and values of the dominant majority. Naturally in societies like those of the Western world, whose strength comes from buying cheap and selling dear, the market economy is taken for granted. Soap characters benefit from it; its casualties are offered access to its blessings, if they deserve it. What you will not see on the soaps is any attack – and certainly not a successful attack – on the market rules of which many fall foul. Thus the viewers are denied, what myth and fairy-tale did not deny them, a critique of social values that might help them to redefine their roles and goals.

Of course it would be silly to expect soap producers to maul with their gums the hands that feed them. But it is a little cowardly to refuse to air controversial subjects by hiding behind the public. The arguments go "Who are we to be so arrogant as to deny the public what it wants?" or "Some subjects – like racism – are far too important to be part of a story that is only one of many in a popular serial." Looked at charitably, such arguments are patronizing; less charitably, they are cynical. Patronizing because it is implied that the audience is interested only in bland escapism; cynical because the producers know they are not offering the viewers a choice. The soaps can be seen as a consumer durable that exists to lure customers into increasing their consumption. You wouldn't expect a detergent commercial to warn you about the allergic conditions and ecological damage the product can cause, so why should you expect a serial to make people uncomfortable by showing the pustules on the backside of their own body politic? Only because the producers themselves claim that their shows are realistic, contemporary and unafraid of tackling any subject. And because television is the medium through which reality is filtered for most of us. And because I cherish this romantic belief that all creative work contains an element of controversy.

Actually, there has been a choice offered within the genre: by those splendidly parodic serials *Soap* and *Mary Hartman, Mary Hartman*. But these were more situation comedy than serial, and made for late-night sophisticates – not the wholesome family viewing offered to day-time audiences. True comedy can change attitudes, where the soaps merely reflect them, and no doubt the airing of such taboos as transsexualism, homosexual love, the suffocating absurdity of family life (made all the more pointed, in *Soap*, by the presence of the omniscient black butler in the Tate household), and the insidious blurring of the boundaries between fantasy and reality fostered by the ads, of which poor Mary Hartman was so notable a victim – no doubt laughing at all these things made them, if not acceptable, then at least topics for conversation. Certainly these shows travelled better than the soaps they satirized, though to non-American viewers I suspect they seemed, not controversial, but a confirmation that the American Way was certifiably lunatic (a judgement backed by the Ewings' behaviour in *Dallas*). Politics were discussed, and those of the Right and the "moral majority" came in for their share of guying. The protests from religious and ethnic groups were enough to show that poking a sacred cow will stir it to make a charge at you: proof of the power of television and the lack of humour amongst fanatics.

Nevertheless these two parodies had little effect on the real thing: not a single soap paid them the compliment of imitation. Obviously that illusory reality which the serials manage to create might have been threatened if they had started to send themselves up – though if sufficiently large numbers of viewers had shown that they liked that kind of thing, no doubt it would have been put on for their benefit. But neither *Mary Hartman, Mary Hartman* nor *Soap* attracted the kind of audiences to make the serial producers take notice, and after a short but merry life, both were discontinued. To the lasting regret, I may say, of those who, without the example of Mary Hartman, would never have admitted their concern about waxy build-up on their floors.

Let us go into a little detail about the organizational hierarchy that controls the soaps. It is corporate structure in a fish-eye lens: a series of little pyramids glued together to form one big pyramid on top of which perch the people with the cash. In England these point-perchers are the BBC, the television companies franchised by the Independent Broadcasting Authority (Granada for *Coronation St*; Central, once ATV, for *Crossroads*; Yorkshire for *Emmerdale Farm*), and an independent production company for Channel 4's soap, *Brookside*. The BBC, being, like Channel 4, a national network, shows its soaps throughout Britain; for the commercial companies, this depends on the Networking Committee and the decisions of the various companies themselves. For instance, Thames thought so little of *Crossroads* that at one point they refused to continue transmitting it in their area (Greater London): only the huge outburst of indignation from the fans persuaded Thames to resume transmission. In fact the early evening soaps are screened everywhere: it is only the day-time English soaps that are confined to regional showings at the whim of the company controllers. (*Soap* itself started this way, being bought by ATV and shown only in the Midlands late at night, until word got out and it was networked nationally.)

The American system is very similar. It used not to be: when they started, soaps were sponsored by individual firms who owned the copyright, and who sold them to the networks. Naturally this gave them total editorial control, and the serials were a vehicle for selling the firm's products. Thus Procter & Gamble, who still own six shows (I believe they are the only firm to retain the copyright in networked serials), used to take up all the advertising slots that opened, closed and punctuated the show, and moreover insisted that, if P&G's products did not actually feature in the homes of the characters, nothing that could conceivably be taken as an endorsement of a rival product would be mentioned.

Things are a little different now. P&G are simply a production company like any other (though no doubt they still prohibit the featuring of somebody else's washing powder, soaps in general have long moved out of the kitchen). They own the show, assume financial responsibility for budgets and payments, and sell it to the networks or to individual companies (usually the network takes on the job of selling the show round the nation). P&G's profit comes from selling dearly to the networks what they have paid cheaply for in production. The network's profit comes from selling advertising space. P&G may advertise during one of its own shows, or it may not: that is a decision taken by their advertising department, of which their programming department is a separate sub-section. P&G's rivals often advertise on P&G-owned shows, and have done for many years. What matters is that the company owns a successful show commanding a high price from those who screen it.

Of course the soaps are still vehicles for selling, as they always have been. But they are not, even in America, selling a particular product (for example, soap). The shows are punctuated by ads for anything from home improvements to vaginal deodorants, and the higher the ratings, the higher the advertising charges. The same is true in England, except, of course, in the case of the BBC, where what is being "sold" is the rest of the evening's programmes on that channel. Ratings matter as much to the BBC as they do to the commercial companies, though there is still a residual sense of shame about this, a hangover from the Reithian Parnassus.

This hangover has dogged the Beeb since its earliest days, when Val Gielgud, as Head of Drama, refused to give *The Robinsons* further houseroom in his department, and was very snooty about *Mrs Dale's Diary*. It doesn't stop the Corporation making and buying popular programmes, but it stops them keeping them going throughout the year. They either have not grasped the fact that it is the continuous nature of soaps that builds a large and a loyal audience, or they wilfully refuse to commit themselves to competing in so vulgar a sphere. Their own standards of soap production are no higher, and certainly no lower, than those of the competition: *The Brothers* was very well done, and could certainly have continued beyond the seven series allowed it (the programme was sold from Abu-dhabi to Zambia, though it didn't travel across the Atlantic). Even the economical melodramas of *Triangle* rivalled, say, *Crossroads* in audience appeal despite not being screened continuously. But the BBC will not allocate the resources to sustain even a little soap through to maturity (they axed the very popular and well written radio serial *Waggoners' Walk* on grounds of economy). They may say that the criticisms advanced of the genre are sufficient grounds to refuse to wade any deeper into the water than the height of their knees, with trousers fastidiously rolled up. But I believe their pusillanimity is financial, not aesthetic.

The way Procter & Gamble organize their commitment to soaps is a fine example of how culture – or put less tendentiously, popular entertainment – is packaged and sold like any other commodity. The company has its own programming department, as I have already mentioned, which is a section of General Advertising. Each has its own little hierarchy: vice-president, division manager, manager, program supervisor. One of the latter sits in on all the important meetings connected with the show, especially those that take place in the offices of the advertising agencies who take charge of the production for P&G shows (a relic from the old days of radio sponsorship). The agency hires the talent and administers the programme on behalf of its client, including overseeing meetings for the show – story conferences and so forth. At these meetings there is generally someone from the network (another hierarchy). And of course the show's production team is itself a little pyramid: executive producer, producer, associate producer.

So major decisions on spending and story progression are made by hierarchs representing every investor: sponsor, agency, network and the show itself. Each takes the responsibility of offering advice and criticism as seriously as their salaries demand: as the P&G house magazine put it, "Our program supervisors watch with the same intensity as that of researchers testing a new product." And while all the working producers I met maintained they were allowed to get on with their jobs without interference from those who ultimately controlled them, I cannot imagine that serious criticism from those who have financial but not creative responsibility for the shows is ever ignored.

In England the system, though equally hierarchical, is less cluttered. The BBC is a bureaucratic mammoth, where initials indicating title and responsibility spread like ground elder. There is television and radio, with controllers for each channel sitting atop departments for Light Entertainment, Features, Drama and so forth. Under the Head of Drama there are the Heads of Series and Serials, and of Plays, and under these notables there are producers in charge of the various slots available, who in turn supervise the work of the producers of the actual actual plays that are bought for transmission. Once a show is in production it is left to the producer concerned to get on with the task, as in the soaps – but long-term decisions about a long-running (i.e. expensive) serial involve committee decisions where the heads of this and that each have their say.

In commercial television the hierarchy consists of the director or controller of programmes for each production company, who has his own board of directors to answer to, and who fights with his colleagues on the Networking Committee for the best slots for his programmes. He too has his heads of department, who in turn oversee the activities of the executive producers, who watch over the producers who are in charge of the programmes. For anyone who has worked in a large company and who is familiar with corporate politics, the whole arrangement is simplicity itself.

Equally, anyone who has done committee work knows what compromises are necessary to get a decision. And this, I think, is the real reason for the creative inertia that lies heavy on the soaps. The larger the committee the greater the compromises. Admittedly day-to-day decisions are taken by a small group of creative talents: producer, writer, director and other key figures. But when the future of a serial is under discussion, each interested party to the decision has to trade off views against those of the others. Those whose voices count for most are those with the most money at stake – and they are usually the furthest from the creative process. The actual creator of the show, who may have an additional credit as associate producer, is only one small voice in a brassy chorus. Most decisions in television are arrived at by committee. That doesn't mean it's the best, or even the only, way of doing things.

The usual alternative to committee decision (which now rules universally) is benevolent (or otherwise) dictatorship, the way of the theatre tzars, the movie moguls and the popes of pop. While that has the advantage of everyone knowing where they stand, it means they are all prisoners of the taste of one person – who is happy to take the credit when things turn out all right, but who starts firing scapegoats when things go wrong.

Another way, always popular with my generation of radicals, is to devolve responsibility, to let each show be run by its own creative team. This is the way television executives *say* the soaps are run. However, even in the BBC, where individual producers are allowed more rein than anywhere else, the shadow of the committee reaches into the furthest corner of the smallest studio. There, as in the corridors of the American networks, the kibitzing of the committee is everywhere heard (kibitzing, for those ignorant of Yiddish, means having someone peer over your shoulder while you're playing cards and offering you unwanted advice). The producers may insist that the buck stops with them, but the buck is carved up in committee.

As an example of committee decision-making, consider Harding Lemay's experience when he wanted to include a story about homosexuality in *Another World*. The Procter & Gamble representative at first encouraged him to include the notion in his story-line, and he also received support from the show's producer and the vice-president of NBC's day-time programming. But back in P&G headquarters doubts began to surface. Viewers, especially women, might be put off. Lemay's argument that prime-time shows and movies dealt openly with the subject, and that day-time viewers were also prime-time viewers, left them unmoved. After months of pressure from Lemay, P&G's programming committee reluctantly agreed to give the idea a try. HQ finally approved the detailed synopsis. The NBC vice-president also approved. After auditions, an actor was hired to come from Hollywood with his family. Everything was ready to give *Another World* another "first", when Procter & Gamble's public relations department overturned the decision taken by the programming department, for fear of causing offence. Since public relations' committee status within the firm was higher than that of programming, their ruling prevailed. Lemay was forced to drop the story, and realized that what he had taken for faith in his creative talent was in fact "a subtle form of manipulation, in which I was cajoled and flattered into agreement, or if that failed, forced to conform to story approaches that would not offend potential purchasers . . ."

Whether it's British or whether it's American, the committee is always at work, especially on the soaps, deciding – as committees always do – according to precedent. What worked in the past is always dragged up as an excuse for not risking anything too novel. Committees consist largely of "No-men", who will not take a risk that hasn't been taken successfully by somebody else. Decisions, especially in television, are commonly taken by default. That it has been ever thus is little comfort.

Where committee bellows to committee across the swamps of broadcasting, the subject is usually scheduling. The time at which a soap is shown makes a difference to the composition of its audience, which affects the ratings, which affects the advertising charges (or in the case of the BBC, lures viewers from the opposition and justifies the licence charge). A mid-morning soap will have an audience of housewives, infants, the retired, the sick and the unemployed. A lunch-time soap pulls in all those who like to relax at home over their sandwich or salad (anyone who cooks seriously in the middle of the day isn't going to be watching television, are they?). This spot has also been shown to attract college kids in America, in their break from class. The 4 pm slot grabs the children home from school. The evening guns start going off around 6 pm, with the prime-time cannon reserved for after 7.30, when it is assumed everyone has finished eating and is slumped in front of the set for the rest of the evening.

Scheduling decisions are taken by the networks, although in commercial television the companies have a certain freedom to juggle with the transmission times. But reliability of scheduling is crucial to the soaps: the fans must be sure that their show is on at the same time on the same channel every day or week or whatever. To the pleasurable tension of the continuous narrative is added the benevolent dictatorship of routine. A soap is something around which you can organize your day.

Naturally each network or television company must think of its rivals, and try either to match their strength or exploit their weakness. In the case of established serials, they don't do this by altering the transmission time, but bear down on the producers to beat the opposition's plots and style. In England the three commercial soaps are so different from one another – and timed not to clash even though they are made by different companies – that imitation doesn't come into it. Only when a new soap is introduced is there any kind of challenge – though *Brookside* was carefully scheduled not to clash with any of its commercial sisters. *Triangle* was one of a number of BBC shows designed to woo the early evening audience from *Crossroads*. Another such serial was the hospital drama *Angels*, but since neither that nor *Triangle* have been allowed to run continuously, comparisons – as far as audience reactions are concerned – are meaningless.

Crossroads itself has been shifted around the schedules a fair bit – a decision taken not by the producer, who resented being messed around, but by the controllers of programmes. Since the audience figures were not much affected – though there were many protests from fans who were forced to rearrange their domestic routines – the reason for switching can only have been to lure and retain a large audience for the rest of the channel's programmes. So despite the contempt with which the commercial companies treat *Crossroads*, they are happy enough to use it to carry their other, possibly more "prestigious" programmes, into the top ten.

A new idea and a radical challenge to existing conventions came when American soaps were extended from half an hour to an hour. Various people are credited with suggesting the change: pride of place goes to Irna Phillips, whose serial *Another World* was the first to expand to the new format, in January 1975, just over a year after Miss Phillips died. (The same serial was the first to expand to ninety minutes, in 1979 – but at that length proved too elephantine to be kept going.)

The idea of an hour-long daily soap appealed to writers and producers for different reasons. Harding Lemay, when head-writer of *Another World*, was frustrated by the limitations of the half-hour script, because the rhythm of the scenes was interrupted by the commercials. As a playwright accustomed to developing scenes at length, he felt that an hour would not only give him more opportunity to deepen the relationship between the characters, but would offer him and the actors more room to stretch. He knew that it would double an already irksome work-load; what he seemed to ignore was that there would be twice as many commercials to interrupt his dialogue, and that favourite scenes would not be exempted from the truncation or distortion made necessary by the demands of the clock. There would be opportunity for the good bits to be better, but with twice the pressure, and the need to bring in an enormous number of new characters and story-lines, the bad bits might be twice as bad.

For the producers the hour meant more power, more studio space, bigger budgets, and greater profits. To cope with more plots and characters they needed more sets, larger technical crews, longer studio hours, and greater expenditure. Though the budgets were still far smaller than those of prime-time shows, they were respectable enough to give the producers increased professional clout. And of course it didn't cost twice as much to double transmission time, since most of the equipment and personnel needed were already to hand. Bigger audiences were expected, who would stay tuned for longer, enabling advertising charges to be raised and thus increase the profits. No wonder people like Procter & Gamble, who owned *Another World*, were keen.

The resistance to extending *Another World*'s transmission time came from the vice-president of NBC's day-time programmes, who was very loath to change the format of the current leader of the network's day-time serials. Her reluctance was no doubt due to the enormous amount of work involved in fiddling about with the schedules, and fear of taking so innovative a step when things were working perfectly satisfactorily as they were and failure would damage her career. After long negotiations during which P&G continued to push for the expansion, the network agreed to allow a one-hour pilot of the new format which, as Lemay described it, was "most dramatic . . . but hardly typical of what would be aired daily". But it had the desired result: the ratings were excellent and letters cascaded in demanding a full hour every day. NBC continued to argue with P&G over rates and figures, but the two most important hurdles – getting the hour transmitted to prove it could be done, and winning the approval of the public – had been cleared. Mr Lemay was allowed to write scenes running on occasion to over ten minutes, which pleased him no end; new players were cast for new characters; and from the first Monday of the new year (1975), *Another World* delivered an hour a day, five times a week, fifty-two weeks a year. Within three months *Days of our Lives* followed suit (so short an interval proving that its change had been planned long before), and within a couple of years an hour was the day-time norm, with a few lower-rated shows like *The Doctors* clinging to the thirty-minute format, because they dared not risk losing what audience they had by stretching an already thin show even thinner.

Within a few months, too, Harding Lemay found himself being pestered by the sponsor for "more plot, which meant, in their definition, murders, trials, surgery, kidnappings, rapes, amnesia – the catalog of melodramatic clichés I had shunned since becoming the show's head-writer." Thus the format that freed him to express himself more dramatically soon became the instrument of his disillusionment. The difficulties of producing twice as much in less than twice the time also told on writers, directors and actors. A decision that was, in the end, taken by the producers and sponsors and network executives, added enormously to the pressures on the creative staff, and underlined the weaknesses of the serial. Far from increasing production standards with the extra money at their disposal, the producers got their employees to labour even harder. There was, if anything, less time to make things work properly, and more temptation to make compromises, to let things pass, in order to complete on schedule. But the audiences loved the hour-long episodes, and soap took a lurch along the road to respectability. Nevertheless you can see why a show that prides itself on its standards, like *Coronation Street*, has always insisted on staying a twice-weekly half-hour serial. "It costs us enough effort to get that right," the producers maintain; "More would only mean worse."

*

Soaps are generally allowed much longer than prime-time shows to establish themselves with an audience. Indeed, there is markedly less interference from above where the serials are concerned, than with the shows that cost the real money.

In England the networks do not allow themselves to be dominated by the ratings to the extent that their American colleagues do. A half-way decent series that is not slaughtered by the reviewers and which receives an average share of the audience is often allowed to go to a second series, and a third, on the principle that if you hit people often enough with the same object, their critical faculties get numbed and they lie back and enjoy it. In America a prime-time series can be taken off after a few episodes if the public or the reviewers show their displeasure. Indeed most get no further than a pilot. Except for the soaps, especially the day-time ones, which are allowed to rattle on from year to year, becoming more difficult to replace the more they are entrenched, until a whole new idea comes along.

Now the odd thing is that the cavalier British approach produces a greater variety of programmes than does American cowardice in face of the ratings – but a far smaller number of soaps. This can only be ascribed to the British tradition of not giving the public too much of a good thing. The BBC, with its upper lip curling discreetly at vulgar popularity, is matched by the commercial companies, who are aware that the IBA wil let them get away with the most generous quota of dross providing that there is a small but clear vein of culture running through it. The key word is "quota", that Reithian relic of rationing the audience to a mixture of high- and low-brow programmes designed to make middle-brows of them all. British broadcasting, both public and commercial, is in fact quite strictly controlled, one of its controls being over the number of programmes allowed to be transmitted of any one type. Soap, being a category programme, is thus restricted in the same way as sit-coms and imported programmes (though you wouldn't think so from the number of these two categories that appear). American television, being free from regulation – within the elastic guidelines of the extremely elastic Federal Communications Commission (FCC) – is free to give the viewers what they want, or (which is not the same thing) what the production companies, basing their hopes on precedent rather than innovation, believe they might want.

The British quota system still does not explain why soaps are so thin on the ground. Quotas, after all, are established by negotiation on the basis of precedent. There was never the danger that Britain would be elbow-high in soap, the way we were once threatened with being drowned in game shows and American imports. The unions represent-ing technicians, actors and writers negotiated controls to safeguard their members, and quite rightly so. But home-produced soaps mean more work for everybody. Why didn't the unions suggest to the compan-ies that more be made? Why aren't more British companies making soaps?

I suspect that the answer is a combination of snobbery and conserva-tism. The soaps are neither glamorous nor prestigious. Nor have we acquired the habit of having the set on all day, though this is changing. There are not, yet, 18 hours to fill daily, as there are in America. Breakfast television will produce no drama (I mean the stuff invented by playwrights), and the mid-morning will continue to be filled by schools programmes during term-time, and old movies. On any one day no British viewer is exposed to more than an hour of native soap. In America a dedicated viewer can watch five hours of day-time serials, and perhaps a couple more in the evening. On the soundly established historical principle that Britain lags up to ten years behind America in most things, we can perhaps anticipate an increase in home-grown soap in the next few years. The problem still seems to be one of respectability: only *Coronation Street* is well thought of by critics *and* audiences, partly because it has survived for so long, partly because it trades in that peculiar brand of nostalgia we like to take for reality, and partly because it is often very funny. *Crossroads* and *Emmerdale Farm* and the few day-time soaps have yet to achieve this kind of respectability – not least because their producing companies do not display that unashamed pride which Granada shows for *Coronation Street*.

Soaps are the ideal weapon for the networks to use in order to keep up with the competition: they fill the hours, hold the viewers, and give the advertisers something to wrap round the commercials. But, though in theory this should mean that a soap, once established, can run forever, there have been casualties. Some, like the BBC's *Compact* or *The Newcomers*, are stopped for reasons of economy masquerading as "running out of ideas" (something that, by definition, shouldn't happen on the soaps). What happens is that a new head of department wants to demonstrate an innovatory zeal, and so axes those shows of his predecessor's regime that have the least prestige, enabling him to talk about "new standards" in the same breath as "new cost-effectiveness" (i.e. cut-backs). Shows limited to a particular setting, like *Emergency Ward 10*, may not so much run out of steam as fall victim to public boredom with their background – in its case, hospitals. To "retool" them would be too expensive.

Again this is a production matter: somebody in the network demonstrating that he or she is unafraid of taking an unpopular decision (as long as the audience is not too big) in the dubious name of "standards". The viewers may protest, but there is a momentum behind a company's decision to drop a show that is virtually unstoppable. Something gets into the hierarchs – the *macho* need for a tough new image, perhaps – and they drop on their uncomprehending victim. It is that mulish brute, the committee, at work. There may be no real reason except a feeling that it is "time for something new". Certainly there seemed little cause for CBS to chop *Love of Life*, which had done very nicely for twenty-eight years, and retain *Search for Tomorrow*, its senior by three weeks. Decisions like that have nothing to do with the merits or otherwise of the show: they come from the politics of the committee, the last refuge, in these recessionary times, of the "mad axeman" who, far from being locked up, gains more corporate clout with every blow.

Of course there have also been failures, pure and simple, amongst the soaps, shows which never took off during the thirteen-week period which is the usual contractual term for those involved. But the virtue of the form is its ability to change in accordance with audience demand. What does not at first meet with viewers' approval can easily be altered, perhaps with a new head-writer or producer. To "tool up" for a soap means a heavy commitment in studio time, space and talent. To enter on that commitment for only a short period means either lack of faith in the form (as in the BBC), or that the sponsor or creator has another idea lined up with more immediate promise of success.

I still think it safe to say that a failure in soap (the big-budget ones aside) is a failure, not of standards, but of nerve.

I have left till last discussion of the prime-time soap that has made the genre internationally respectable. In a word, *Dallas*.

Dallas is the Prince Charming who owes everything to Cinderella. It has taken all the elements of the humble day-time serial, and added large amounts of money. The show is not studio-bound, but full of location filming, helicopter shots, and all the paraphernalia of the movies. All that takes time – the weather and the light have to be right, and each shot has to be set up for one particular camera position, which means everyone hangs about a lot. Time costs, and *Dallas* budgets are the same as most glossy prime-time dramas, which is to say about seven times as high as day-time soaps. With all that money, the shots are still repetitive, predictable, mechanical. And behind the look there is the old formula, the continuing narrative featuring stereotyped characters in plots familiar to serial watchers everywhere. True, *Dallas* is only shown once a week, and made in batches so that there is a gap between one series and another – a gap during which the addiction may be broken, after which disbelief is less willingly suspended. That alone prevents it from being considered a "real" soap. But it still has a professionalism and polish which have attracted audiences who had long sneered at the genre. The wonder is it hasn't happened before.

Irna Phillips tried her hand at evening soaps, but she was too tied to the day-time formula – and wasn't allowed the budgets – to succeed. In England, where most of the soaps are on in the early evening, the nearest equivalent to *Dallas* was *The Brothers*, which was extremely successful, both in production standards and in audience figures, but which remained tied to the naturalism that has always distinguished British television drama. Where *Dallas* scored was where it went Over The Top. Had *The Brothers* been allowed to continue, no doubt it would have had to be more outrageous in its search for plot. Perhaps this influenced the BBC's decision to axe it. But the more outrageous *Dallas* has been, the more the audience appear to like it. The reason isn't just a fashionable jumping on the bandwaggon. *Dallas* allows all the family to indulge their taste for the soap formula that critics of the cheaper serials have made them feel guilty about – and moreover in weekly portions, "instant" soap rather than the slow-cooking kind. For its domestic audience, *Dallas* is a fairy-tale about the princes and princesses, the ogres and thugs, who act out the morality the viewers have been taught to revere. Their heroes embody old-fashioned chivalric values which have died out almost everywhere but on the soaps. For its foreign audience, the serial offers a double bonus: a narrative like fly-paper, produced with enviable polish (on the kind of budgets only American producers can afford) – and the chance to feel superior about the idiocies of American plutocracy. There are few things more satisfying than to be able to sit back, having been absorbed in someone else's troubles for an hour, and indulge in a little smirk.

Dallas has done a lot for soap, even though its pace is too rapid for the genuine article. Old-fashioned soap junkies may look on it with suspicion, like a gaudy dude coming into the old saloon and buying everyone a drink, but the allure of its undoubted success has rubbed off on the entire genre. Internationally it has penetrated markets denied to other soaps (it is more popular abroad than even *Bonanza* was), by virtue of being a weekly serial — day-time drama on any scale is almost exclusively an American phenomenon. Other nations don't allow or can't afford to make or buy many day-time programmes for the house-bound audience. Yet the need for soap is universal, which means that the slot was there, in prime-time, to be filled by Lorimar, the imaginative (and imitative) independent producers of *Dallas*.

I wouldn't say that *Coronation Street* or its peers have done anything so vulgar as to imitate the *Dallas* style – but there has been a bit of splashing out, a little more location work (known as "remotes" in America), a touch more extravagance, just to show that we aren't all fuddy-duddies this side of the Atlantic. No doubt these improvements would have been made anyway, in line with inflation or the changing expectations of the audience. But equally there is no doubt that a programme as popular as *Dallas* has an effect that is almost universal: the "Who Shot J. R." episode was watched by more people throughout the world than any other drama. As Gilbert Seldes pointed out, you don't escape just because you don't listen. *Dallas* has become a part of culture and conversation. Whether or not its popularity lasts – and I can't believe it will – soap production will never be quite the same again.

THE CRITICS: FROM DERISION
TO ADULATION

There are critics, and there are reviewers. I would define a critic as someone who takes a leisurely and reflective look at a subject, and who makes a judgement of its worth on the basis of carefully defined standards. There are precious few of those writing about television.

A reviewer has a few hours, or at best a few days, to scribble down his or her subjective thoughts on a piece, with precious little time for reflection. There is no shortage of those when it comes to writing about television.

It will readily be seen that my choice of words is more respectful to critics than to reviewers. This is simply because I admire those who possess what I lack myself, the ability, patience and confidence to take infinite pains over making carefully considered judgements. Some critics, of course, write absolute rubbish. Many reviewers – and I was one for years – write marvellous sense with absolute clarity. Their opinions are often better informed than those of the critics, and they frequently have wide knowledge of, and a keen sympathy for, their subject. I tell you these things so you will know how I grind my axe.

Most of those who write about television are reviewers or journalists. One reason why there are few critics of television is that the form itself is young. Two generations – fifty years – is almost too short a time, by academic standards, for the stalagmites of critical judgement to have grown to a respectable height. Another reason is that television is a popular medium, in the most vulgar sense of the word. The critic is more often concerned with what is excellent, with the works of art created by and for an élite. The discerning critic is an élitist – which needn't be an insult – who can see merit in what vulgar prejudice condemns. Television is by its nature anti-élitist. Of course it influences our tastes and attitudes, but it does this more by its *form* (its perpetual glittering in the corner of our living rooms) than by its *content*.

The critic is concerned with form as well as with content, but is more at home with the form in which artists express themselves (how they use paint or prose) than the form in which these messages are conveyed (through galleries, publishers, or whatever). The artist can do things in a thousand ways, but television, because of the way in which it is financed and controlled, ensures that these ways all seem equal – or equally forgettable. The critic, therefore, feels at a disadvantage in the face of a medium that reduces so much to so little.

In television, the artist has less control over the means of expression than in any other medium. What is said, and even more important how and when it is said, is decided by those who control the networks – broadly speaking, the commercial interests – not by the artists whose work appears on the screen. This is because television is still a medium of limited access. Though there is scarcely a country without it, the cost of the hardware is such that those who want to appear on television have to please the controllers. Of course this is true of theatre, of painting and of books. But there are lots of theatres and galleries and publishing houses. Those who are rejected by one stand a good chance with another. On television, despite the plethora of channels available, there is only a limited number of networks, and these are run on strictly commercial lines. For a critic such limitations are anathema

Having said which, I cannot deny that there *are* critics of television, in the sense I have described. Most are housed within universities, with courses in Communication Theory and the like. There is a small but flourishing school of semiologists who have turned their formidable vocabulary loose on television. There are historians whose study of the growth of the medium has led them to make critical judgements of its output (I am thinking particularly of Eric Barnouw, author of *A History of Broadcasting in the United States*). Lastly there are those whose years of exposure, either behind the cameras or as long-serving reviewers, have given them a perspective which can be called truly critical. Of these, the number who have turned their gaze on soap opera is remarkably small.

Why this should be is curious. I think it is a matter of snobbery and ignorance. There is one addict amongst the critics – Raymond W. Stedman, whose history of *The Serials: Suspense and Drama by Installment* is detailed, dramatic and the definitive work covering all American serials up to the early days of television. There are those, notably the semiologists, who devote their attention to the genre in order to make political (and cultural, sociological and structuralist) points about the nature of television. But most critics give little time to the soaps, I believe, because the serials are in a sense immune to critical pressure (that is, their audience remains unmoved by what the critics say); because they look inferior to other forms of drama on television; and because the critics are unaware of the pressures – most of them, as we know, stemming from the commercial nature of the beast – that bear down on the soap makers.

Critics, on the whole, do not spend time on the trivial, on works without redeeming artistic merit. Occasionally they go slumming, like George Orwell when he wrote about "The Art of Donald McGill" or "Boys' Weeklies". But usually the purpose of these little jaunts is to return with some sociological conclusions about the audience, rather than to analyse the artistry of whatever is under consideration. Sociologists have had a rewarding time with soaps ever since they began, but sociologists are not critics. They are academics who draw conclusions about behaviour from statistics carefully assembled to appear as objective as possible. A critic will maintain that he or she tries to be objective and to adhere to a set of agreed principles. But in the end it is his or her personal judgement that counts (the difference between the critic and the reviewer being that the latter is confessedly subjective). The sociologist does not deliver judgements: he or she draws conclusions from the data provided. That's why sociologists are not much use when it comes to criticism.

They have, however, come up with some facts about soap watchers – most of them blindingly obvious. In the 1930s a team headed by Herta Herzog interviewed American radio soap addicts and came to the conclusion that the audience consisted mainly of housewives who identified with some of the characters. Some listeners used the shows to solve their own problems: the genre is at its most powerful when it gives people a reflection of their own experience. But most found in their favourites an entertaining release from the tensions engendered by the Depression.

A New York psychiatrist, Dr Louis Berg, listened to eight serials for eight weeks in 1942, and emerged fuming against what he regarded as an addiction that was as dangerous as the "opium pipe that brings momentary surcease with drugged dreams". For Dr Berg the soaps created the very anxiety that Herzog's research found they allayed. But then Dr Berg was a psychiatrist, not a sociologist: his ideas, lunatic or not, were based not on research but on his own reactions. The American NBC network was nevertheless sufficiently concerned about his opinion to hire three doctors to report on the serials they pumped out. Their conclusion was, you will be amazed to read, the very opposite of Dr Berg's: "Since the tendency of all dramas studied is towards the solutions that are generally accepted as ethical in our social existence, the effect of the dramas tends towards helpfulness." In other words, the soaps repeat the message taught in school and Scout and Guide camps, that good will triumph and evil will be punished.

British sociologists have been amused rather than exasperated by soap opera, which no doubt is proper in a broadcasting culture which, for all its faults, offers a wide choice of quality goods. What has exercised them most has been the portrayal of female roles, but here too there are two mutually contradictory schools. One maintains that women in the British soaps are contemptible stereotypes of downtrodden consumerism; the other that the serials offer "a complete validation of women" in that they are pictured as forthright and articulate fighters for their own points of view.

After a considered study of sociologists, I can offer a couple of conclusions of my own. The first is that their statistics can be used to prove anything. The second, which follows from the first, is that they display a strong tendency to find whatever it is they are looking for. A third conclusion is that what they tell you, you knew already.

My conclusions are hardly academically sound: they are not the result of exhaustive and properly weighted surveys, but the cogitations of an amateur observer. I have no wish to dismiss or denigrate the discipline of sociology – but I do think sociological ideas about the soaps must be seen in the context of the sociologists' role, which is surely to investigate the assumptions, principles and methods of the establishment. As the broadcasting establishment is a fine example of a corporate structure, and soaps, as we have seen, are a solidly established structure within it, the serials are a natural target for sociological fire.

There are of course sociologists and other specialists who defend the soaps. There are those who find any popular programme worthwhile, as a counterweight to the "élitism" of the more demanding offerings. There are those who see the broadcasting establishment, not so much as a top-heavy *Titanic*, rather as a leaky trawler, dragging a collection of sagging nets within which various fish are able to jostle for position. The soaps, according to this attitude, are packed sufficiently loosely to allow good fish and bad to co-exist: in other words, there is much to condemn but enough left to praise. And then there are those, mostly psychoanalysts of one stripe or another, who find fantasy such as that featured on the serials beneficial to their patients, and who believe that the shows' (relative) lack of violence – at least when compared with most prime-time series – does no harm and may even do good. But considering that most of these learned critics are not addicts, but droppers-in to the soaps, their judgements may be treated circumspectly. As all judgements should be, including mine.

To a critic, originality is as important as the effect the work will have on others. Since no one could claim that the soaps are original –

that, indeed, is one reason for their popularity – many critics have found them beneath proper notice. Likewise with their effect. A good painting stimulates the imagination of the viewer in ways unconnected with its subject; as does a good book, and all good music. Soaps, however, are written to be forgotten – a point made by Gilbert Seldes, the first and almost the only member of his tribe to consider the soaps seriously. No wonder his colleagues, then and since, believed that a form so reminiscent of the planned obsolescence that has disfigured modern society was not worth their attention. Many writers feel the same about television as a whole.

The serials are also parasitical, which is not in their favour if they are to be thought of as an art form. They are based on pulp fiction, on the romantic and narrative tradition that, however ancient, has usually been scorned by serious artists. Moreover the soaps' influence outside the genre has been negligible: they have given birth, not to new forms, but merely to more of their own.

The clone that has attracted the attention of the critics is of course *Dallas*. It is odd that respected professors of this and that – not just of Communications Theory – have been prepared publicly to declare their admiration for this series, when not one in a thousand of them would admit to being soap opera fans, let alone to watching television during the day. I believe the reason for this has less to do with the merits of *Dallas* itself than with the position of "experts" in our society, amongst whom professors and critics must be counted. The early 1980s has proved to be a time when the status of "expertise" has sunk lower than at any time in half a century (by a curious coincidence, the same thing happened in the 1930s. There is obviously a link between Depression, Recession, and the respectability of soap). Not only do expert forecasts, analyses and prescriptions turn out to be wrong in general and particular, but the experts who utter them have no shred of public esteem with which to shelter their shrivelled reputations.

Nobody likes being a pariah. Even artists who claim not to care what the public thinks do not relish being ridiculed or reviled. And critics have to have some following, or they would not survive. At this point it might be useful to quote James Agate, who described the four stages through which a critic passes. First is the ignorant confidence of youth; second, the period of invincible knowingness. Then there is the long and mellow middle period, "in which, finding nobody to hold up his arms, he tires of maintaining the standard and desists from giving battle". Lastly comes the senile period – which Agate described as the only one in which anyone believed a word he said. No doubt he felt himself to be senile when he was writing this – and perhaps the same is true of those critics who have praised *Dallas* (a programme I much enjoy, though I admit to preferring *Dynasty*, which resembles the "real" soaps more). But I prefer to think that our pro-*Dallas* critics are in their third, mellow period. Finding no one to hold up their arms, there they are, lying on their backs and waving their legs in the air. What they want is to have their tummies tickled by a loving public. One way of showing how close they are to public taste is to adore what the public has long enjoyed without their help – especially when the public's favourite has gained the glamour and respectability of big-budget prime-time television.

I have to say that *Dallas* has not yet inspired any notable additions to the stately embonpoint of critical literature (Gilbert Seldes said it all in the 1930s). I am merely trying to explain why so many critics have publicly endorsed *Dallas* when their previously published opinions gave no hint of serial addiction. But those few critics who *have* examined soap opera – for example Renata Adler in the *New Yorker*, Professor Horace Newcomb, former critic of the Baltimore *Sun*, the contributors to the British Film Institute's Television Monograph on *Coronation Street* – have all found in the genre a seriousness of purpose worthy of respect.

For Horace Newcomb the soap opera is "organic rather than formulaic and repetitive". Through its shifting pattern of sub-plots the serial grows and changes. Though the characters are stereotypes and the outcome of the plots predictable, the form ages with the viewer:

> The world of the soap opera is more painful, more harsh, more unrelieved, than the world of the audience, and yet the characters always survive. The values are not those of overwhelming success in which right always conquers. They are those of pure survival, complicated by ambiguity and blurred with pain even in its most sought-after accomplishments. The values are not ambiguous in the false sense of the situation drama, in which right is sometimes painful in its success, for the characters in those dramas never remember the following week that they were faced with a dilemma a week before . . . By contrast, the characters of soap opera must live for years with their mistakes and watch the implications multiply with each passing day. (From *TV: The Most Popular Art*, New York: Doubleday, 1974.)

Professor Newcomb – who, in passing, points out the importance of music in establishing mood in the soaps – concludes that "human frailty and human valor are the province of all complex art". The soaps embrace the nuts and bolts of "frailty" and "valor", and do so without the "veiled and not-so-veiled cultural assumptions about ways in which human problems can be eliminated by heroic action, gentle advice, or slapstick resolutions". Therefore they "stand between most of television and a number of new television productions that are reaching for a newer version of popular art".

Renata Adler, like James Thurber before her (and he also wrote for the *New Yorker*), started watching soaps when confined to bed. She too found them to be the very opposite of escapist: indeed, they brought home the "most steady, open-ended sadness to be found outside life itself". For these critics, as for their British colleagues (who are fewer in number – but then we have fewer soaps), it is the way in which the soaps use artifice to convince their audience that they are true-to-life that is the most remarkable – the most artful – thing about them. Like those *naif* artists who so excite critics by painting like children, it is the remorseless clarity of the soaps' vision, and the primitive but undeniably effective way in which they convey their imagery, that arouses critical admiration. Of course you will think that I have only chosen examples that suit my book. Be fair. Most reviewers rubbish the soaps, or at best are baffled by them. Those critics who deign to notice them do seem to get captivated. I ascribe this to the need to submit themselves wholeheartedly to the grip of the serial. Reviewers can and do drop in occasionally on a soap, and find enough to fill a column without becoming addicted. Critics need longer exposure in order to arrive at measured conclusions – and it takes a very strong will indeed to resist the desire to know what will happen next, once you have become familiar with characters and plot. I reckon three months is more than enough to contract the habit. That's how long it took me.

For the structuralist critics, soap is a political issue: "the politics of the representation of class and gender", as the Television Monograph on *Coronation Street* put it. These critics analyse, in a language much mocked for its opacity, how the serials pander to the "dominant cultural assumptions" about the roles of men and women, rather than challenging them. What is notable about the study of the *Street*, however, is the evidence of the contributors succumbing to the charm of the form. I am not accusing them of being unrigorous in their analytic method – indeed I am relieved that, for all their tortuous verbiage, their conclusions agree, more or less, with mine. (Incidentally, they claim to have had to invent a new vocabulary and style of writing to cope with a new analysis of a new phenomenon. Be that as it may, their conclusions do not seem to me to differ materially from those of the excellent Seldes, writing fifty years ago, in a prose of enviable lucidity.) These conclusions are, to summarize with rough justice, that within the stereotyped characters and predictable plots of the popular serial, there is room for more complexity and growth than the ignorant reviewer imagines; that the limitations peculiar to the genre constitute an important part of its appeal; and – perhaps most significant – that the pleasure the form gives to its devotees can be understood and shared (though not without an element of bafflement) by intellectuals of the highest brow.

The critics, with their considered objectivity – or at any rate their tranquil reflections – seem to feel that it is part of their brief to enquire whether the effect the soaps have on their audience is for good or ill. Here they put on all sorts of other hats – those of sociologists, psychoanalysts, cultural anthropologists. It seems proper to deal with these questions here, in the section devoted to all the kinds of criticism the soaps are subject to. The questions, which I have touched on in other sections, come under four basic categories: artistic ("why do the shows look so mediocre?"), cultural ("what is so appealing about these stereotyped characters?"), emotional or psychological ("does escapism make you short-sighted?"), and political ("are soap audiences being brainwashed?").

We know why the soaps look mediocre: time and money. Soaps do not look like anything else on the screen, and nothing else has anything like the same effect, achieved with the same economy of means. So much for the artistic question.

The cultural question concerns the effect of stereotypes. Take the treatment of women: there are those who feel that the serials do them (in particular) an injustice, by presenting them as subordinate to men; there are those who maintain that the soaps present "real" people "realistically"; and those who rejoice that soap women are predominantly strong types – so strong that they may upset the serials' predominantly male critics. What cannot be denied is that most of the women in the serials closely resemble many of their real-life viewers in what they suffer, endure and fight for.

If there were feminists writing the soaps, would this liberate the audience? Alas – and I say alas because I try to avoid sexist stereotyping in my own writing – I think not. Stereotypes are central to soaps, the foundation of the narrative structure which forms the basis of the genre's appeal. Peripheral characters who are "liberated" frequently appear in sub-plots, but their politics are dashed to pieces against the stereotypical rocks. Their effect is negligible compared with that of the central characters. Only when the liberated woman has become a stereotype herself will she be able to take her place in soap opera. There are some who say this is already happening – for example Tony's wife Pat in *The Archers*.

Other critics raise the issue of class. All right, they say, you've got to have stereotypes – but why should these always be the bourgeoisie?

Most writers are middle-class, but that shouldn't stop them writing about classes other than their own (or that to which they have risen or fallen). Most directors, producers and network controllers – indeed, the great majority of those who work in television – are also middle-class, if we define this in terms of money, status, security and the estimation of others. Nevertheless it is part of their job to cater for the whole range of classes, attitudes and tastes of their audience. What makes them concentrate on the vast and spreading middle when it comes to the soaps?

Because the middle is the Highest Common Factor of their viewers. It embraces average experience and average expectations. It is a terrain too familiar to need explanation: it can be taken for granted as a background to passion, melodrama, suspense and romance. It offers instant easy identification even for those who do not belong to it. For most, it is "reality".

Of course the soaps are not exclusively concerned with middle-class characters. There is a scattering of poor, a smidgeon of blacks, even a family or two of poor blacks. *Coronation Street*'s regulars all boast of being working-class (with the exception of publican Annie Walker, whose snobbish airs were much mocked behind her back). I have mentioned the curious fact that in class-conscious Britain the soaps are more egalitarian – that is, they feature more workers than bosses – than their counterparts in the Land of the Free. The heroes of American soaps are, by virtue of earnings alone, upper-class, at least by English financial standards. But in America everyone says they are middle-class – part of that flattening process that democracies seem to create.

The cultural critic can find a mirror of the times in the soaps. They may only *suggest* the realism of everyday life, via the shorthand they have made their own, but they present, if not a map, then a faithful portrait – executed with due artistic licence – of our attitudes and ambitions. What the critic sees in this picture of course depends as much on his or her perceptions as on what the picture contains. There is greed, and malice, and lust; there is sacrifice, selflessness and heroism; devotion and aspiration on the highest spiritual plane. All this within a context that is predominantly middle-class – just as we find it around us.

It is true that there is a certain cosiness about life on the soaps: life there may get hard – *very* hard at times – but integrity wins through and survival, for those who deserve it, is always assured. This, say some critics, is not true to life. But if you substitute "afford" for "deserve", you surely have a true-to-life description of our society: life is often very difficult, but those who can afford to struggle through. Not always, any more than on the soaps, but often enough to make the generalization stick. Most of us admire, or want to be, winners, and the soaps are the same. Many critics admire those artists who favour the underdog, the person with few redeeming qualities. Such people do not fare any better in the soaps than they do in real life. The virtues that the soaps emphasize are those of middle-class morality. The uncomfortable truth is that everyone can feel safe in the middle – and though the soaps may titillate the fright buds, safety is what they're selling, the safety of the stereotype and the happy ending.

The psychological question of whether the soaps are peddling a harmful escapism does, I believe, little justice to the common sense of the viewers. Those who confuse the events they see on the little screen with life as they actually live it are very few – they may well benefit from psychotherapy. Those who confuse the *actors* they see with the characters they play are a much larger group, but this confusion is understandable. What most viewers are perfectly capable of doing is separating fact from fantasy.

The public is well aware that the soaps are fiction. They are caught up in the narrative, but they know it is only a story. Certainly there are some who, when they see a favourite character faced with a problem they themselves face, are influenced by, and may even imitate, the solution adopted by that character. But such imitation is, I believe, on a par with imitating the fashion, appearance, style or quirks of any hero. You can stand in a cinema queue and watch people emerging from a John Wayne movie, and see lots of people walking like Big John. The effect wears off after a while and proves only that they have temporarily submerged their own style in somebody else's. I am often influenced by what I read of other writers' habits and working methods, and give theirs a try, especially if I am stuck. My problem becomes their problem, and if they have an answer, I'll give it a whirl. This is not escapism, or confusing fact and fantasy: it is enlarging your own experience by borrowing from somebody else's, something one does all the time with one's friends, and even more with one's mentors. To the soap addict, the characters *are* friends and mentors, invented though they may be. Of course they exert a behavioural influence.

Nevertheless most critics overestimate the power of popular television to affect viewers' behaviour. There is some evidence to prove that violent behaviour in children is encouraged by the repeated violence they see on television – but there is no gratuitous violence in the soaps. Because of their very nature, with plot-lines planned months in advance, and proceeding at their own special stately pace, nothing happens that is not grounded in character. More important, nothing happens without the repercussions echoing through the serial for weeks and months. If there is violence, it will be punished – as the viewers know. Half the pleasure of watching is waiting for the inevitable to catch up with the characters. Nobody could claim that the soaps transmitted anything to encourage anti-social behaviour.

But the psychological criticism goes deeper than that. It is concerned not so much with behaviour as with attitude. It argues that those who are addicted to television fiction somehow lose control of reality. Those who, rather than do something themselves, prefer to watch fictional people come to terms with their problems, will be less able to cope with their own. Television, these critics argue, is not only the most powerful and popular medium in the world, it is also the one people accept as authoritative.

Now everyone who has studied the subject knows that the picture of the world presented by television is angled, shaped, coloured and filtered by those who control the medium, no less than by those who actually make the programmes. Viewers are not getting an objective picture: they are receiving a perspective distorted to suit the tastes and purposes of those in charge of transmission. This distorted perspective, according to some critics, makes it even harder for some viewers to distinguish fact from fantasy.

This argument is itself subjective, and as difficult to prove as to disprove. If I say that I have never met anyone who believed that what they saw on television was the literal truth, I have no other grounds than my personal experience for asking you to believe me. I am, of course, talking of television fiction (though the expression "I saw it on the News" has never been taken, in the circles in which I move, as conclusive proof of anything). When I was a regular TV reviewer, there was much debate over the status of what were called "drama-documentaries", or "faction", programmes written as fiction but based on fact and recorded in the "realistic" manner which had become associated with documentaries. Some people complained that "the public" would be unable to tell where fiction took over from fact – and behind that bland assertion was an attack on the politics of those who created these "factions", who were characterized as radicals. Now I always mistrust critics who claim that "other people" will be affected by something that has left the critics themselves uncorrupted and unconfused. Special people they may be, with a vision more acute than that given to ordinary folk, but experts on other people's behaviour or reactions they are not. It is not criticism, but speculation, to predict the effect a work will have on others. Those who indulge in this game enter the dank tunnel of censorship.

People see what they want to see in television, and take from it what they want to take. You know how listening to two people discussing a programme often gives you the impression that each was watching something different. Whether expert or amateur, everyone picks out of a programme the bits that suit – or contradict – their own particular experience and attitudes. This is truer of television and radio, which have to vie for attention with so many other distractions, than of any other medium. To a woman scared of being mugged, seeing a young man on her favourite soap being arrested by police as a suspected thief may make her feel thankful to the agents of law and order. To a kid who has been harassed by the police, the same incident will reinforce his or her prejudices against them. This simple example is meant merely to illustrate the process whereby whatever we watch sticks to the burrs of prejudice with which all our minds are cluttered. Television reinforces those prejudices rather than creates them. What it does create is a climate of expectation, for consumer goods and the values of a consumer-oriented society. But that is a political question.

To answer the charge that the soaps may cause psychological damage to their audience by allowing them to take the soft option of escape into fantasy – or, a different charge, that the serials present the viewers with a false "reality" – I maintain the audience takes an altogether more robust attitude to what they see and hear. My evidence is based on the way people watch soaps, their reactions to them – and the total failure of the detractors to provide any kind of proof that viewers' behaviour is affected, for better or worse, by what they see.

Watching the soaps is a routine – daily, weekly or whatever – on a par with domestic chores or the mid-morning cup of coffee. It is one of a series of pegs on which the day's events are hung – and if the peg remains empty on occasion, if, that is, an episode is missed, all is not lost. Such is the nature of the genre that it is easy to catch up with events: as we know, each episode contains plenty of reminders of what has happened to enable new, forgetful or distracted viewers to grasp what is going on. It may be a valid criticism to say that such endless repetition does little to stimulate the frontal lobes. But there is a difference between providing easy entertainment and peddling material that actually impairs the viewers' ability to think for themselves.

Viewers' reactions, even in sociological surveys, provide overwhelming evidence that they are aware that what they are watching is invented by writers and impersonated by actors. They get involved in the doings of their favourite characters, and criticize those parts of the story which seem to them inconsistent with what they remember of what has gone before (there are many more people who appear to have total recall than those who watch and remember nothing). They enjoy identifying with their chosen subjects, and waiting for what they know to be inevitable to happen – but they also know there is a camera between them and what they are absorbed in.

Even allowing for the inflated importance attached to interviews with sociological researchers – the person being interviewed is anxious to make the most of it, and wants to give the answers he or she thinks the interviewer desires – I have not read of anyone who admitted going out and doing something he or she would not normally have done, just because they saw it on their favourite soap. What people do admit to is reading their own problems and attitudes into those of the characters – bereavement, illness, trouble with the children or parents or lovers. That the characters resolve these problems satisfactorily is of great comfort to the viewers. But the state of being comforted is surely more a source of strength than of weakness. Whatever the case, there is no proof that it actually affects *behaviour*.

Intentions, perhaps – something on which psychologists are very strong. No doubt that is why those therapists who actually use the soaps on their patients to encourage them to fantasize claim the effect is beneficial. Indeed, recent research conducted by Professor Jib Fowles of the University of Houston concludes that most people *need* television as a medium of escapism and fantasy. They use it to clear their minds of accumulated tensions, not to learn new anxieties. That is all they expect of it.

The charge of presenting a false reality is serious, and carries political connotations. What the critics are saying here is that the picture of society presented by the soaps is not only warped, it is also dangerously seductive. Dangerous because viewers are, in the opinion of these critics, brainwashed into believing that the solutions to personal and social dilemmas featured on the soaps can and should be adopted in reality. These solutions, which emphasize the values of a consumer-based economy – that is, good people get the good things because they deserve them, and everyone should try and be good so that they too may enjoy these good things – are nothing but propaganda for false values, false because they are based on the acquisition of objects rather than on the dignities and virtues which civilized people have long struggled to maintain.

This is a version of the conspiracy theory of politics. According to this theory, the legitimate aspirations of the majority are thwarted by small numbers of powerful people conspiring together to make things go their way. Whether it is the directors of multi-national corporations or a discreet gaggle of civil servants, they find a way to bend the rules to their advantage. And in television, the object of the conspiracy – apart from the universal one of making money – is to keep off the screen opinions and images that might subvert the consensus, in which soaps play so loyal a part.

I do not for a second deny that soaps act very successfully as selling agents for the values promoted by their sponsors (using the term to cover all those who put up the money and cream off the profits without being involved in day-to-day production). Nor do I deny that television is adept at presenting the consensual view under the guise of objectivity, and is a subtle censor of opposing viewpoints. Television is part of the consensus: it helps to form it and ensures its vitality. The problem I have is in seeing this as a conspiracy. It seems to me that anything as costly and as powerful as television is bound to fall into the hands of wealthy and powerful people who want to preserve their position. This surely has always been so. If and when television ever becomes cheap to produce, access will become freer. Then audiences will fragment, which means that fewer people will watch each programme, which in turn means that whatever message is being propounded will have its strength diluted. These are inescapable facts in a capitalist society.

In Britain the government does not exercise direct control but the consensus is safe. It is just as safe, if not safer, in America where pride is is taken in the lack of control, which is left to the operation of the commercial market. In theory, anyone who can get the money together and who stays within the law can put out a television programme. In practice the people who do so support the status quo. Is this a conspiracy? If so, who are the conspirators? Are there locked, sound-proofed and bug-proofed rooms off the corridors of the BBC or Procter & Gamble where anonymous executives plot a new campaign to brainwash the hapless public? Of course there are, and they are discussing ways of grabbing even more viewers for their programmes. Do their deliberations include a measure of political propaganda for each programme on behalf of the system? No, because they don't have to. Popular programmes, designed as entertainment, do not challenge the assumptions of their audience. If they did, they wouldn't be popular. Therein lies their power, and the power of those who put them on.

The crucial question is, would a different sort of popular programme affect popular attitudes? Nobody knows, because it hasn't been tried. If one asked why They didn't put on a radical soap – one that challenged the consensus, that attacked the dominant assumptions of consumerism, that put forward alternative ways of organizing and behaving – there would be two simple answers. One, those who hold these views have failed to make them dramatic and popular (not to mention their failure to gather together the resources to put them across); two, why should the current sponsors of popular programmes bother to promote anything that might rock their gilt-bottomed boats?

What exercises the critics is the willingness of the viewers to accept what they are given. Worse, the public actually likes it. Never mind that the soaps are easy viewing or listening, entertainment produced with a degree of polish and a generous measure of professional honesty. The public appears eager to swallow, in huge quantities, the bromides that render its members, as it were, intellectually impotent. But all this is more a criticism of the public than of the programmes or the medium under scrutiny. I myself doubt whether television can be used to alter basic attitudes: the agents of change have in my opinion to appear outside the living room. Television, I have said before, is a reflective rather than a creative medium, as far as politics is concerned. It is a bit like your friendly neighbourhood bar, where you go to relax, gen up on the gossip and, if you like, engage in argument which, however heated, is forgotten soon after you have left the premises. In my experience, people who get serious in bars are soon avoided as bores, and much the same seems to be true of television. Its importance in the size of its audience, more than in its power to persuade this audience of anything.

Certainly it both reinforces existing prejudices and refuses to challenge them seriously. But I believe that many critics confuse numerical size with intellectual importance. If someone were allowed to harangue a football crowd on the evils of the social system, would there be a riot? Yes, because they came to watch a game – which is all television is, in political terms. It is not the right medium to persuade people of new ideas. Its own persuasive power lies in repetition of what its viewers are already persuaded of (I cite in evidence political broadcasts and debates, in which more people are swayed by the appearance of the candidates than by the content of their speeches). The soaps are the most repetitive of all television genres, but all they persuade people of is what those people already think and feel. The serials enlarge their viewers' experience in certain, carefully limited areas which have nothing to do with party politics. I would almost say that the soaps don't have *time* to engage in politics, so pressed are they for time to unravel the myriad threads that make them popular. To want them to be otherwise may be honourable for some critics, but I believe it to be unrealistic. If these critics were honest they would castigate the public rather than the programmes they watch. But that is biting the hand that turns the page.

Let us now look at the reviewers, who are read by far larger numbers than the critics, though their influence is small. Not that even the critics make much difference, at least to the makers of programmes: they contribute to an intellectual climate that may, in time, affect what goes on, but they do not make or break programmes the way theatre reviewers can close shows. But television reviewers usually work retrospectively, writing about what has been shown and is rarely repeated. There are of course *previewers*, who pick out programmes they think worthwhile, ahead of their transmission time. Though they are more widely read than any of their colleagues, and probably have the greatest influence of all, they are the least regarded (except by the programme makers, who woo them assiduously), no doubt because all they have to do for their money is list their likes and dislikes, with little rhyme and less reason.

The role of television reviewers is odd, undefined and isolated. They come to the job with no particular qualifications, and there are no rules to guide them. Those who acquire celebrity do so through "knocking copy", a mocking style that takes a dead programme and shakes it so vigorously it looks almost alive. Now destroying your targets has long been a way of achieving fame, from Dr Johnson through Bernard Shaw to Kenneth Tynan and Clive James. In America the Mencken tradition lives on in the pages of *The New Yorker* which, however, rarely stoops to dealing with television. But of all targets, television is the easiest. There is so much of it, for one thing, which inevitably means there is far more dross than gold. It is also free, or virtually free, to the viewer, which means that less value is attached to it than those forms of entertainment that cost money. (Though British viewers have to pay a licence fee to support the BBC, the cost of it is negligible when set against the output offered – grumble though we all do.) Television is thus a sort of sitting turkey at which reviewers feel impelled to blast away.

The chief reason, I believe, that people bother to read television reviews of programmes they have already watched is to see if their views correspond to those in print. It is a matching of amateur judgements against those of the professionals – except that the reviewers are only professional in that they are paid for their opinions. There is no evidence that viewing habits are affected by what reviewers say – no correlation between a good press and good audiences that exists in theatre, cinema and publishing. American network executives terminate (with extreme prejudice) projected series if a pilot show has been badly received by the public, but they base their decision on viewing figures, not on what is said in the press. From all of which I conclude that television audiences make up their own minds – when indeed they exercise positive choice.

There are probably few programmes which people deliberately choose to watch. News and sports programmes are amongst them, and so are the soaps. For the rest, it is a matter of chance, distraction or apathy.

Very often the set is simply on, chattering away to itself like an elderly relative by the fireside, and members of the family drop in every so often to see and hear what is going on. If nothing interests them, they may change channels, or more likely they drift away themselves. No one knows for sure how people watch: one can only judge by one's own habits and those of the people one knows. Obviously sports fans will hog the screen for those events that interest them, and a big film will probably draw everyone in (even if they've seen it), at least for a while. But the watching pattern, according to audience research methods pioneered by Nielsen in America and the BBC's Audience Research Department, remains fragmentary and haphazard. The soaps and the news pull them in regularly in reliable numbers (though even the news is falling off a bit). The rest is more or less mystery.

Reviewers like making people's minds up for them (an ambition they share with programme planners). They see their role as dispensers of sound advice and wise counsel, warning against the false and meretricious (which seems to include most of what they see). They find themselves addressing a public which appears to pay them no heed. Is it any wonder, poor souls, that they shout themselves hoarse in an effort to be heard? Perhaps they see themselves as sharing that honourable journalistic tradition of knocking the establishment (the ownership of newspapers and television stations having much in common). No doubt they can be righteously outraged at the enormous sums of money lavished on what they see as rubbish (and the enormous profits derived therefrom). But the worst part of the whole business is that their rage is impotent. They are only quoted in books about television, and when they have said something nice or humorous about a programme. It's a job, of course, and one that may even get them on television itself if they scourge wittily enough, but its satisfactions are few. Reviewers of the other arts go on forever, but TV reviewers have a high turnover rate, and are either transferred to lighter duties like writing books or fronting chat shows, or are carried away babbling.

These limitations have to be borne in mind when considering what the reviewers say about soap opera. Not that they review them often, since the soaps are there all the time, and the reviewers' attentions are drawn to the "new" shows which start each season. When reviewers do dip a toe into the soapy water, they tend to emerge either baffled or distraught. "Why do people watch this rubbish?" These reactions are in part due to ignorance, in part to the pressures under which they – like the soap people – are forced to work (tight deadlines, no time to revise or refine, let alone research), and in part to the mischievous desire to slash at the neck of the sacred cows of popular choice.

Rarely do the reviewers go into the mechanics of production – and when they do it is even more rarely the soaps they concern themselves with. Oh, they'll do it for *Dallas* – everybody has something to say about *Dallas*: it's even news when the girl who plays doe-eyed Pam Ewing reveals the troubles she has with her co-stars in the dressing room. But investigation of the home-grown staples, the *Guiding Light*s and *Crossroads*, is left to the columnists of the specialized magazines like *Time Out* or *Soap Opera Digest* (incidentally one of the fastest selling journals in America). With some honourable exceptions, daily or weekly reviewers have too much to cover in too little time to enable them to do proper research.

But it's the audience, and its presumed taste (or lack of same), that really baffles them. Few reviewers watch as ordinary people watch, that is, casually and with distractions. Ordinary people talk through important dialogue, soothe or shout at children during moments of extraordinary tension, time the loudest part of the washing-machine cycle to coincide with a scene of most tender romance, and fall asleep before the dénouement. Certainly they don't take notes. A reviewer watching (as I did) at home surrounded by family may spend as much time bellowing at those nearest, if not dearest, as in watching the screen. Except during the soaps. There is something so compelling about those familiar characters squaring up to their daily grind that even the noisiest child falls silent (or flees the room yelling "Yuk"). But what does a reviewer see who sits down for the first time (or the first for a long time) before this phenomenon? Actors hamming up clumping dialogue in cheap sets. At least, that's what it looks like when held against the best of the rest the reviewer turns to in order to find something to write about. No wonder they are confused when looking round at the unblinking eyes and slack jaws of the addicts. The soaps, being proof against criticism, are safe and easy windmills for the reviewer who fancies a gallop with a lance.

When they find something good to say about the soaps, it usually concerns those things the shows have in common with the rest of the stuff they watch. Reviewers still like to feel that they are ordinary folk armed with a notepad and a gift for articulating snap judgements. Being unfamiliar with the soaps, it comes as a great relief to them when they at last stumble on something they recognize: the "realism" of the serials that allows comparison with other "realistic" programmes that make up the majority of TV drama.

What the reviewers identify as realistic on the soaps is their concern for Social Issues: breast cancer, sterility, foster care, and so forth. Not being addicts, the reviewers miss the significance of that special brand of coded "realism" that the soaps have made their own. Instead they discover that, amongst all the romance (which itself is coming in for critical reappraisal), the soaps can and do concern themselves with serious issues – and, moreover, try to resolve them, which is more than the heavier dramas usually do. Complex plotting and the resolution of all doubts are scarcely in vogue amongst contemporary dramatists, so the presence of both on the soaps comes as a surprise to the reviewers. This gives them something good to say about a form whose niceties otherwise escape them.

Romance is something else. Previously derided as outmoded, trivial, and – in the last decade – demeaning to women, it has quite suddenly begun to receive attention bordering on respect from journalists and reviewers. The chief reason is its enormous success in books and films – a success romance writers have always enjoyed in their own quiet way, but whose commercial dimensions have now attracted media attention. What has for generations been derided as "women's stuff" – though many of the best practitioners are men – has suddenly become fashionable.

The insistent clamour of the cash register has always fascinated the papers, especially in a time of recession, and romantic books, like the soaps, have been coining it. Some reviewers have found merit in this fact alone, rather than in the actual stuff the public have been buying in their millions. (The question "Can the public be all wrong?" usually implies the answer "No".) But also articles about the *need* for romance amongst women – as a creative expression of sexual need unsatisfied by contemporary men – have had their effect, and this has spilled over into consideration of the soaps. Some of the shows, the American day-time ones especially, portray stuff as hot as any romantic novel, and certainly hotter than the prime-time shows. The bed is possibly the most important piece of furniture in the soaps, seen or unseen, but when they feel it is about to become respectable, the reviewers will sprawl all over it.

Their attitude to the genre has changed a lot more than the genre itself. Looking through the files of reviews of the soaps from the 1930s on, knocking copy predominated, indeed overwhelmed all else, until very recently. From the *New York Times* to the British broadcasting weekly *The Listener*, the tone has been *de haut en bas*, along the lines, "Hello, I'm a stranger here myself, but I thought I'd just drop in and see the extraordinary things you good people get up to when no one's looking." Certainly none of them would admit to being regular watchers, the implication being that *they* only watched television during the daylight hours out of duty, that nothing so undemanding could be any good.

Part of the reason for this attitude was fashion – that is, the soaps were very unfashionable among the intelligentsia, and remained so until the beginning of the 1980s. Another part of the explanation lies in the working method of the reviewer, who is forced by the demands of deadlines and the limitations of space at his or her disposal to distort, compress and wrench out of context. The reviewer has to seize on something that will make good copy, and seize on it quickly. With something as huge and amorphous as the soaps, what they seize on will invariably be those elements that "good" television avoids – all those clichés of characterization and plot that are an intrinsic part of the genre.

To the reviewer in a hurry, the outrageous coincidences (the long lost lover turning up at the wedding of the almost redeemed heroine), the melodramas (kidnappings and crimes of passion), the bolts from the blue (amnesia, a mysterious crippling illness) are always good for a laugh. If you are not familiar with the conventions of the genre, and have not witnessed the careful build-up to these situations, of course they look a little ridiculous. If you want a giggle, summarize the week's story-lines: "Tom, who unbeknownst to his wife Jane has a son by Ann, who is Jane's long-lost sister, has been found in the Australian desert suffering from amnesia . . ." Out of context, and without the resonance that long-term viewing brings to them, naturally they sound crudely incredible (as do the plots of grand opera or Jacobean tragedy). It's no trouble to knock out a piece that is at best witty, at worst condescending, to demonstrate the reviewer's fearless independence of popular fashion. That he or she is also ignorant and prejudiced is no crime: many are the reviewers who are prepared actually to boast of these qualities in defence of what they like.

But this boorishness is currently out of fashion. The soaps, which have carried on in their own sweet way regardless, have recently become respectable. (If I say I was unaware of this when I began this book, you won't believe me, but I swear it's true.) Nor is it just *Dallas* which has made them so, though of course it has helped. In America the discovery of the youth market is even more important, commercially, than the export market: young people actually buy the goods advertised between the acts, whereas foreigners merely buy the show. Excavating the attitudes and motives of the young has always been a favourite pastime for sociologists and critics, and their little cries of discovery have in turn influenced the reviewers, who do not make trends, but have to be damn quick at scenting them. Proof lies in a whole clutch of articles in the popular press – for instance *Newsweek*'s long study of *General Hospital* in the autumn of 1981 – in which there is no mockery, only awe at the power the shows have over their audience, an audience which can no longer be dismissed as middle-aged dowdies, but which is composed of the very consumers whose taste will decide the future of the reviewers and their organs.

In England the glamour of the American prime-time imports has had its effect, but there has also been a small but respectable academic industry puttering away to alter the reviewers' conceptions. Seminars on soap opera run in conjunction with the British Film Institute (who also put out a kit for schools encouraging awareness of the form's conventions), serious papers on the genre and its implications presented at the Edinburgh TV Festival, the nagging persistence of the semiologists – all these have had their effect. The growing respectability of courses in communications and the media at colleges and universities, and the soaps' own astonishing (to the reviewers) survival, have all gnawed at the reviewers' complacency towards the genre.

Survival has always affected criticism. On one level the work of someone like Ian Fleming, which scarcely developed in a literary sense from book to book – that is, it did not exactly grow even if it matured – garnered increasing acclaim as James Bond survived everything imaginable, and several things unimaginable, such as the death of his creator. On a different level the work of the structuralist school of critics, which was ridiculed and despised when it first stumbled on the literary scene in its pebble-glassed prose, has since gained respectability simply through its staying power. Not that more people understand its vocabulary or share its views, simply that these are no longer dismissed as fads or irrelevancies.

Western civilization reveres survival almost as much as does the Eastern. Whether they are politicians or public enemies, those who live long enough with their marbles intact find themselves encrusted with the barnacles of public affection. Reviewers, in their ceaseless search for something new, often stub their toes on the old and dig it up with wonder. All of which works in the soaps' favour: the tide of academic approval (or at least research – and if public funds are devoted to the study of the genre it must surely have some merit?), combined with simple endurance have attracted the attention and often enforced the respect of the reviewers. They even claim the genre's changelessness and total consistency as part of its merit.

You, discriminating reader, will have noticed that this fit of approval consorts ill with the reviewers' need to provide knocking copy. But reviewers are not consistent. They damn a soap for not leaving enough to the imagination, and praise a documentary for a "hard-hitting conclusion that leaves the viewer in no doubt of what to think". They commend as "sprightly" a comedy that relies on the world's oldest jokes, and are sniffy about a serial that contains nothing "new". That is why I have carefully tried to discriminate between critics and reviewers. The former owe it to their profession to provide a sort of rope-rail to

hold onto as one skirts the cliff edge. The latter are far more concerned
to get their copy in on time. Which is one reason why they treat all
soaps as if they were the same – or worse, damn as "soapy" those
programmes which appear to use some of the genre's conventions to
put across a "serious" message. An example is the way some British
reviewers knocked *The Day After*, the American programme about the
nuclear bombing of a small town. What the reviewers did not realize
was that the banality of characterization did not make *The Day After*
a soap: while in my view it made what happened all the more terrible,
if it *had* been a soap there would have been a happy ending. Soaps are
banal for an uplifting reason and *The Day After* wasn't that, any more
than was the serial *Holocaust* – also derided as soap-like. But reviewers
are all too often incapable of such informed discrimination.

There is a whole industry, small but flourishing, devoted to analysing,
understanding and criticizing soap opera. Ever since the Rockefeller
Foundation set up the Office of Radio Research at Columbia University,
New York, in 1937, there has been a distant rumble of critical thunder
on the subject. What started as research projects for university sociologists has taken over entire departments, whether it be the Centre for
Mass Communication Research in Britain's University of Leicester, or
the course "Inside Day-time Television" offered by the University of
Southern California. This reflects not so much a growth in soap's
popularity – the audience has remained fairly constant over the years
– as an attempt by modern universities to offer their students "relevance". Academic discipline in the abstract is no longer enough: what
matters is the subject to which it is applied. The study of dead languages
and cultures is thought to be less relevant, and certainly less appealing,
than an "in-depth look" at what is readily available.

In England, lest it be thought we lag behind in the pursuit of the
relevant, there have been published detailed studies of both *Crossroads*
and *Coronation Street*, academic in tone, at least when compared
with the gossipy but informative books like Noele Gordon's or H. V.
Kershaw's. I have mentioned the seminars that have taken place on
television fictions, and these included several serious papers on soaps
and their attitudes to "reality", women, audiences and the like. All
this proves that even if we only have a handful of soaps, compared with
the dozen or more available to Americans, our academics are as aware
of their importance, and anxious to pin it down, as anybody's.

Nothing in England, or anywhere else for that matter, compares with
the scope of "Project Daytime", a "comprehensive research endeavor
based in the Department of Communication at the State University of

New York at Buffalo". This was founded on the premise that "Daytime television celebrates the American condition: Game Shows inform and provoke us. Soap Operas involve and addict us. Talks shows entertain and socialize us." Research in progress at Buffalo included "an analysis of the impact of Soap Operas across various cultures and continents", "the development of an *Emotional Index of Television Viewers* [their italics]: Daytime vs Prime-time", "a comparative study of sexual behaviour in Prime-time's portrayal of the family in American society". The Project Director edited a symposium on soap for the *Journal of Communication*, and herself produced a paper on illness and disease in the serials. Which only goes to show that when the Americans go into a subject, they have the determination and the funds to do it thoroughly.

Allowing for my own prejudiced view that sociologists go to enormous lengths to prove the obvious, what can we learn from all these academic effusions? Is their aim to celebrate the form and bring even more millions to appreciate its complexities, or to change it by sharpening the perceptions of its viewers, whose opinions have so much influence on the makers?

I candidly admit that I learned a fair amount. I found out how to identify the stereotypes, and their role in a narrative structure whose roots went down to antiquity. I discovered that what to me was simple entertainment, was to many a therapeutic experience. Being myself a fan of only a few shows (and a dropper-in to others), I was led to look at many more serials and to see what they all had in common (which was good for my critical faculties). I read with horror how some critics regarded the soaps as sexist, which had simply not occurred to me. I learned that the addictive desire to know what will happen next was historically respectable, and had links with folk myth and epic narrative (not to mention the romantic novels and pulp fiction that I used to read under the bedclothes).

From the semiologists I learned that it is possible to pin down the narrative structure of soap opera with terms like "the hermeneutic code", which my dictionary defines as a code concerned with interpretation, and which that seminal semioticist Roland Barthes explained as a code that functions by making "expectation . . . the basic condition for truth". Tania Modleski, in an article published in *Film Quarterly*, Fall 1979, put it succinctly: "The narrative, by placing ever more complex obstacles between desire and its fulfilment, makes anticipation of an end an end in itself." She goes on to link, in her essay whose subtitle is "Notes on a Feminine Narrative Form", soaps and "a possible feminine aesthetic", pointing out that the works of "many innovative women artists", such as Nathalie Sarraute, are "antiprogressive" in form, just as soap opera is. The postponement of climaxes, the interruptions that allow each character time to consider the consequence of others' speech and actions, are "opposed to the classic (male) film narrative, which, with maximum action and minimum, always pertinent dialogue, speeds its way to the restoration of order".

Ms Modleski quotes a comparison made by Marsha Kindler between soap opera and Ingmar Bergman's *Scenes from a Marriage*. The "open-ended, slow-paced, multi-climaxed structure" of the serials is "in tune with patterns of female sexuality" and thus might be more capable than other forms of dramatic narrative of showing feminine growth and self-awareness. Taking on the feminist critics of the genre who feel that it offers women fulfilment only through family and domestic bliss, Ms Modleski points out that this implies that the soaps offer the female viewer a mirror-image of her own family, whereas what she sees, and perhaps longs for, is a kind of *extended* family, "the direct opposite of her own isolated nuclear family". To call for women to embrace solitude and self-sufficiency, as some critics do, is, according to Ms Modleski, quite wrong: "for too long women have had too much solitude and, quite rightly, they resent it." She points out how watching the bitch – the one character who "tries to gain control over her feminine passivity" – forever being thwarted and trying again, may help the woman viewer reconcile herself "to the meaningless, repetitive nature of much of her life and work within the home". And she ringingly concludes that "it is crucial to recognize that soap opera allays *real* anxieties, satisfies *real* needs and desires, even while it may distort them."

What distinguishes Ms Modleski, and some of her structuralist colleagues, from the critics and the reviewers who spend more time analysing – in terms that range from pity through amazement to contempt – the audience than the soaps themselves, is that her final words are a call to feminists to *use* the serial form (amongst others). "We have," she says "a responsibility to devise ways of meeting these needs (that is, the ones that soap opera satisfies) that are more creative, honest and interesting than the ones mass culture has come up with. Otherwise, the search for tomorrow threatens to go on, endlessly."

What that means to me is that the serial form is important enough and flexible enough to accommodate the serious ambitions of its most creative critics. The form is in no danger of dying, but if critics like Modleski can galvanize writers to make it work to their advantage, and, more important, get the audience to *demand* more from it, its future can only be more exciting. That there are enormous difficulties in attempting such improvements, and that they are unlikely to succeed, I know from my analysis of how the genre works. But that there are some critics who are unafraid of calling for the effort to be made is in itself a celebration of its importance.

8

THE PUBLIC: PRIDE
AND PREJUDICES

Soap fans are something else. They are not hysterical like pop fans, though they like to show their appreciation. They are not violent, like sports fans, though they defend their heroes with passion. They do not surrender themselves uncritically to the show, but enjoy playing an active role in shaping its future: in this they are, uniquely, partners in the production process.

Nobody who is not of their number understands their addiction, but their ranks are open to all. Indeed, they welcome fellow converts, and bear with fortitude the jeers of the uncomprehending.

They can no longer be dismissed as a collection of bored, lonely and frustrated housewives. Though women have always been in the majority, they were joined by children (either truanting or home from school), the unemployed, shift-workers, invalids, retired people and the self-employed. Those who own up to their passion include the Queen and former President Carter's late mother, professors, college graduates and homemakers (note, in passing, how the terminology of domestic choredom has changed over half a century). Each is an individual, making generalizations suspect; but each has in common a love – sometimes shameless, sometimes restrained, sometimes close to loathing – for the genre.

Before the age of mass communications, news and story were matters shared in public. But radio and television, along with newspapers and best-sellers and pulp fiction, are public media received in private. The same programmes enter millions of different homes in millions of different circumstances. The public itself is a mass of privates: the soaps, almost alone, unite them in a society of shared enthusiasm and feelings. True, sports and state funerals or weddings and some news programmes have a similar unifying effect. But though these play on our feelings, they lack the peculiar power of fiction. Sport may be cathartic, the news may be engaging, shocking and even hopeful, but though newscasters, like sporting stars, are figures of national importance, the audience is not engaged with them as *characters*. It is their *role* – as authorities, winners, or whatever – that counts for more than their personalities. If they fall from grace, whether through drunkenness, corruption or simple failure to keep scoring, that is the end of them. With soap characters, it is just the beginning.

The soap fan is served in a different way from other publics, and watches differently too. In prime-time, programmes of entirely different styles succeed one another, so that the effect of, say, a play or a comedy is effaced by what succeeds it. Unless of course the viewer or listener turns off in order to digest what has been transmitted, which very rarely happens.

The soaps, however, are screened in blocks, at least in America. Even in England there are nights, and regions, where two or even three of the early evening serials follow close on one another's heels. Whatever the case, they are always reliably there in the same slot. This means that the fan is allowed a wallow, where with other programmes no more than a quick splash is permitted. You can really get into the feel of the soaps, wrap yourself up in their world without fear of interruption (except from the ads). If, as in America, the soaps continue from mid-morning to the time school comes out, you can turn off – interrupted by the children, say – without having seen anything else. Your impressions and feelings will remain whole, unbattered by the distractions of comedians or variety artistes or game shows. Soap can provide all you need.

Americans get more undiluted soap (to coin a phrase) than anybody else, which explains the extraordinary tenacity and involvement of their fans. Yet in England, as in other countries who are not offered soap in blocks, the fans are as loyal, and feel themselves to be as special, as the Americans. They may watch in families, but they feel they are individuals – individuals who often have to brave the scorn of other members of the household, or who are forced to make special arrangements (like preparing meals well in advance of their being consumed) in order to have the time to themselves that will allow them to see their serials in peace. Naturally, making this special effort allows them to feel special. I would not want to make too big a thing out of this, for serial fans do not *behave* any differently from other members of their community. They are special only in their loyalty to a particular type of programme, and in their reactions to that programme. Soaps are a phenomenon, but that does not make their audience freaks.

Soap fans are not zombies in thrall to invented characters whose life styles they pine for. On the contrary, they have a healthier response than most other viewers and listeners to the things that move them:

they answer back. Marshall McLuhan pointed out in 1964 that the TV viewer was involved as participant. There is more mail received about the serials than about any other programmes by the television companies, who welcome the letters and calls not just as a sign of appreciation, but as a guide to what the fans want. What stirs the public out of what is usually perceived as its torpor in face of the box? The simple fact that they have come to know their serial characters well enough to feel free to criticize. They are as involved as they are with friends. Familiarity breeds comment.

The comments are by no means all friendly, but they are all informed. Here is an example from a 1982 *Guiding Light* file:

> Number 9 [in the ratings], well, how do you like that? Five from the bottom. Do you want to know the reason – Boring!! *GL*, you are boring, boring, boring. The writers must be tapped out . . . Nola's fantasies – boring – she was more fun when she was at the hospital, being a bitch. Bea and Henry? get serious. The super-rich do not hang out with the super-poor. The tycoon and the boarding-house frau? Reads like a bad soap opera!

From the same file there are complaints that there are "too many kids" jumping in and out of bed, regardless of whether they are or aren't married. This is a rare note of censoriousness, since the moral climate of the soaps is renowned for its hygiene. Such a grumble would scarcely occur in England, where the soaps are the last place one would look for the gratification of lust.

But what is striking about the letters of those who take the trouble to write in – who are, of course, but a fraction of the soap audience – is the degree to which they feel personally involved in their serial. They are not just writing routine letters of complaint about something that has offended them: to justify their praise or blame, they offer the most personal details about *themselves*, as if to persuade the producers to think of them as individuals, not an undifferentiated mass of viewers. Anyone who thinks the age of writing letters is dead ought to consult the soap opera files.

> "Oh yes! I happen to be 75 years old, but not a prude."
> "I represent 50% of our population – good, honest English wives and mothers."
> "Every morning at coffee time in the laboratory a furious argument rages over (a) what should happen next and (b) what will happen next. We may disagree but we are always interested and despise the lesser breeds who do not listen."

"I am 13 years old and just started to subscribe to *Soap Opera Digest*. I love to watch soap opera and if I miss any episodes, as I do a lot because of school, I read up on them. My favourite is 'General Hospital'. I'm really getting fed up with the show, though. They've had Luke and Laura split up long enough! . . . The whole show is becoming totally stupid. I may just stop watching it altogether until Luke and Laura's wedding!" (21 July 1981)

The first of these reactions is from a *Guiding Light* fan (many of whom mention the fact that they have been with the show since its radio days). The second is from a *Crossroads* fan angry at the disappearance of Meg Mortimer. The third is from a BBC Audience Research Report on *The Archers* (1954). The fourth is typical of a pubescent pundit. All of them demonstrate the soap audience's self-awareness. More than that, the viewers have, if you like, a political sense of their own power, and its limitations. They know that it is on their loyalty that the programme makers rely – and yet (as Dorothy Hobson points out in her book on *Crossroads*) the older viewers at least are aware that they are not a strong enough market force to have a great influence on the producers. They play on sympathy instead:

"I live alone and over 70 and look forward to seeing Crossroads. I feel she is a friend come into my home. I do hope that you can do something to save her."
"I know I am old 88 years but I am a good judge of people. All I can say keep going Meg we will miss you."

All this is to disprove the myth that soap fans are mindless, passive, and uncritical of what they see and hear. Their responses show that they understand the sophisticated process by which soap opera is brought into their homes, and that they are not so in awe of it that they are afraid of arguing their case. They are also pleased to make their enjoyment plain. They care enough to want to influence what will happen. They know that it is all "just a story", but it is *their* story, and they feel they have every right to see that it turns out properly.

Of course they are not always listened to. Meg Mortimer was not saved, despite the thousands of letters and a nation-wide campaign orchestrated by the popular papers. The death of Grace Archer was sprung upon a shocked and unsuspecting populace who complained, too late, that the "murder" (by the producers: Grace was in fact destroyed by a falling beam in a stable fire) was planned purely to distract attention from the opening of commercial television (which it did, very successfully). Those devotees of *All My Children* who pleaded that, despite their differences, Phoebe and Charles Tyler should stay together, were grievously disappointed. And whole soaps can be slaughtered without regard to public outcry: the massacre of the radio serials that took place on both sides of the Atlantic almost wiped out an entire genre (save for *The Archers*), while the loss of CBS's long-running *Love of Life* was proof that nothing and nobody is ever completely safe.

But the fans, though they mourn, accept that producers are as cynical as politicians, and listen only when it's expedient. This doesn't stop the public exercising its right to complain, advise and warn. Nor does it prevent viewers and listeners making demands they know, or at least suspect, will go unsatisfied. Their chief wish, repeated so often it's almost a litany, is for a happy ending for their favourite characters. They know – who better? – the ambivalence of the genre towards endings of any sort, but they are unashamed of their desire for wedding bells, silver-lined clouds, and gilt-edged sunsets. They know that soap is almost the only genre to offer such delights, in an age when neither art nor politics dares speak much of hope, let alone satisfaction. Does this make them fantasists? No, because they accept that only rarely do they get what they demand in the way of happy endings. We are programmed from conception to expect things we never receive. The soaps realistically reflect this permanent disappointment – but they and their fans remain optimists.

More curious than complaints or demands are the warnings issued by the public to characters they know to be fictitious. Contract actors and actresses have to get used to receiving sheafs of letters addressed to the characters they play, putting them right on matters which, if the correspondent paused for thought, are patently ridiculous. A character might be falsely accused of a crime witnessed by another member of the cast. Letters will flutter in beseeching or ordering the witness to tell the police the truth. The letter-writer knows that it is all part of the plot, and that to have it put right too soon will rob both audience and characters of a story-development on which their mutual enjoyment depends. The explanation usually advanced for this confusion is that the viewer or listener has become so involved that he or she has muddled fiction with reality. I think it is a lot more subtle than that. I believe that the fans are involved not just with the *story*, but with the whole *process* by which it is told. It is like a treasure hunt where everybody can join in. Those who spot the clues rush to claim the prize, which is recognition of their cleverness. It is a sign of their influence, not just over the characters, but over their fictional destinies.

The audience becomes not simply viewers and listeners, but story-tellers too.

I wouldn't claim that soap fans are unique in the degree of attention they pay to what is going on, but it's no relaxation for the real addict, who concentrates ferociously on every detail. And this despite the slow pace and frequent repetition of story details, that are designed for the "distracted" viewing the makers assume is normal. The true fan can pick out the tiniest mistake or inconsistency, which more casual listeners or viewers – and some writers and directors – are happy to let pass. As proof of involvement, the fan will whip off a letter. Now if you are involved in a story – any good story, be it novel, film or serial – you are involved as an individual, not as a member of a group. You forget yourself in what is happening to the characters whose actions and attitudes fascinate you, but your reactions are yours alone, and you feel them strongly. If you are not moved by the story, you will allow yourself to be swayed in what you think by what others say or feel. soap opera fans are so wrapped up in the show that their opinions are completely their own. This strength of personal feeling is rare, especially in television. The fans know it and want to share it. It can be shared with others who feel likewise, if there are any in the household. More often the soap fan watches or listens alone. What could be more natural than the desire to share his or her feelings, and anxieties about what might happen, with those who are even more involved than they – the characters, and through them the people who control the story? Especially when the viewers are encouraged to believe they know things that the characters don't, which gives the audience that all important feeling of being insiders, privy to crucial secrets – and helps to bind them even more tightly to the serial.

Viewing television in this manner, or listening to the radio, becomes a sort of private game. Now the appeal of game shows is well known, but there the involvement or complicity between audience and those taking part ends when the transmission does. True there are often puzzles and competitions for the home audience to take part in, but these involve merely answering set questions. There are also the immensely popular 'phone-in shows. But the soap opera issues no such direct invitations to its audience to participate. Such is its peculiar hold that the viewers and listeners go on thinking about the characters when they have faded from vision or sound. More, the fans prolong their favourite imaginary lives by writing about them as if they had an existence outside the transmitter.

Such a response has a long history (Dickens experienced it too). In America, the early sponsors were staggered by the volume of replies they received when they invited listeners to send in box-tops in order to receive free gifts. One thing this proved was that the audience was paying close attention. Another was that radio was a great selling device. But a third thing was that the audience was eager to grab the opportunity to answer back. By writing in they were putting their mark – in a more sophisticated way than dogs and cats – on a territory where they were invited to roam, though only within strict limits. They were personalizing the impersonal.

Soap opera, of course, prides itself on personalizing everything. Yet it is, as we know, a corporate structure overshadowed by bigger corporate structures. The audience is well aware of this, and makes it pretty clear when roused by some corporate decision. The refrain, "Why should these people in charge of programmes tell us what *they* think we should like?" runs through all the complaints, in England as in America, at the deaths of characters or serials. The fans know where the power is hidden, but that doesn't stop them marching round its walls blowing trumpets when they feel like doing so.

The sending of gifts and cards congratulating invented characters on birthdays, engagements and weddings is, I believe, done in much the same game-like spirit. The actors and actresses at the receiving end of public generosity are naturally delighted. And why should the showering of presents on made-up heroes and heroines, who are so well known to their audience they have become close friends, be a sign that the donors have lost their marbles? The Prince and Princess of Wales were flooded with gifts from complete strangers when they got married, and again when they had a baby. Presidents, pop stars and even politicians get messages, telegrams, cards and souvenirs from fans they have never known or even corresponded with. Nobody thinks the givers are loony. And yet Princes, Princesses and Presidents are as much fantasy figures to their subjects as are the characters in the soaps. They are there to be seen and heard (though not as often as the soap people are available to their fans), but the vast majority of those who go to the trouble of buying them something are not personally affected by what they say and do. What affects the public is the image, the glamour, the fantasy – just as with the soaps.

Lest it be said that *I* am now confusing fact with fiction, let me state clearly that I do not deny that there is a difference between the Princess of Wales and, say, Krystle Carrington of *Dynasty*. Both play demanding roles with enormous grace, both use the power that their husbands have conferred on them with the best intentions, both incarnate the fantasies of a substantial portion of humanity. Both are, in the best sense, consummate actresses, radiating charm even when they may not feel like it. Both always appear immaculate, neither can turn round without their every word and gesture being reported and commented on, both are now public property. The difference is that the Princess of Wales *is* the Princess of Wales, whose next part is likely to be that of Queen of England, whereas Krystle Carrington is an actress named Linda Evans, who can play anything she wants to.

Which is more real, to the person who watches and marvels and is captivated by their every action? Of course there's a difference, but is it a difference that matters? Princes may have lost their power – but they and their Princesses retain the power to fascinate. Indeed, the plethora of serials about the very rich argues that royalty, whether crowned or levied on an oil barrel, has returned (if it ever altogether vanished) as a subject of popular fantasy. The fact is that the Princess and the Actress are equally desirable to, and remote from, most of us. The desire to bridge the moat that separates them from us takes the form of sending some small offering. This links us to them, and in some little way makes them beholden to us. I cannot understand why when we do this to Princesses, everyone thinks it's sweet and terribly patriotic, and when we do it to actresses who play Princesses, everyone (that is, everyone who doesn't do it) thinks we're mad. Hollywood stars once accepted such adulation as a matter of course. Pop stars do so now. Why on earth shouldn't soap stars, who have a larger and more faithful public than either?

I am more puzzled by those who write to soap characters, using their fictional names, and ask for favours or advice about personal problems. One character on *Crossroads* was required to turn the collar and cuffs of another character's shirt. The actress concerned, on receiving a large parcel, naturally assumed it was an exciting gift from a fan. But it was only a load of old shirts, accompanied by the request that she turn the collars and cuffs as she had on screen. Even more common are requests for help in dealing with family rows, adultery, broken love-affairs, or inadequacy.

In one sense there could be nothing more natural than writing in to somebody whom you know so well you forget they don't know you. Nobody makes adverse comments when people write in to "Agony Aunts" with a public plea for help with a private difficulty. These "Aunts" are as fictional as soap characters, since they usually write under assumed names, and they reveal a good deal less of themselves than the soap hero or heroine who is a regular guest in their correspondent's home. But what happens when either the soap character who has been written to, or the production office of the show in which they appear, takes pains to write a reply in character, that is, under the name of the person they play? What is the reaction of the soap fan who receives a genuine letter offering genuine (or at least general) advice, bearing a signature the fan knows to be that of a made-up person? I would guess this sets up a certain confusion. Nice of the actor, actress or production secretary to show that they care – maybe their advice, if offered, is helpful – but does this whole game keep the charade going, or undermine it?

Certainly it is the stated intention of the production office to preserve the bubble of illusion unpricked for as long as possible. Since the earliest days of radio soaps the (obviously unseen) stars were forbidden to make public appearances except when made up to fulfil the public expectation of their characters. Television stars have no need for such disguise – except that they, like their radio forebears, are sometimes required to sign letters in character. (I distinguish those who write for advice from those who write in for pictures and autographs of people they know to be actors and actresses.) The players perform this odd task with more sympathy than cynicism for those members of their public who seem to them so confused. Many stars take pride in the fact that they put on so convincing a performance people will turn to them for help. Of course this phenomenon could be used to attack inadequate or uncaring social services, the isolation and stress of modern living, and so forth. If people have to turn to invented characters in a serial, things have reached a pretty pass. But are the soap producers actually doing harm by encouraging the fantasies of those who need help, or are they indulging their audience's taste for a bit of harmless – and commercially profitable – game-playing?

If there is no profit in it, the producers won't do it. Obviously they maintain the illusion to keep the fans happy and watching, and to demonstrate what a caring company they belong to. So sensitive are they to public feeling that they would undoubtedly react with horror if it were proved that their actions were actually harmful. (This has never been proved, and is only advanced to make a critical point about illusion and reality.) Such advice as is offered is carefully considered and, like that of the "Agony Aunts", usually directs the correspondent, where necessary, to the local doctor, priest or guidance clinic. No one knows whether or not the advice is followed. Maybe it was enough for the letter-writer merely to put his or her problems down on paper, to be read by a friendly eye. Maybe getting a letter from a fictional character is like getting the "autograph" of Lassie or Champion the Wonder Horse: a joke which, when you think about it, makes you realize how silly you were to ask in the first place. Maybe these fans are nuts. I must admit that this aspect of the relationship between public and soap characters concerns me. Perhaps it's another one of those games people play with their television sets, goading those electronic phantasms into a flesh-and-blood response. I'm not sure, and I worry about it.

One thing soap opera provides for its public is the opportunity to gossip about the characters. Some critics maintain that the way we live now has killed gossip stone dead. I believe that to be rubbish. Toss in a fact or a conjecture where any two or three are gathered together, and it will be browned with gossip as surely as if it were a battered prawn lowered into hot fat. Gossip, the embroidery of facts, is as much part of modern life, wherever it is lived, as it always has been. The soaps are simply a marvellous vehicle to enjoy it in. As the biologist said, quoted earlier in the Audience Research Report on *The Archers*, what should happen to the characters, and what will happen, becomes the subject for enthusiastic debate.

Again, this is part of the game enjoyed by all those who watch the soaps. These players (that is, the listeners and viewers) do not win or lose, which makes a change, but they are united in their knowledge of their subject, which sets them apart from those who, not being addicts, haven't the faintest idea what they are talking about. This sense of apartness is the lifeblood of gossip. Knowing what someone else doesn't know, and sharing your knowledge with those who do, is the whole point of the exercise. It is never boring, at least not to insiders, to dissect and discuss the motives and futures of characters with whom they are intimately involved, and yet whose actions will not actually affect their own. It may be the purest irresponsibility to take somebody apart and reassemble them according to your own fantasies – but this is one of the great pleasures of gossip, and when you do it to a fictional character, you need feel neither guilt nor shame. Couple that with the fact that the gossipers share with their subjects all sorts of common experiences and attitudes – unhappy love affairs, miserable marriages, problems with sex and children and money – and you have a teeming pool to dip into. It is also a pool whose waters are murky enough to be interesting, without being treacherous enough for danger.

Gossip's concerns are intensely and exclusively personal: not what such-and-such a person will do about the great problems of our time, but what he or she said or should have said to or about the person he or she was sleeping with. The soaps have refined gossip into a high-octane fuel on which they run forever. Without it, they are nothing: whole plots revolve around, not what A actually did, but what B thought A did. B gives a garbled version to C, who complains to D, who enmeshes E ... the process is as elastic as it is familiar. It offers unrivalled scope to its fans, who can continue it in private or public.

Apart from being personal, soap gossip is reassuring in its subject matter. There are sundry sexual shlemozzles, but violence is rare, and politics non-existent. One of the chief reasons given by the public for its addiction to soaps is that they avoid the tawdry, the squalid and the gratuitous shedding of blood. Some American shows of late have been trying to spice up their content by going in for preposterous adventure, and their files bulge with complaints as a result. Soap fans are on the whole a peaceable lot, and peace usually gets short shrift on television. The viewers grumble, with justice, that there is enough sex and violence, on television and off, without the soaps going in for it too. They turn to their favourite shows to get away from all that, to immerse themselves in the slow development of characters whose dramas are domestic rather than sanguinary. One of the most comforting things for the soap public is that they can always lose themselves in their favourites' problems and know that they will, in the end, turn out to be manageable. It is true that there are an astonishing number of murders on the soaps, not to mention rapes, injuries, fatalities from disease, accidents and the smashing of crockery to mark displeasure. But these are not dwelt on, nor indulged: they are incidental to the truly important story, which is how the characters will react. What counts is how misfortune is endured. That it *is* endured, by the deserving, is what repays the viewer's or listener's devotion.

I don't think this argues that the members of the soap public lack material to gossip about in their own lives, or that they bury their heads in soap to avoid "real" issues. What the soaps do is to extend their range – give them more to gossip about – as well as occasionally providing a small oasis, offering temporary shelter from the harshness of the rest of their world. It goes without saying that the lives of most people are rarely touched by actual violence. The soaps offer a world where people are affected by events they can come to grips with, not by random terror from unknown assailants. Soap life turns chaos into a sort of order, sees through the mysterious and pursues the game of consequences to its inexorable conclusion. Gossip tries to do much the same.

The subject of gossip – personal failings – never changes, though the taste or tolerance of the gossiper may. Mind you, when it comes to personal taste, or rather, attitudes towards others, I would maintain this has changed a lot less than many social historians seem to think. We may believe we are pretty tolerant these days about who sleeps with whom, but what is our tolerance compared with that of the age of the Borgias? Those who complain about alleged goings-on – and who add to their number and importance, for gossip multiplies things quicker than any calculator – are often those who do not get enough of what is complained about. The soaps provide a steady supply of tid-bits that have nourished the gossips since the gods took themselves off to Valhalla: fornication, neglect of duty, greed. Like knitting patterns, they offer an alternative to the ready-made scandals of real life, in a variety of traditional styles.

And yet the style and attitudes of the soaps *have* changed over fifty years, in accordance with, or a little behind, that of their public. Clothes have altered, of course, but although most of the young characters are swathed in denim like their flesh-and-blood contemporaries, none of the older players are exactly "with it". They dress, on both sides of the Atlantic, like our own dear Queen: expensively, in good taste, a little dully for the most part, but with the occasional astonishing flourish. They all, even the young heroines, tend towards the conservatism of middle age, in fashion and attitudes, rather than indulging in the exhausting attempt to bend with the trend. I am not sure if this makes them lazy, reactionary or more confident of themselves than those who wouldn't be seen dead draped in last month's fad. All I know is that the clothes soap people wear closely resemble those of the successful chain-stores the world over, where a gesture or two is made to current hemlines or trouser widths, but where you can get essentially the same gear as was obtainable a decade ago.

Of course it is difficult for the soap stars to dress in the height of fashion, because – with all that planning months in advance – by the time they came to wear it, it would probably be *passé*. There is also the fact that quite a lot of the shopping for clothes and props is done in the chain-stores whose influence on mass fashion is greater than anything else. It is said that the soaps influence fashion, but I see no evidence of it. At the top end of the range, nobody could afford to dress like a Ewing or a Carrington, assuming they had either the desire or the opportunity to do so. In the middle part of the social register, shown off in *Crossroads* or *All My Children*, everyone looks like the people who watch them. What the viewers copy, apparently, is more likely to be *décor* than *décolletage*: it is alleged that there are scores of rooms in Britain decorated *dans le style Meg Mortimer*, just as there must in America be quite a few attempts to get a lounge looking like Phoebe Tyler's.

It is not hard to understand why this should be. To doll yourself up to look like a fictional television character is to expose yourself to ridicule, whereas it is a sign of taste to select certain features of someone else's interior decoration – even from a set that has been seen so often in the background you would recognize it almost without identifying it. Fashion is based on imitation: individual style is shown in the items selected for copying. The stars themselves dress, not to be models for others, but to enable their viewers to identify with the parts they play. Like their audience, they want to look much like others of their age and status, while showing off just a touch of individuality. Their taste is that of their fans: given the nature of soaps, it could not be otherwise.

Much the same is true of attitudes to the kind of problems dealt with in the serials. That misleading expression applied to the soaps, "a mirror for our times", misleads precisely because anyone can find in a reflection whatever it is they are looking for. Those anxious to prove that ordinary people are decent and common-sensical can find an abundance of evidence to support their case; those who are concerned to find vindictiveness, chauvinism and small-minded pettiness can also go away happy. The point is that soaps deal with the whole range of emotions and attitudes by simplifying them into the reactions of people to events. Soap people react the way their audience would like to react, if they had the opportunity. There is nothing abstract about them, never any question of dealing with hypothetical issues. Attitudes are shown translated into action: what will be done about a lover, a foundling, a legacy. Real life is a lot more iffy than that.

That the soap public likes simplicity cannot be denied, even if – in response to the growing complexity of modern living – it has become accustomed to more sophisticated responses from its heroes and heroines. The reaction of the 1930s serial character to a dilemma seems laughable today: archaic in language, crude in action. Now we see much more havering over the right thing to do, much more weighing up of pros and cons, more agonizing and temporizing before the final commitment to the "right" course of action. The outcome is still not in doubt: it's the way they approach it that has grown more subtle.

But in fact this sophistication is more a matter of vocabulary than of action. What I mean is, people talk about things differently, even if they act the same way. Take rape. For the soaps' first thirty years, this never actually happened, at least not to nice girls – but it was always there as a possibility. Its victims automatically became fallen women and were rarely heard of again. But now we *define* rape differently. In the 1980s it is accepted that rape can occur within marriage, or between so-called lovers. A woman who is forced to submit to the brutal lusts of a man she has lived with for some time has been raped. And that sort of thing was always happening, even to radio heroines. The consequences were the same, then as now: trauma, loss of love and respect, an unwanted child who grows up to become a Problem. Or painful miscarriage and subsequent sterility, as happened to Krystle Carrington on *Dynasty*. The rapist can only atone for his dreadful act by showing himself capable of true love, devotion and tenderness. And his victim will not only take a hell of a lot of convincing – she will know, and the audience will know, that there is always the possibility of it happening again. Such a possibility can keep the story going for years and years.

Though nice girls didn't go to bed before marriage at least before the 1960s (and bad girls always did), sex was always on their minds. From Ma Perkins' daughter to Mrs Dale's, the great question was not Should I? (to which the answer has always been No), but When? Television soap heroines simply ask different questions: Why Shouldn't I? (knowing the answer was Because It's Wrong), or Where? They still keep out of other people's beds (on the whole), but their approach is phrased differently. Extra-marital sex on the serials still has dire consequences, but I'm not sure people *do* it more now. Deirdre Barlow's adultery with Mike Baldwin on *Coronation Street* was whipped up into a froth of publicity by the press, and led to heated national debate, but her action was exceptional. Most soap characters are content to talk around the subject, endlessly.

I would argue that the same is true of the public's experience. No doubt statistics can be produced to prove that, of the generation that preferred the Pill to their morning cereal, more of them slept together than did their predecessors. What is certain is that conversation about the subject changed. No one had to worry about little bastards: the important questions concerned happiness, love and self-esteem. But promiscuity offered no solutions: the level of frustration did not fall with the bedsprings, nor post-coital misery vanish with the coil. The whole subject is still as much of a problem as it was when Eve discovered there was more growing on the fig-trees than laxatives. On the soaps and off them, people are no more confident about their sexual behaviour that they were half a century ago. The most active organ in the human body remains the tongue.

This is not to say that attitudes to some things haven't altered. Working women are now as acceptable on the soaps as in reality, where a generation ago they were considered suspect. The public is now less reticent about discussing matters that were once private and personal, and the soaps have done a lot to encourage this. Whether it be breast cancer or infertility, the serials have helped to rob these subjects of their terror by talking about them. In this they are following public concern reflected in other media. But it is also a process they have fostered from the start. The matriarchs and philosophers who were the central characters in the radio soaps helped people by getting them to talk about their problems. The appeal of the genre was like that of the confessional, with the added bonus that you got advice as well as penance. For every letter complaining about bad taste in spilling such things all over the hearth rug, there are a hundred encouraging the good work.

I realize why I am having such difficulty in trying to think of ways in which the soaps have altered. It is because they deal with people's problems, and these have altered hardly at all. Or rather, everything may have altered, but nothing has changed. We may talk about them differently, but we don't *look* at them very differently. It would be surprising if we did, in a mere fifty years.

What has not altered is the nature of the genre and its effect on the audience. With other forms, constant exposure serves only to show up weaknesses, and the public slides away through boredom. But with the soaps, the opposite occurs: the audience stays for, and grows fat on, a familiar and consistent diet, which is eagerly swallowed as long as its premises and promises remain credible. This fidelity contains all the signs of an addiction, of a craving for more of the same. Some soap fans, indeed, have remained with a show for thirty years or more. But the addiction is not unbreakable. Like reformed alcoholics, former fans publicly proclaim their renouncing of the serial habit, usually because the plotting and characterization of a show that has kept them in thrall for years have finally become too preposterous to bear. And of course those who become addicted while of school age find that changes in circumstances and working schedules disrupt their soap viewing: once the habit is broken, the compulsion to pick it up again steadily weakens.

If soaps kept their audience for life their viewing figures would not be in millions but billions. Instead, they rely on picking up new viewers for all those who fall off through boredom, death, lobotomies, marriage, night-work or lack of access to video recorders. The serials manage this because they are clever enough, flexible enough, and responsive enough to keep in step with their new viewers as well as with the old. They perform the extraordinary feat of appearing everlasting and up-to-date. They do this by listening carefully to what their public says it wants. Like politicians, the soap-makers take their soundings, and then appear to lead. But of course they are only leading in the direction their public has said it is willing to go. Which is towards simplicity.

We all hanker after simplicity (which doesn't imply we are simpletons). We live surrounded by complicated machinery designed to make life easier, we are numbed by complicated analyses of our conditions offered by experts in obfuscation. We are delighted when anyone offers a simplistic solution to get us out of the maze. The soaps dangle such a solution before our eyes and ears, but, like us, their characters never quite adopt it. They know as well as we do that there are simple ways of extricating themselves from the messes they have plunged themselves into, but they never actually take them. Like us, they shilly-shally, and get in deeper. But always before them is the obvious course that somehow they never get around to following.

Much of drama concerns itself with the gap between what could or should be done, and what actually happens. But the soaps are rare in offering even a hint or a promise of simple answers. It is the chief reason for their popularity. They exist by filling the gap between promise and delivery with delightful expectancy. The audience is cheered by the expectation of something good happening, and at the same time intrigued by when and how it will happen. This is one of the hardest things to explain to non-addicts. They cannot understand how anyone with imagination could sit down knowing exactly – or as near as makes no difference – the outcome of what they are seeing or hearing. To them, knowing the answer means there is no challenge. But what they miss is the beauty of seeing the sum being worked out.

The non-addict is also puzzled by the way the fans watch. If, they might ask, you're all up to date and you know what is going to happen, why pay such close attention and go round shushing everyone? Especially when anything you might miss is going to be repeated in some form or another for some time to come.

The addict can reply that it is the *little* details that count, the ones that don't get repeated. The small gesture, the off-hand reply: these are things that mean everything to those in the know. The better you understand people, the more significance you can read into their tiniest signals, those that are meant only for the most intimate friends.

Soap-watching allows involvement at all sorts of levels, from the addicts with their preoccupation with minutiae to the more distracted viewers who only want to keep up with the story. And just as everyone watches in a different way – college students in groups cheer and boo their favourites, senior citizens knit and weep silently – so each watches the serial that caters best for his or her concerns. No one watches all the soaps – that would be impossible, not to mention confusing: they would dribble one into another. The public is not hooked simply on the genre, regardless of what each show offers. On the contrary, they discriminate markedly between what they do and don't like, and are both vociferous and particular in what they defend (or attack).

Research in the 1930s showed that listeners twiddled their radio dials to find the right mix of serials that would satisfy their own emotional needs. One explained how she listened to a certain show because "the son there turns against his father just the way our son does", but, finding the boy's mother "too submissive", she turned to another serial for the satisfaction of hearing "the woman is boss". The same process is still at work, with some viewers identifying closely with Laura Spencer, the *General Hospital* heroine who was raped by the man she subsequently fell in love with and married, and others refusing to approve the show's trendiness, and finding more pleasure in *One Life to Live*, or *Guiding Light*, where the heroines manage to remain unsullied until the Church's blessing permits all hell to break loose. But each soap tries to mix its incidents and attitudes so that there should be something for everybody. In Britain, *The Archers* – according to correspondence published in the *Guardian* – lost several fans who had had enough of what they saw as endorsement of Tony's reactionary views at Bridge Farm: no doubt reactionaries (who always grumble at being ill-served) rushed to the programme, to join those for whom politics is just another form of swine fever. There are those who cannot stand the "cosy nostalgia" of *Coronation Street* and prefer the "everyday realism" of *Crossroads*; and those who develop a rash at the mere sight of David Hunter and who would prefer a night with Fred Gee at the Rover's Return any time. All of which proves that the soap public doesn't just sit there in a trance, but does precisely what the critics accuse them of being incapable of doing, and exercises the power of choice.

By exercising this power, the audience has also earned, to an unparalleled degree, the right to be listened to. Of course broadcasters have always been subjected to audience pressure, but outside the soaps they have bowed to the best organized and most powerful, which is to say the lobbying of the censorious "Moral Majority". Soap fans are only rarely organized into lobbies, and when they are it is by the popular press or fan magazines, to save a dying character or serial. Such organized pressure is usually unsuccessful. Where the fan is most effective is in writing to demand changes in a story-line – provided there are enough other fans to agree with them.

The popularity of 'phone-in programmes is surely founded on the callers' desire for a quick flash of fame for themselves and their opinions: a huge number of people will thus learn that they exist. But soap fans are different. Public glory, however brief, is not the point, which is to influence something already dear to them, and make it even more satisfying. The fans identify so completely with their own favourite show that they regard it as personal property, to be disposed of in whatever way they think fit. This is unique in the mass media. People are always writing in praise or criticism of programmes, but they don't expect the makers to take much notice. Soap fans do: indeed, they insist on it. And when, unprompted, large numbers of them demand the same thing, they usually get it, whether it be a change in characterization, or a shift in a story-line that has yet to be resolved. Because they get results, the fans take their responsibility seriously. Their demands are consistent with what they know is possible. (Of course there are some cranks, but they are usually ignored.)

What makes possible this extraordinary identification between public and programme is the permanent nature of the soaps. Anyone who stays around long enough in broadcasting – DJs, commentators, even weather forecasters – starts to receive mail. But that merely shows that the public likes to cluster round the odd beacon of permanence in an ephemeral medium. There is more than that in the audience's involvement with the soaps. The fan's role is not simply that of commentator or casual critic: it is, or it can be, actually *creative*. Those who write in want to do that which in all other spheres (real and fictional) is usually denied them: to influence the lives of those near and dear to them.

In what directions do they want to influence their favourites? Mostly they are in favour of stability. They want, at least the majority does, the lovers to settle down, families to stay together, and victims to be recompensed by happiness. But it is by no means as simple as all that. Most of the letters I have read show a keen appreciation of the conventions of the genre. They know precisely what can and can't be achieved. (Those who don't usually reveal themselves to be new to the form, or extremely hostile to it – like the disgruntled husband who wanted his wife's favourite man killed off so she would pay more attention to her marital duties.) Even though they know it's fantasy, they stick to the rules. Without them, what would be the point of playing the game?

Television-watching as a game is, I believe, something of a new idea. Electronic games (all those awful things lurking in space or the deep), and "inter-active" television (where you play games with your bank account or bookie), are all very vogueish, but not what I am talking about. The soap game is something that has been invented by the players. The programme makers capitalize on it, of course, but if they started to organize things so that the game lost its spontaneity, I believe it would collapse. Like the British Constitution, the rules have grown over the years to become almost sacred, without ever being written down.

Readers who have followed me this far will know what the rules are: consistency in characterization, credibility in plot. The object of the game (which is never achieved, so the game goes on forever) is to ensure that Good triumphs, Evil is punished, and Happiness rules. The game itself is far older than the mass media. It is not recorded whether or not Homer was besieged with requests to get Helen back together with

Menelaus – but the pair were in the end reconciled and lived happily ever after at Sparta. Certainly writers like Dickens and Trollope were "honoured" (Trollope's word) by hundreds of letters seeking happy endings for their heroines and heroes. It would seem that once the public's sympathy is engaged in a story, there are any number of them anxious to play the game of securing a satisfactory outcome.

The television (and radio) public has not been given much credit for this kind of active participation. Indeed, all the studies of the mass media – with the exception of Marshall McLuhan's and those by soap researchers – have concentrated on the audience's passivity. Television – and radio before it – has been blamed for killing conversation, ruining family life, brainwashing an apparently listless public into accepting false values, encouraging mindless acceptance of violence. But soap fans (or at least a substantial minority of them) are activists, and moreover activists in a Good Cause. Even those who do not approve of the (morally impeccable, if old-fashioned) values of soap opera could not deny that its fans answer back. They are neither numbed nor awed by the medium. Soap-watching is a spectator sport as healthy as any other.

Like any sport, the soap watchers have their fan clubs. In England, where such notions are regarded with suspicion, and associated either with organized hooliganism (as in soccer) or with the mindlessness of adolescence (wetting themselves over pop stars), the organization is amateur and limited in scope. There are jokey groups like the Ogden Appreciation Society, but while the British fans will flock to a fête or charity affair where one of their favourites is making an appearance, they do not expend much energy or money on subscriptions and paraphernalia. New Zealand fans once organized a Great Coronation Street tour, lasting seven weeks and costing £1500 a head, which culminated in the Kiwi addicts – who were five years behind the Mother Country in transmission of the show – getting a special tour of the Granada studio. But such devotion, never mind expense, is an exception. The British prefer to do their worshipping, like so much else, without fuss. They'll hang about in groups for a glimpse of a star, if they happen to be in the vicinity, but that's as far as it goes.

Or almost. When Meg Mortimer got married in Birmingham Cathedral, thousands jammed the area ready with confetti. And, on another occasion, when news got out that the *Coronation Street* cast was to attend the wedding of the show's stage manager, local police tried to take adequate precautions. Special car-parks were organized, with special stickers for the guests. Even so, police on motor cycles had to escort the stars – not to mention the bride and groom – through streets packed with more people than had turned out to see the Queen the year before. Even when the reception was over, the crowds would not disperse until they had seen the face of every star they knew to be present. The stiff upper lip softens for soap opera. The vaunted privacy of the English falls easy victim to the crowd fever of the fans.

In America the fans are far better organized. Many of the stars have their own fan clubs, equipped with voluntary secretaries who inform members when their idol will be on public view, feed them items of gossip and mail them signed photos and other memorabilia. More than that, they arrange parties and luncheons where the public may mingle with the gods, often on a regular basis. Those who manage to obtain tickets for these affairs (and who of course pay for the privilege) queue up to have their pictures taken with their heroes, obtain autographs and, most of all, express their appreciation. This is the key to their attendance, the reward for their devotion: being able to say a thank-you for the pleasure they have got from watching. It is the same process as sending the stars gifts: a way of crossing the divide, of emerging, however briefly, from anonymous obscurity, of making *them* feel grateful by showing gratitude. There is also the pleasure of being able to say "I met him (or her)" when next watching the actor or actress at work.

Of course watching somebody regularly allows you to know them so well you feel they must know you too. It is easy to stroll up to a famous face and claim acquaintance: being public property, the stars are used to it, and besides you might easily mistake them for a close relative, so certain are you that you know them. I once did this myself at a party, when there was a lady standing alone, like me without a drink, and with no one to talk to. Being convinced I knew her, but having forgotten her name, I strolled over and was about to introduce myself, when our hostess rushed up. "Your Majesty," she said, "may I present Peter Buckman?" A true story – and of course relevant, for the Queen is known to be as avid a fan of *Coronation Street* as her mother is of *Crossroads*.

The great majority of soap watchers, of course, does not join fan clubs or write letters or hope to press the flesh of their fantasies. They watch for the pleasure of relaxing into a good story, of submerging their own problems in someone else's invented ones. But we English-speaking readers and viewers and listeners must not forget that many of the soaps to which we are addicted are also sold to other nations, with cultural attitudes very different from our own. Most countries, indeed, have their own native soap operas, this side of the Iron Curtain, anyway. As a way of attracting large audiences, the genre's profitable appeal has not been lost on programme makers wherever they are to be found. Nor are the home-grown products mere imitations of Anglo-Saxon successes like *The Brothers* or *Dallas*. Some are, of course, just to show that their culture can do anything Hollywood can – or downtown

Burbank – but most are true reflections of the nation's own culture.

The clips that I have seen, from Japanese, Spanish, Indian, Egyptian and other sources, were too short, too incomprehensible, and frankly too risible for me to form much of a judgement. But the whole point of the genre is to involve its audience with everyday problems over an extended period. You cannot succumb to a two-minute clip: you need to immerse yourself in the story. Once you begin to understand who the characters are, and what they represent, it doesn't matter that they act, look and talk differently from those with whom you are familiar. What matters is how they behave, and here soaps are the same the whole world over.

This sameness is the only explanation for the world-wide success of programmes like *Coronation Street* or *Dallas*. The flavour of their speech will be lost in dubbing or subtitles, their backgrounds and the appearance of the players may be as exotic as a grass-skirted Hawaiian would seem in Piccadilly Circus, their daily doings must bring a smile to the faces of those whose most precious luxury is the TV set itself. And yet the stereotypes are recognizable, their destinies predictable yet engrossing, and there is the narrative to carry them along. They cater, with enormous professional expertise, for the universal appetite for a good story. That is why they sell everywhere.

There are those who maintain that the Anglo-Saxon soaps are foisted onto innocent foreign audiences and used as subtle (or crude) sales vehicles for the Western way of life. In the true spirit of the dialectic, there is an opposing view which holds that the socialist countries who buy our soaps use them as anti-capitalist propaganda, showing the corruption and misery engendered by the decadent accumulation of wealth. I don't buy any of that. I do not deny that the soap producers make a hefty profit on their foreign sales, and that they are standard-bearers for American (and English) television values. But these values are more technological than spiritual.

It is possible that the subtle differences in class betrayed by whether you sit in the snug or in the bar of the Rover's Return, and whether you drink mild or bitter, might be lost on the people of, say, Singapore. (Who, according to H. V. Kershaw, are fans of *Coronation Street* though they receive it with its original dialogue accompanied by Chinese sub-titles running up the left-hand side of the screen, and a simultaneous commentary in Tamil on the local radio.) But the people of Singapore cannot fail to notice the quality of acting – and, if they cared to think about it, the design, lighting, pace and direction – that distinguishes the Anglo-Saxon soap from the native dramas. I do not denigrate the drama productions of other nations: I simply note that, since England and America have had television longer than anyone else, and since they have spent many millions over the years on refining their techniques, it would not be surprising if the quality of the product (even so economic a product as soap) was, well, different. Which can only be an advertisement for our television output.

Of course, the oily doings of the billionaires of Texas or Colorado are as foreign to the British as they are to the Malays. We the public are happy to settle down in territory we do not recognize, with people whose accents are almost impenetrable. The luxury or poverty of the setting is immaterial: it is the roles and reactions of the participants that involve us. A bastard is a bastard the whole world over: the Algerians and East Germans (to take two examples of J. R.'s fans) are fascinated not because the Ewings represent a class enemy (everyone knows money doesn't bring happiness, which is a message shared by all the soaps), but because they want to see how long the villain can stay a grin ahead of destiny.

I don't want to overdo the complexity or sophistication of soap opera, because it is basically a beautifully simple process. Indeed, its simplicity is part of its charm. But just as American fans of *One Life to Live* or British *Emmerdale Farm* nuts enjoy the resonance that their background knowledge of the characters gives each situation, so foreign fans of exported serials must feel a little superior if they know something more than their peers. The Japanese who speaks English and knows something about American business methods will respond with greater awareness to the shenanigans of *Dynasty* than will the Japanese fisherman, though for both (if they watch) the basic appeal of the story is the same. And yet (again I quote H. V. Kershaw) a Brooklyn viewer of *Coronation Street* found every one of its characters in his New York apartment block. This proves that soap stereotypes transcend nation and class, not to mention audience barriers. We live, of course, in an age of homogenized culture, where television attempts to make the whole world kin by broadcasting space walks, royal weddings, games and beauty competitions to hundreds of countries at once. But the selling powers of the medium are limited by the discrimination of the viewers, and soap viewers have shown themselves to be amongst the most discriminating audience of all. As consumers, they may be suckers for whatever is advertised between the parts of the shows they favour, but as viewers they can tell a false note in their own or in imported serials, as surely as they can detect a chip in crystal.

It is because of what they expect and accept of the genre that I will hazard a prophecy (I should mention that my record as forecaster is dismal). I believe the prime-time weekly soaps – *Dallas, Dynasty, Falcon Crest* and others as yet uncloned – are merely a passing fad. *Dallas* has been top of the ratings for some years as I write (despite being described by *Variety* as "a limited series with a limited future": I'm not the only one who gets things wrong), but it is showing signs of plot fatigue. That in itself is not enough to sink it: what I believe will happen is that those who were attracted to this beautifully made but essentially imitation soap will in the end tire of it, while those who are addicted to the real thing will continue to find their kicks elsewhere, in the less prestigious but more evenly paced serials that have been running forever. The addicts need their fix more often and less cut with trendiness than prime-time can give. The prime-time watchers are mere amateurs.

The real thing is built up like a coral reef, sharp little corpse piling prettily on sharp little corpse until you have a structure capable of tearing the guts out of any audience. The once-a-week soap is really a set of melodramatic highlights strung together and hurled at the viewers. Without the careful construction, the *pointilliste* background, the slow (my god it can be slow!) development of character and situation, each drama becomes at best incredible, and at worst laughable.

The prime-time public is more fickle than the reliable (but discriminating) soap audience. They will one day (I will not say soon) get bored with this "instant soap" that can so easily be shown up for the gewgaw it is by some rival form of drama in the same slot: a well-paced thriller or an adult comedy. Day-time and early evening soaps have no such rivals. Their strength is in their reliability and their continuousness. The public that likes them remains faithful and involved, forgiving much and receiving much pleasure. It is a *different* public from the rest, with different expectations. Its members could be compared, for a change of metaphor, to wine connoisseurs, happier with the more mature vintages, which they prefer to sip at regular intervals. They would never gulp down the whole bottle at a go. Those who think themselves soap fans on the strength of a fondness for *Dynasty* are not, in my view, being schooled in appreciation of the real stuff. When the sparkle goes flat they will rush off in search of a new taste. But the inevitable decline of the "instant soaps" will not affect the genre. Once the media spotlight has moved on, and the glamour-soaps have been worn to rags, the true soap public will settle back, with a sigh of relief, in the welcome obscurity it prefers.

The defensiveness of the true soap fan – although it is less now than it was – says a lot about our attitudes to leisure and pleasure. Why should anyone feel guilty about listening to or watching an entertaining programme regularly? That the programmes can be ridiculed on account of the writing, acting and direction is only a small part of the answer.

Much more significant are our puritanical attitudes to work, which made (and still make) sitting still and doing nothing (though one is listening or watching) something to feel guilty about. Those who don't do housework (that is, most men) don't consider it a "proper job" from which breaks are needed or justified. Those who are stretched on the rack of domestic choredom feel, or used to feel, the need to be forever "doing something" to prove their worth. Listening to the radio or watching the television does not qualify as "doing" anything. It is, or was, akin to idleness, and many of those who did it felt bad. Indeed, they tried to carry on "doing things" while listening or watching, so that they'd look busy.

The notion that a person's worth can only be judged by the work they do, whether productive or not, is only now beginning to lose its grip, even for a generation who are finding it impossible to get paid jobs. The whole notion of the work ethic is being undermined by new technology and the threat (for that is what it is) of leisure (as unemployment will soon be euphemized). The expectations that have sustained Western societies for five centuries – schooling followed by work for five or six days a week until age forces retirement – now stand no chance of being fulfilled. People will start work at a later age, and they will finish at an earlier one. They will change jobs several times. Their working week will have fewer and fewer hours. Sooner or later this must force a change in attitude. If work as we presently understand it is going to become a scarce resource that will have to be rationed in some way – which is what I think will happen – it is of course possible that people will value all the more such work as they manage to get. I would hope that we find some other measure of a person's worth. What is certain is that our approach to, and opportunities for, leisure are going to change.

Soap-watching is always going to be a leisure pursuit for millions. For some – students in communications courses, for example – it is also work, for which academic credits may be gained. Making work out of pleasure is in the puritan tradition. But the students who regularly watch *General Hospital* or *Guiding Light* also do it for pure entertainment. They watch in groups, which makes their addiction more of a cliquey thing than a passion strong enough to be indulged alone. As with all orgies (so I am assured), the excitement is heightened by the presence of others, and this tends to swamp or drown the refined critical sense of the individual. Nevertheless, the fact that kids share with their elders a taste for a genre that has become critically acceptable is a bond between the generations (it is more common for the young to worship what their seniors despise). The young might move on to something else, but they will always retain a residual, or nostalgic, affection for their early passions. Indeed, in Britain the long-established shows have found a new audience amongst children. *Coronation Street*, for example, is more popular with those under 16 than most of the programmes produced specially for this age group.

I'm not entirely sure what conclusion to draw from this fact. Does it mean that today's children are ready for more adult fare than that which is offered to them? Does it mean that, although children's programmes are made to the same high standards as adult ones (and often higher), their intended audience's well developed critical sense leads them to prefer soap ? Does it imply that the soaps are really kids' stuff? Or does such a statistic merely mean that school-age children like watching television as late in the evening as they can get away with, and are hooked, like the rest of humanity, on the continuing story?

I opt for the last, which also explains how a new audience comes into being as the old hands in its cards. What is interesting is whether children see the serials' chief concerns differently from their elders. Girls, like their mothers, are acute observers of fashion, and comment instantly on any change in clothes, hair styles or accessories. This attention to personal detail, with appropriate commentary ("doesn't she look *awful*?"), is what makes gossips of us all. Boys pick up on jokes, and the attitudes of the male characters to the female. (Girls pick up on these things too, of course, whereas boys noticing fashion is so rare as to be statistically unmeasurable.) But adultery and its implications are lost on most children. So what are they getting out of the serials, if they miss out on that central piece of furniture, the bed?

No doubt they have their views on the soppiness of much of adult behaviour confirmed. Certainly they absorb a moral code which is basically that of their great-grandmothers. *If* (and I emphasize the "if") children are more influenced by what they see on television than by what goes on in their homes – which I very much doubt, even though they spend more time in front of the set than they do in school – then the teeny soap fans are going to face an adult world decked out with the prejudices of their ancestors.

But then, new challenges – such as those of adulthood – tend to reinforce old prejudices. We are a conservative species, to the point when the "radicalism" of one generation is invariably succeeded by the reaction of the next. The soaps are a testimony to that simple fact, not an obstacle to change. And children are conservative creatures, hostile or at best indifferent to change unless it means an improvement in otherwise intolerable circumstances. So they can respond instinctively to the conservatism of the soaps, even if they are unmoved by their play of lusts. Since the genre is so clever at providing for involvement at all sorts of levels, children can easily be catered for. After all, they are still at the age when they are encouraged to bury themselves in a good story.

I wonder if girls watching the soaps will pick up, earlier than their non-soaped sisters, the fact that their sex has problems only they can solve. Will they learn, ahead of their own experience, that men will always let them down, that they have only themselves to rely on? If so, will this affect their attitude to the opposite sex – to sex generally? I don't know, and no research has been done on this interesting topic. On the basis of my own observations, I would say it might affect or advance their attitudes, but not their actions: when it comes to love, nobody learns from experience, or from others' mistakes, much less their own. This too is a lesson taught by the soaps. It is unthinkable that they could be responsible for a decline in the standards of romantic behaviour, when that is their whole ethic.

What about women watching? Basic attitudes may not have changed, but their roles have certainly come in for reassessment. Now that working women are a majority in the serials on both sides of the Atlantic, there must be a certain tension between women viewers whose labour is confined to household duties, and the more independent and perhaps more fulfilled soap heroines. Soap women, strangely enough, are never shown watching television: for them, entertainment always involves the opposite sex. For women watching, is that pleasurable fantasy, or a grim joke? As for working women who come home and have to prepare meals and do housework, fitting this in while watching the soaps must lead them to reflect ironically on how little has actually changed. While choredom is much less in evidence now on the soaps than it was – soap women rarely have the time for a gossip over a cup of tea or coffee: they are much more likely to chat at work or at the shop or restaurant – those who watch the shows still suffer under its yoke.

This is a sign of our hypocritical attitude to liberation. We can accept working women, on and off the screen, as long as they continue to do all the tasks they used to do when they remained at home all day. That they can take on this double burden is a sign of their strength – and one reason some men dislike the soaps' influence is precisely because they show women to be stronger and more capable than such men perceive, or want, them to be.

The right to enjoy entertainment, to relax, still has to be earned in our homes. Escapism is still not something responsible adults readily admit to indulging in. Millions of regular fans are still a little on the defensive, after all these years. Perhaps this is part of the pleasure they get from the genre: that feeling of being apart, of indulging themselves in something a little wicked, something that gives delicious shivers of harmless guilt. They belong to an amorphous but powerful fan-club, with their own rules and rituals which mark members as "Us" against "Them". There is, as there has always been, a strong need to belong to a tribe, to feel rooted in certain common assumptions and bound by shared convictions. This need is stronger now than ever, when previously accepted boundaries are being torn down and private territories opened up to commercial exploitation. Which is why soap has always found a public.

And I would guess it always will. The future of both radio and television promises programmes for every conceivable minority, through cable, cassette and satellite. Though this promise will bear a pretty tarnished look as the offered programmes come to resemble each other more and more, soap will always be amongst them. It will not be always cheap: on radio now, which you would think was the perfect medium for it, being so portable and versatile, it is being kept at arms' length by the planners, who point out that it is infinitely cheaper to have a single presenter in a studio with a pile of records and a telephone, than to have to pay several writers, scores of actors and actresses, and umpteen studio crew. Even so, the BBC's External Services launched a new soap, set in a London hotel, with their sights aimed at an audience of ten million overseas listeners. And on television, of course, the form flourishes as never before (in the opening week of the British Channel 4, their new soap *Brookside* scarcely a classic example of the genre, topped the Channel's ratings). The unchanged devices of half a century's entertaining experience are as effective now as they have ever been.

That means there will always be millions prepared to watch others do what they long to do, and offer to sacrifice all for love. Will he do it? Will she accept? What will happen? If those questions are ever finally answered, that *will* be the end of civilization as we know it.

NOTES ON SOURCES

Introduction
Maurice Nimmo of Haverfordwest suggested to me that the sung jingle is responsible for the "opera" part of the title.

Chapter 1
p 5: For the history of the BBC I relied on Asa Briggs' three volume *The History of Broadcasting in the United Kingdom* (Oxford: OUP, 1961-1970), and the *BBC Yearbooks* to which he led me. For the history of American radio and television I consulted Eric Barnouw's equally absorbing triple-decker, *A History of Broadcasting in the United States* (New York: OUP, 1966-1970). I also used the latter's definitive study of *The Sponsor: Notes on a Modern Potentate* (New York: OUP, 1978).

p 7: Milton Shulman's phrase "the least worst television in the world" was applied to the whole of British television, but I have taken the liberty of using it to bolster my argument about the BBC.

p 8: The famous introduction to *The Romance of Helen Trent* can be heard on *Golden Memories of Radio*, a series of six records produced by the Longines Symphonette Society, Larchmont, New York, and introduced by Jack Benny.

p 9: Frank Hummert's modest disclaimer is in Raymond W. Stedman's *The Serials: Suspense and Drama by Installment* (Norman: University of Oklahoma Press, 1971, 1977).

p 10: The story of the romance between Frank and Anne Hummert is in Robert Metz's study of *CBS: Reflections in a Bloodshot Eye* (Chicago: Playboy Press, 1975). The Manya Starr story, with many other illuminating anecdotes about radio soaps, can be found in Robert LaGuardia's *From Ma Perkins to Mary Hartman: an illustrated history of soap operas* (New York: Ballantine Books, 1977).

p 11: *Backstage Wife* can be heard on *Golden Memories of Radio*, op. cit. Radio soap addicts can also get a fix from a record simply called *Soap Operas*, which contains episodes from four Procter & Gamble serials, *Ma Perkins,*

Road of Life, Young Dr Malone and *The Guiding Light*, complete with commercials (produced by Mark 56 Records, Anaheim, California, copyright Procter & Gamble, 1974).

p 13: Research into the American soap audience in the 1930s and '40s is in Herta Herzog's "On Borrowed Experience" (*Studies in Philosophy and Social Science*, IX, 1; New York: Institute of Social Research, 1941), Paul Lazarsfeld and Patricia Kendall's *Radio Listening in America* (New York: Harper, 1948) and Paul Lazarsfeld and Frank Stanton's *Communications Research 1948-9* (New York: Harper, 1949). Procter & Gamble's experience is covered in the company's history by Alfred Lief, *It Floats* (New York: Rinehart, 1958). On Irna Phillips, I consulted the State Historical Society of Wisconsin, to whom Ms Phillips presented an extensive collection of scripts, outlines, and correspondence.

p 14: Procter & Gamble kindly allowed me to visit the *Guiding Light* studio, where Executive Producer Allen Potter gave generously of his time.

p 16: The pressures on those who worked in radio soaps are outlined in LaGuardia, op. cit., and in *Molly and Me*, by the creator of *The Goldbergs*, Gertrude Berg (New York: McGraw, 1961).

p 17: Gilbert Seldes' entertaining views on soap are in *The Great Audience* (New York: Viking, 1950), and are quoted with permission.

p 18: Statistics about listeners to Radio Luxembourg, especially Sunday ones, are from "The Story of Pop Radio", in *The Listener*, 14 October 1982.

p 19: The history of the genesis and growth of *Front Line Family* I owe to its creator, who told me all in July 1981. Details of its public popularity and the prejudices it had to surmount within the BBC from BBC Written Archives.

p 20: For American soaps and the war effort, see Barnouw, op. cit.; John K. Hutchens, "Are Soap Operas Only Suds?", *New York Times Magazine* 23 May 1943; George A Willey, "The Soap Operas and the War", in L. W. Lichty and M. C. Topping, eds, *American Broadcasting* (New York: Hastings House, 1975).

p 21: The BBC's Director of the North American Service's warning about the proposed "Russian interlude" for *Front Line Family* is from the BBC Written Archives Centre, file reference R19/1047, and is reproduced with permission.

p 27: The battles within the BBC's Drama Department over soap opera are also in the Written Archives, as are Val Gielgud's views (14 June 1945, file reference R19/1047, reproduced with permission).

p 28: *Mrs Dale's Diary*'s "Editorial Policy" comes from the BBC Written Archives, file reference R19/779, and is also reproduced with permission.

p 30: The full history of *The Archers* is contained in William Smethurst, ed., *The Archers: The First Thirty Years* (London: Eyre Methuen, 1980).

p 31: For the early history of television, see Barnouw, op. cit.; Briggs, op. cit.; and *British Television Drama*, edited by George W. Brandt (Cambridge: CUP, 1981). Soap on American television is well documented by Stedman, op.cit; LaGuardia, op. cit; and M. Edmondson and D. Rounds, *The Soaps: Daytime Serials of Radio and Television* (New York: Stein & Day, 1973).

p 33: For the demise of American radio soaps, see Stedman, op. cit., who also carries the CBS Press Release of 22 November 1960 which tied up the loose ends of *The Right to Happiness* and *Ma Perkins*.

p 35: On *Waggoners' Walk* see David Wade, "Popular radio drama", in *Radio Drama*, edited by Peter Lewis (London: Longman, 1981).

Chapter 2

p 50: Harding Lemay's experiences in serial writing, on which I have drawn heavily, are contained in his *Eight Years in Another World: The Inside Story of a Soap Opera* (New York: Atheneum, 1981), and quoted with permission.

p 55: The effect of *The Young and the Restless* in "youthing" the soaps is detailed in Manuela Soares' *The Soap Opera Book* (New York: Harmony Books, 1978), from which I have (with her permission) plagiarized much useful background information on American soaps I never saw.

Chapter 3

p 67: I got a year's worth of American soap plotting from my subscription to *Soap Opera Digest* (New York: Network Publishing), which is also full of anecdotes, gossip, interviews, analysis, criticism and the reactions of the fans.

p 69: It was in the pages of *Soap Opera Digest* that I learned of the view of the *New York Times* that *The Young and the Restless* handled rape better than the movies.

p 70: An analysis of "social issues" in American soaps is contained in Manuela Soares, op.cit. I owe my knowledge of the Australian soap *No. 96* to Peter Grose, and to "Double-Decker Soap Opera Sandwich: Number 96 and The Box" by Stuart McPherson and Colin Slow in *Media Information Australia*, no.6, November 1977.

p 71: The complications of *As the World Turns* were explained in *Soap Opera Digest*, which often unravels family knots for confused viewers.

p 74: *Soap Opera Digest*'s views on pregnancy are in the issue dated 2 February 1982.

p 76: The relationships in *As the World Turns* were detailed in a paper by Louise Spence called "Life's Little Problems . . . and Pleasures: The Beginning of an Investigation into Narrative Structure of Soap Operas", prepared for a course at New York University in 1981.

p 77: I am grateful to Independent Television Publications Ltd, publishers of *TV Times Magazine*, for permission to quote the *Crossroads* summary; and to *Soap Opera Digest* for *The Doctors* quote.

p 78: For permission to quote from the story-line of Episode 5017 of *The Doctors* I am indebted to the National Broadcasting Company, Inc, and to the Writers' Guild of America, East, Inc.

p 87: The idea that the interrupted method of soap narrative reflects the interruptions and frustrations of mothers and housewives is mentioned by Tania Modleski, among others, in her penetrating article "The Search for Tomorrow in Today's Soap Operas: Notes on a Feminine Narrative Form", in *Film Quarterly* (University of California Press), Fall 1979.

Chapter 4
I have talked to many soap writers on both sides of the Atlantic about their craft. Some love the work and are proud to say so – for example Peter Ling, Peggy O'Shea, and H.V. Kershaw in his book *The Street Where I Live* (London: Granada, 1981). Others prefer to keep their criticism anonymous. Harding Lemay, op.cit., is the one head-writer who has committed his doubts and difficulties to paper.

p 101: These outrageous plots can be found in the pages of *Soap Opera Digest* (1981).

p 102: I got the background information on Phil Redmond's *Brookside* from the British magazine *Broadcast*, 1 March 1982. There was an interesting discussion of the serial on the BBC2 programme *Did You See . . .?*, reported in *The Listener* of 18 November 1982.

p 104: The early history of *Coronation Street* is in Kershaw, op. cit., who was one of the original contributors to the programme.

p 106: I am indebted to the American Broadcasting Company and to the writers for the excerpt from Episode 3552 of *One Life to Live*.

Chapter 5
Most of this chapter was based on personal interviews.

p 121: Linda Gray mentioned how effectively she used her eyes during the programme "Angela Rippon Reporting on The Soap Opera Business", BBC1, 3 September 1980.

p 122: My knowledge of *Crossroads* comes from Peter Ling and from Dorothy Hobson's book *Crossroads: the Drama of a Soap Opera* (London: Methuen, 1982).

p 127: Ruth Warrick details her career in *The Confessions of Phoebe Tyler* (written with Don Preston. Englewood-Cliffs: Prentice-Hall, 1980).

p 130: Background information on *One Life to Live* from Alex McNeil's astonishingly complete reference book *Total Television: A Comprehensive Guide to Programming from 1948 to 1980* (New York: Penguin Books, 1980).

p 130: Lee Rich was also interviewed by Angela Rippon.

p 131: I owe the *Young Dr Malone* anecdote to Hugh Franklin.

p 134: Information on American stars being reborn in soap is taken from *Soap Opera Digest*.

Chapter 6
I am delighted to thank Jacqueline Babbin, producer of *All My Children*, not only for our long and revealing conversation, but for allowing me the freedom of the studio.

p 144: I gleaned these facts about what happened during the American writers' and technicians' strikes from bar-room gossip.

p 145: For *Crossroads*, see Hobson, op.cit.

p 150: For the organization of Procter & Gamble's Programming Department, I am grateful to the company for sending me articles that appeared in the house magazine *Moonbeams.*

p 152 and p 154: See Harding Lemay, op. cit.

Chapter 7

p 162: Semiological or structuralist criticism of the soaps can be found, for example, in the British Film Institute's Television Monograph on *Coronation Street* (1981), with contributions by Richard Dyer, Christine Geraghty, Marion Jordan, Terry Lovell, Richard Paterson and John Stewart.

p 163: The state of research on American radio soaps in the 1930s and 40s was reported by John K. Hutchens, op.cit.

p 164: The British argument over soap operas and women was aired at the 1977 Edinburgh Television Festival, reported in *Broadcast*, 12 September 1977.

p 165: I got the James Agate quote from a review of a book about drama criticism. Unfortunately no provenance was given.

p 166: I am grateful to Doubleday for permission to quote from Professor Newcomb's book.

p 167: Renata Adler is quoted in Soares, op.cit.

p 170 On what, if anything, television does to people, see *Television and Human Behavior* by George Comstock, Steven Chaffee, Natan Katzman, Maxwell McCombs and Donald Roberts (New York: Columbia University Press, 1978).

p 173: People must know that there is a camera between them and their favourite characters since they always write to them care of the television studios.

The American psychologist Dr Joyce Brothers is amongst those who use soaps as a teaching device (*Soap Opera Digest*, 2 March 1982)

Jib Fowles, Professor of Humanities at the University of Houston, Texas, was quoted in *The Standard*, 5 January 1983. He argued that television does not put things into our brains, but takes them out, as do dreams and fantasies, "sponging the mind free from tension". As for the fear that violence is induced by watching it on television, a study at the University of Chicago has shown that TV addicts are *less* fearful than non-viewers.

p 180: *Newsweek*'s cover story on *General Hospital* was in the issue dated 28 September 1981.

p 181: The British Film Institute sponsored, with the Institute of Contemporary Arts, the seminar on soap opera on 29 September 1982.

p 182: Noele Gordon wrote *My Life at Crossroads* (London: W. H. Allen, 1975). I am indebted to Dr Mary Cassata, Director of Project Daytime, for information on its scope and the state of its research. Papers on soap have appeared in the *Journal of Communication* (published by the Annenberg School Press, Philadelphia) in Autumn 1979 and Summer 1981.

p 183: Roland Barthes' *S/Z* was translated by Richard Miller (London: Cape, 1974). Modleski, op.cit.

Chapter 8

p 188: Marshall McLuhan's pioneering work *Understanding Media* was published in 1964 (New York: McGraw-Hill).

p 188–9: I am grateful to Procter & Gamble and the producers of *The Guiding Light* for these comments from their fans. The comments on *Crossroads* are taken from Hobson, op.cit.; those on *The Archers* from a General Report from the Audience Research Department, 18 August 1954; those on *General Hospital* from a correspondent to *Soap Opera Digest*, 21 July 1981.

p 193: Kathy Staff, who plays Doris Luke in *Crossroads*, told Dorothy Hobson the story about the cuffs.

p 202: For the 1930s research see the note on Chapter 1, p 13. Contemporary attitudes are demonstrated in letters to the production companies and the television magazines. *The Archers* correspondence ran in *The Guardian* during July 1982.

p 203: The husband who wanted his wife's attentions returned to the household was an American, writing to *Soap Opera Digest*.

p 204: The facts about *Coronation Street* fans are in Kershaw, op.cit.

p 209: American college soapers were the subject of the already cited *Newsweek* article, as well as a piece in *Rolling Stone* of 1 October 1981, entitled "Daze of Our Lives" by Lisa Birnbach. See also Manuela Soares, op. cit. Incidentally, research findings from the 1930s to our own times reveal that there is remarkably little difference in educational background between those who love the soaps and those who disdain them. This fact, noted by Lazarsfeld and Kendall, op.cit., has recently been confirmed by statistics showing that, amongst American audiences at least, there is a gap of less than one per cent between the viewing habits of the best and least educated (quoted in *The Standard*, 5 January 1983). In other words, all those snobs who say they never watch popular programmes like soaps are lying.

p 210: The facts about children watching adult programmes have been noted by, amongst others, Christopher Dunkley in his "Research" columns in *The Listener* during the spring of 1982.

SELECT BIBLIOGRAPHY

Barnouw, Eric. *A History of Broadcasting in the United States*,1 A Tower in Babel. 2 The Golden Web. 3 The Image Empire. (New York: Oxford: University Press, 1966, 1968, 1970).

Barnouw, Eric. *The Sponsor: Notes on a Modern Potentate* (New York: Oxford University Press, 1978).

Barthes, Roland. *Mythologies*, trans. Annette Lavers (London: Cape, 1972.

Barthes, Roland. *S/Z*, trans. Richard Miller (London: Cape, 1974).

Berg, Gertrude, with C. Berg. *Molly and Me* (New York: McGraw-Hill, 1961).

Brandt, George W. ed. *British Television Drama* (Cambridge: Cambridge University Press, 1981).

Briggs, Asa. *The History of Broadcasting in the United Kingdom*, 1 The Birth of Broadcasting. 2 The Golden Age of Wireless. 3 The War of Words. (Oxford: Oxford University Press, 1961, 1965, 1970).

Buxton, F., and Owen, B. *The Big Broadcast 1920-1950* (New York: Viking, 1972).

Comstock, George, and others. *Television and Human Behavior* (New York: Columbia University Press, 1978).

Drakakis, John, ed. *British Radio Drama* (Cambridge: Cambridge University Press 1981).

Dyer, Richard, and others. *Coronation Street* (London: BFI Television Monograph No. 13, 1981).

Edmondson, M., and Rounds, D. *The Soaps: Daytime Serials of Radio and Television* (New York: Stein & Day, 1973).

Fiske, J., and Hartley, J. *Reading Television* (London: Methuen, 1978).

Harmon, Jim. *The Great Radio Heroes* (New York: Doubleday, 1967).

Hobson, Dorothy. *Crossroads: The Drama of a Soap Opera* (London: Methuen, 1982).

Hoggart, R. *The Uses of Literacy* (London: Chatto & Windus, 1957).

LaGuardia, Robert. *From Ma Perkins to Mary Hartman: an illustrated history of soap operas* (New York: Ballantine Books, 1977).

Lazarsfeld, P., and Kendall, P. *Radio Listening in America* (New York: Harper, 1948).

Lazarsfeld, P., and Stanton, F. *Communications Research 1948–9* (New York: Harper, 1949).

Lemay, Harding. *Eight Years in Another World: The Inside Story of a Soap Opera* (New York: Atheneum, 1981).

Lewis, Peter, ed. *Radio Drama* (London: Longman, 1981).

Lichty, L. W., and Topping, M. C., eds. *American Broadcasting* (New York: Hasting House, 1975).

Lief, Alfred. *It Floats: The Story of Procter and Gamble* (New York: Rinehart, 1958).

McLuhan, Marshall. *Understanding Media: The Extensions of Man* (New York: McGraw-Hill, 1964).

McNeil, Alex. *Total Television: A Comprehensive Guide to Programming from 1948 to 1980* (New York: Penguin Books, 1980).

Metz, Robert. *CBS: Reflections in a Bloodshot Eye* (Chicago: Playboy Press, 1975).

Newcomb, Horace. *TV: The Most Popular Art* (New York: Doubleday, 1974).

Seldes, Gilbert. *The Great Audience* (New York: Viking, 1950).

Silvey, Robert. *Who's Listening? The Story of BBC Audience Research* (London: Allen & Unwin, 1974).

Smethurst, William, ed. *The Archers: The First Thirty Years* (London: Eyre Methuen, 1980).

Soares, Manuela. *The Soap Opera Book* (New York: Harmony Books, 1978).

Stedman, Raymond W. *The Serials: Suspense and Drama by Installment* (Norman: University of Oklahoma Press, 1971, 1977).

Sterling, C. H. and Kittross, J. M. *Stay Tuned: A Concise History of American Broadcasting* (California: Belmont, 1978).

Thompson, Denys, ed. *Discrimination and Popular Culture* (Harmondsworth: Penguin Books, 1964).

UNESCO. *Television Traffic: A One-Way Street?* A survey and analysis of the international flow of television programme material by Kaarle Nordenstreng and Tapio Varis (Paris: Reports and Papers on Mass Communication, no. 70, 1974).

Warrick, Ruth, with D. Preston. *The Confessions of Phoebe Tyler* (Englewood Cliffs: Prentice-Hall, 1980).

Whelan, Kenneth. *How the Golden Age of Television Turned My Hair to Silver* (New York: Walker, 1973).

White, L. *The American Radio.* A report on the United States Broadcasting Industry from the Commission on the Freedom of the Press (Chicago, 1947).

Williams, Raymond. *Television: Technology and Cultural Form* (London: Collins/Fontana, 1974).

INDEX

91; children, 75–6; confused
identity, 67; death, 21, 67, 70;
destiny, 90–1; drug addiction,
70; family, 76–7; illnesses, 66–
67, 70–1, 91; incest, 71; love,
67–8, 71–4; marriage, 71–2,
92; power, 53; prison, 69, 70;
rape, 59, 67, 69–70, 198–9;
romance, 73–4, 179; sex,
72–4, 199; surrogate
motherhood, 92; taboos, 71;
youth and age, 75–6
Post, Emily, 9
Procter & Gamble, 9, 13, 14, 20, 32,
33, 149, 150, 152, 154–5
producer, 99, 136, 139, 143, 146
Project Daytime, 182–3

Queen's Messenger, The, 31

radio, 5–8
  soaps on, 8–24, 27–31, 32, 32–4,
    212; *see also programme titles*
Radio Dealer, 5
Radio Luxembourg, 17, 18
Radio Manufacturers' Association, 5
Radio Normandie, 18
Redmond, Phil, 102–3
Reeve, Christopher, 133
Reith, Sir John, 5, 6–7
reviewers, 126, 161, 163, 167, 175–82
Rich, Lee, 130
Right to Happiness, The, 33–4
Roache, William, 133–4
Road of Life, The, 14
Robinsons, The (formerly *Front Line
    Family, q.v.*), 27, 28
Rockefeller Foundation, 182
Rogers, Tristan, 130
Roosevelt, Franklin D., 20
Rosenthal, Jack, 96
Ryan's Hope, 70, 135

Search for Tomorrow, 32, 101, 158
Second Mrs Burton, The, 33
Second World War, 18–23
Seldes, Gilbert, 17, 165, 167

Shulman, Milton, 7
situation comedy, soap opera
    distinguished from, 9
Soap, 147–8, 149
soap opera
  appeal of, 13, 25, 26–7, 41
  art, craftsmanship and, 95–7
  basis, form, conventions, 8, 17,
    23–4, 26, 34, 83, 85–7, 89,
    93, 102, 200–201
  birth of, 7–10
  Britain, first in, 18
  camera work, 137–8
  chic, fashionable, 114, 134,
    180
  and class, 169
  and committees, 151–3
  conservative, old-fashioned,
    60–1, 114
  conspiracy theory, 24, 25–6,
    173–4
  disparaged, 5, 28, 163–4, 168–75
  early, in America, 10–17
  editing, 142
  in foreign countries, 205–7
  future for, 212
  good and evil in, 11, 26, 44, 66, 82,
    89–90, 146
  and government, 20–1, 174
  length, 14, 35, 43, 131–2, 154–5
  longevity, 14
  medical, 14, 92
  and money, wealth, 52–3
  moral tone, conventional
    morality, 11, 12–13, 24–6, 48,
    114
  and myth, 38, 146–7
  organizational hierarchy, 94,
    148–53
  and politics, 22–3, 65, 146–7
  production, 16, 24, 35–6, 136–46
  purpose of, 17, 25, 64, 87–8
  and ratings, 156
  and "reality", realism, 28, 29,
    45–6, 172–3, 178–9, 198
  in Second World War, 18–23
  situation comedy distinguished, 9